Fifth Edition

The Career Adventure

Your Guide to Personal Assessment, Career Exploration, and Decision Making

Susan M. Johnston

Marine Corps University

PEARSON

Boston • Columbus • Indianapolis • New York • San Francisco • Upper Saddle River
Amsterdam • Cape Town • Dubai • London • Madrid • Milan • Munich • Paris • Montréal • Toronto
Delhi • Mexico City • São Paulo • Sydney • Hong Kong • Seoul • Singapore • Taipei • Tokyo

Dedication

To my husband Jack, and my sons Charlie, Mitch, and Russ . . .
my deepest gratitude for your love and support.

Editor-in-Chief: Jodie McPherson
Executive Marketing Manager: Amy Judd
Acquisitions Editor: Katie Mahan
Editorial Assistant: Erin Carreiro
Senior Production Project Manager: Beth Houston
Editorial Production Service: Electronic Publishing Services Inc., NYC
Manufacturing Buyer: Dennis Para
Text Printer: Edwards Brothers Malloy
Cover Printer: Lehigh-Phoenix Color
Electronic Composition: Aptara®, Inc.
Senior Designer: Beth Paquin
Interior Design: Electronic Publishing Services Inc., NYC
Cover Design: Studio Montage
Cover Image: Philip and Karen Smith/Getty Images

Library of Congress Cataloging-in-Publication Data
Johnston, Susan M.
   The career adventure : your guide to personal assessment, career exploration, and decision making / Susan M. Johnston, Marine Corps University.—Fifth Edition.
      pages cm
   Includes bibliographical references and index.
   ISBN-13: 978-0-13-248119-9
   ISBN-10: 0-13-248119-7
   1. Vocational guidance.   2. Vocational interests.   3. Self-evaluation.   4. Job hunting.   5. College students—Employment.   I. Title.
   HF5381.J574 2014
   650.14—dc23

                                                                                                    2013015068

10 9 8 7 6 5 4 3 2 1

ISBN-10: 0-13-248119-7
ISBN-13: 978-0-13-248119-9

About the Author

With approximately thirty years of experience in career development and counseling, Susan M. Johnston has had the opportunity to work closely with hundreds of students and clients who have chosen to take on the challenge of career planning. As an instructor in career planning and a private practice career advisor, she has guided individuals through the process of self-assessment, career exploration, and decision making to achieve their career goals. Prior to her classroom and private practice experience, she held positions at Sinclair Community College in the area of Cooperative Education and with the Career Planning and Placement Center. In addition to her teaching and counseling services, she is Director of Institutional Research, Assessment and Planning at Marine Corps University, Quantico, Virginia, the graduate professional military education school of the Marine Corps.

Susan graduated summa cum laude from Wright State University with a B.A. in Communications and holds an M.S.Ed. in Counseling from the University of Dayton. She holds a Ph.D. in Workforce Development and Education from The Ohio State University. In past positions, she has been on assignment with the State Department in India for the U.S. Information Agency, and prior to her experience as an educator, she was a contract negotiator for the U.S. Air Force. She is an active member of the American Counseling Association and the National Career Development Association. Her research interests include psychological factors influencing career transition and the factors influencing performance in high-stress, high-stakes settings.

Susan is a resident of Fredericksburg, Virginia, whose oldest son, Charles, is a major in the United States Marine Corps and the father of three daughters. Susan's middle son, Mitch, is a CPA currently pursuing a Masters in Business at Purdue University. Her youngest son, Russ, is an investment banker in Chicago.

Contents

PART II Career Exploration 47

LEARNING ABOUT THE WORLD OF WORK

4 Exploring the World of Work 49

Networking   71

Establishing Contacts and Support

Decision Making and Goal Setting   89

PART III The Job Campaign   103

ORGANIZING YOUR SEARCH

7   Designing Your Resume and Cover Letters   105

8   Interviewing with Confidence   133

9 Developing Job Leads   149

Continuing Your Adventure   163

Appendix   167

NOTE: Every effort has been made to provide accurate and current Internet information in this book. However, the Internet and information posted on it are constantly changing, so it is inevitable that some of the Internet addresses listed in this textbook will change.

NEW TO THE FIFTH EDITION OF *THE CAREER ADVENTURE: YOUR GUIDE TO PERSONAL ASSESSMENT, CAREER EXPLORATION, AND DECISION MAKING*

■ *Offers strong foundational information* with opportunities to use tools that accomplish career goals, so students are encouraged to implement knowledge and methods available to see immediate results.

■ *Builds on students' experiences* as a base for development and decision making by referring to their own context as a frame of reference for processing new career perspectives. The internal dialogue sets the stage for social communication that informs and validates the career planning experience.

■ *Shows how to set up social media outlets* that connect students to the larger real world in which their actual career goals will be achieved. They are guided through using powerful tools of communication to frame career accomplishments.

■ *The Career Adventure Café* is a unique social networking tool that leverages the power of peer interaction and engagement to inform and encourage career development and enables students to work collaboratively to move toward individual goals. The CA Café is an option created through Facebook that invites students into a shared adventure in which they pool their experiences and pace one another's progress. It allows students to support each other through the difficulties and celebrate the successes.

■ *The modular format* allows students to focus on the aspect of career development most important to their immediate growth.

Choosing a career is an exciting process of self-discovery. It draws you out into the world to explore careers and sets your path with decisions that will result in insight, growth, and reward. This journey is most fulfilling when undertaken with a belief in yourself, a willingness to risk, and a sense of humor! The adventure does not end when a career is chosen—the career is always a work in progress and continues to change as the adventurer grows and changes.

The most important resource in any career adventure is you—the person who explores new vistas and makes the career choice. *The Career Adventure: Your Guide to Personal Assessment, Career Exploration, and Decision Making, Fifth Edition*, is designed to actively engage readers in planning their own careers. The exercises and activities found throughout the book make the adventure an interactive one; you are encouraged to consider thoughtfully each step of the journey, building confidence as you see your decisions yield results. This edition expands the process to include the power of social networking, connecting each person as part of a unique collaborative community supporting the goals of each member.

The book is divided into three parts. Part One, "Self-Assessment: Learning About Yourself," focuses on self-knowledge and discovery. Students explore career dreams, motivations, values, life stages, abilities and skills, personality, and interests. In this edition, the opportunity to share aspects of the assessment process offers a way of expanding your understanding of who you are and how you function in the world. Examining these areas begins the process of discernment that is critical to making a meaningful career choice.

Part Two, "Career Exploration: Learning About the World of Work," guides you through the career market and trends and investigates government resources and other publications. Important discussions of networking and decision making and "trying out" careers, accompanied by practical exercises, help readers set goals and then formulate plans and develop skills to achieve those goals. Throughout, you can leverage the power of social networking to expand your world and reach out beyond the limits of conventional career and job exploration through digital connections.

Part Three, "The Job Campaign: Organizing Your Search," looks at the job search, examining the details of resume writing, interviewing, and marketing skills. You will have an immediate opportunity to apply new skills when working through the exercises. Even students who do not plan to enter the full-time job market immediately will benefit greatly from the information in Part Three. The power of social networking is fully available in this section of this edition by connecting you to sources of information and forging relationships that will jump-start your search for the right career opportunity, the right opportunity for growth as a professional.

This fifth edition of *The Career Adventure* takes a fresh look at the adventure of career planning and the influence of technology and globalization on the process and landscape of career development. Perhaps no field has been influenced as profoundly by the explosion of information and digital tools as has career planning. Finding information is easy. Indeed, we're buried in data. Developing the critical-thinking skill to understand your priorities and move decisively is at the core of the fifth edition.

All of the resources available from prior editions are amplified in this edition with a new and powerful option—the use of social networking tools to connect and expand your range as you move through the phases of career development. Options to create social networking sites individually and as a class connect you to your fellow students and to the people outside the class as allies and sources of information for development and decision making. Whether you are a digital native or a digital immigrant adapting to the new methods of connecting, you will find tools to help you navigate self-assessment, career exploration, and job seeking with help from Facebook, LinkedIn, Twitter, and a number of information outlets. As in prior editions, search techniques that minimize "Web wandering" are included. This precludes the temptation on the part of career explorers and job seekers to stray from the main path and avoid information cul-de-sacs.

The economic meltdown that reconfigured the career landscape has left an impact on our understanding of jobs in the United States. Careers have become increasingly volatile, and the ability to gather data and analyze information will become more and more important in influencing career decisions. The transition from an amped-up growth economy to a job marketplace fraught with uncertainty left many career and job seekers feeling anxious and uncertain. The challenge to take responsibility for managing your own career has never been greater nor has it required more intelligent evaluation of career data and economic trends. The global economy and the technology that fuels information transfer will continue to influence the factors that create jobs and wealth. The fifth edition of *The Career Adventure* emphasizes the use of analytical skills and digital connectivity to make your own success in a volatile marketplace. Practicing the skills associated with this model will put you miles ahead of your career competition. This edition builds on step-by-step growth, with practical guides that allow you to progress in a calm, self-directed way toward your goal, aware of economic swings, but far from intimidated by them. And the connections and relationships you build now will be a resource on which you can rely as you continue your career.

Suggestions for group discussions appear throughout the book, giving you the opportunity to interact with peers, instructors, administrators, and the community both face to face and in digital space. Internet resources and pertinent digital content are offered throughout the book to expand your information base and help you take full advantage of electronic resources, necessary skills in today's career/job marketplace. This real-world exchange connects the classroom to the larger world, in preparation for the actual job campaign and career demands.

The world around us plays a dramatic and constantly changing role in our career adventures. However, it is the adventurer who guides the journey and determines the outcome. Recognizing what information is needed, knowing how and where it can be found, and understanding what can be done with it are the keys to achieving any and every goal. *The Career Adventure* was written to help you acquire the skill and confidence to see the goal and achieve it!

ACKNOWLEDGMENTS

This book could not have become a reality without the generous support and encouragement of the following people. I would like to thank them for their efforts.

Dr. Lamarr Reese, Terry Maiwurm, and Leonard Banks supported the development of particular ideas for the book. Brenda Krueger and M.L. Smith shared with me ideas about personality development, and I would like to extend my deepest appreciation to LaDon McFadgen, Chrystan Coleman, and Tony Allen, who were invaluable in helping me more fully understand the significance of diversity in career issues. A big thank-you goes to Bruce Anderson for guidance on electronic transmission of resumes. My thanks also go to Jon Sargent at the Bureau of Labor Statistics for assistance with labor trends data.

My thanks to the following career-planning professionals for their generous guidance: Dr. Ana C. Berrios-Allison, The Ohio State University; Sheryl S. Ken, Wright State University; and Dr. Stephen Richey-Suttles, University of Dayton. I would also like to thank Del Vaughan and Dr. Priscilla Mutter for the opportunity to work with them in serving students. My special thanks to Dr. Jean Cook Purcell for her active promotion and support of my goals and her continuing belief in me.

I am very grateful to the following reviewers, who read this material in various stages of its development and offered ideas as to how it might be improved: Dr. Carolyn W. Kern, University of North Texas; Lance Erickson, Idaho State University; Allison Kay Bell, Ivy Tech Community College; Roselie Bambrey, Ivy Tech Community College; Dr. Kevin J. Jones, Ivy Tech Community College; Mikel J. Johnson, Emporia State University; Carole J. Wentzel, Orange County Community College; Jan L. Brakefield, University of Alabama; Pat Joachim Kitzman, Central College; Eve Madigan, Los Angeles Trade Technical College; Dave Sonenberg, Southeast Community College; Pablo Cardona, Milwaukee Area Technical College; Katy Kemeny, Lansing Community College; Cliff Nelson, Hinds Community College; and Maria Mitchell, Reading Area Community College. Students will find the book more readable and more helpful as a result of their efforts.

I would also like to thank Jodi McPherson, Katie Mahan, Beth Houston, Lauren Hill, Erin Carreiro, Sande Johnson, Susan Kauffman, Susan Hannahs, JoEllen Gohr, and Gay Pauley for their guidance and support as editors and production coordinators of this book and its preceding editions.

I would like to thank my parents, Claude and Marcia Kelnofer, for instilling in me a strong work ethic and a basic respect for all types of work and my husband, Jack Johnston, whose loving support and belief in me has sustained me for the past 30 years.

Introduction

Welcome to the exciting, chaotic process of career decision making! We are all involved in our own real-life career adventure. We are constantly challenged to understand more deeply who we are and what we are looking for in our lives and our careers. This process of choosing a career is an adventure—a discovery of *who you are*. Understanding yourself is an important aspect of growing and becoming an adult in our culture. The real you has a voice that seeks expression in a variety of ways, one of which is through your career.

A career is a primary path for personal growth, a way to define and expand yourself at the same time. It is a source of economic support, emotional strength, and a means for self-discovery. Making a career choice involves finding an arena that will meet your needs and offer you opportunities for continuing growth.

This book offers a model for career development. It will guide you through the process of career decision making and start you on the path toward a satisfying career. The steps in this process are summarized below:

- *Self-Assessment:* Learning about you, your motivations, values, skills, interests. You are the starting point in your career development.

- *Career Exploration:* Finding out about the world of work and how you might fit into careers that interest you. This step involves taking a look at careers and the job market.

- *The Job Campaign:* Preparing yourself for available opportunities and the challenges of entering the world of work.

Achieving your career goals requires organization and preparation. Let's start by taking a closer look at the process you will use as you begin your journey.

SELF-ASSESSMENT

In the first three chapters you will begin the exciting and challenging process of self-assessment. The self-assessment process is similar to exploring a room in which there are a huge number of interesting objects, all related to one another, like pieces of a puzzle. As you wander through the room, you see that each object represents some aspect of your life. You may recognize many of the objects from past experiences. Some of them may prompt memories of joy, sorrow, satisfaction, or any number of emotions. Some may evoke no feelings at all, but may simply reflect something about yourself that you have always known and accepted. Whatever your reaction, you realize that each of these things is a part of you and has contributed to who you are now and to what you may eventually become.

Making career decisions begins in almost the same fashion. You examine aspects of your life, values, personality, motivations, interests, and skills in order to understand yourself better. Once you have assessed your needs and interests, you will then identify occupations and careers that correspond with those needs and interests. Finding out more about potential occupations and careers is the next phase of career decision making.

CAREER EXPLORATION

After discovering what careers most appeal to you, the next step is to learn as much as you can about them. In Chapters 4, 5, and 6, you will learn how to research the career market and explore available jobs. Most career information resources are now available digitally. A key aspect of this edition of *The Career Adventure* is the opportunity to work together with other people who are seeking information about careers through social networking relationships. The links of social networking are embedded throughout the book and offer ways to inform your experience as your process informs others in your network. In addition, you will obtain much useful information by networking with professionals who have firsthand knowledge of the field in which you have an interest.

Networking for career information gives you an inside look at a career and the people who have chosen that discipline before you have to make a commitment to that career. Through networking with professionals, you begin to develop your own set of contacts, some of whom may remain a valuable resource throughout your work life. Ways to "try out" a career before making a final decision are presented as well.

At this point in a career adventure, you will be ready to make concrete decisions about your career and begin to commit more formally to your career goal.

YOUR JOB CAMPAIGN

Chapters 7, 8, and 9 cover the tools and techniques for organizing a job-search campaign that will lead you to the career of your choice. Having knowledge and skills in a particular field is only one component of career success. In addition, you will learn how to showcase your abilities so that when you begin your job search, you will have a competitive edge. A well-written resume, an organized marketing campaign taking advantage of conventional and digital search tools, and a comfortable interviewing style all are proven methods for job marketability.

The final chapter encourages you to rely on this career planning model as a resource for your continuing development as a professional and member of your community.

Finding your career is a lifelong process—increased self-awareness and knowledge of this process allow you to grow, learn, gain insights, and make satisfying decisions as your career unfolds.

BEGINNING THE ADVENTURE

Learning about yourself and the work world, researching options, making decisions, developing the resilience and flexibility to adapt with changes—all of these steps are challenging and may create anxiety for many people. It may feel at times as if you are about to leap off a cliff into the unknown. Make up your mind that you are *ready* to jump into your career adventure. As you do, your strength and confidence will increase because you know:

- *You will be doing everything possible to ensure a soft landing.* You will do the homework and the research, and you will feel secure with the information that you gain. You are a bright person who is learning to make the right choices. You are ready and well prepared.

- *Even if your worst fears become reality and you are not satisfied with your choice or the field changes in ways you couldn't predict, you can always change your mind, reset your path, and keep going.* You will be prepared to handle any obstacle that comes along. Besides, you have plenty of time to "wiggle your way" toward your ultimate goal. Your effort now will put you ahead of the game later.

And remember . . . this is an adventure! The freedom to examine who you are and the world in which you live and then to move toward a personal goal is a precious privilege—one that countless people around the world would risk everything to have. Ever since we were children, we've all been asked, "What do you want to be when you grow up?" That question presumes free choice and its accompanying responsibilities. Cherish the freedom and excitement that this discovery process offers you. Whether you are 18 or 50, the career choices you make are the living reflections of who you are. Yes, the process may be chaotic and confusing at times. But it is the adventure of your lifetime. Go after it and enjoy the freedom and fun of *your* career!

COLLEGE CAREER PLANNING YEAR BY YEAR

FRESHMAN YEAR		COLLEGE RESOURCES	CAREER ADVENTURE
Academic Activities	▪ Take a variety of courses, explore various majors	Academic Advisor	Ch. 4
	▪ Visit the campus career center	Career Center	Ch. 4
	▪ Learn the basics of the Career Planning Model	Career Center	All Chs.
Campus Community	▪ Research volunteer opportunities	Student Activities	Ch. 4
	▪ Join a club or an organization	Student Activities	Ch. 4
	▪ Get involved in service learning	Academic Advisor	Ch. 4
Networking Activities	▪ Get to know professors, advisors	Academic Depts.	Ch. 5
	▪ Interact with upperclassmen, classmates	Resident Hall/ Clubs/Classes	Ch. 5
	▪ Create Facebook page for your Career Adventure and visit the CA Café	Online Community/ CA Café	All Chs.
Career Activities	▪ Investigate career blogs, Twitter feeds like Career Rookie	Career Center	Ch. 5
	▪ Attend career fairs throughout the year	Career Center	Ch. 4
	▪ Begin summer job search in early spring	Career Center	Chs. 7–9
Personal Activities	▪ Explore values, skills, and interests	Career Center	Chs. 2–3
	▪ Schedule time on computerized guidance systems	Career Center	Chs. 2–3
	▪ Identify preferences through personality assessments	Career Center	Ch. 3
	▪ Recognize skills necessary to success in the workplace	Career Center	Ch. 3
	▪ Develop behaviors expected in the workplace (i.e., punctuality, reliability, and conscientiousness)	Career Center	Ch. 4
	▪ Broaden your vocabulary	Library	All Chs.
	▪ Develop good personal management skills	Resident Advisor	

SOPHOMORE YEAR		COLLEGE RESOURCES	CAREER ADVENTURE
Academic Activities	▪ Continue strong academic work and curriculum planning	Academic Advisor	All Chs.
	▪ Consider a study abroad program option	Academic Advisor	Ch. 4
	▪ Learn about the world of work	Career Center	Ch. 4
	▪ Decide on a college major	Career Center	Ch. 4
Campus Community	▪ Play a larger role in campus groups	Student Activities	Ch. 4
	▪ Continue volunteer activities	Student Activities	Ch. 4
Networking Activities	▪ Continue to build working relationships with faculty and staff	Academic Advisor	Ch. 5
	▪ Start a list of prior/current contacts who may be available as possible sponsors or mentors in the future	Career Center	Ch. 5
	▪ Start gathering letters of recommendation	Career Center, All Contacts	Ch. 5
	▪ Use your Facebook page to share your Career Adventure	Online Community/ CA Café	All Chs.
College	▪ Begin narrowing career focus to three industries, three jobs, three places	Career Center	Ch. 6
	▪ Meet with co-op coordinator to explore internship/co-op opportunities	Co-op Office	Ch. 4
	▪ Write a resume	Career Center	Ch. 7
	▪ Learn about interviewing and practice good interview techniques	Career Center	Ch. 8
	▪ Explore graduate school options	Academic Advisor	Ch. 4
Personal Activities	▪ Continue to develop strong oral and written communication skills	Faculty	All Chs.
	▪ Broaden cultural perspectives	Student Activities	Chs. 4–5
	▪ Develop healthy life habits	Resident Advisor	Ch. 10

JUNIOR YEAR		COLLEGE RESOURCES	CAREER ADVENTURE
Academic Activities	▪ Meet with academic advisor to plan remaining curriculum choices	Academic Advisor	Chs. 4 & 6
	▪ Choose course electives that add value to your career goals	Academic Advisor	Ch. 4
	▪ Study abroad	Academic Advisor	Ch. 4
	▪ If planning on graduate school, register for graduate school admission tests	Graduate School Academic Advisor	Ch. 4

JUNIOR YEAR		COLLEGE RESOURCES	CAREER ADVENTURE
Campus Community	■ Assume leadership roles on campus	Student Activities	Chs. 4 & 10
Networking Activities	■ Join student affiliates of professional organizations	Academic Advisor	Ch. 5
	■ Read professional journals	Academic Advisor	Ch. 4
	■ Conduct informational interviews with professionals from college major advisory boards or community sources	Academic Advisor	Ch. 5
	■ Gather specific information about jobs or graduate schools	Academic Advisor	Ch. 5
	■ Use your Facebook page to share your Career Adventure	Online Community/ CA Café	All Chs.
Career Activities	■ Attend career workshops/career fairs	Career Center	Chs. 5–9
	■ Develop effective job-search strategies	Career Center	Chs. 7–9
	■ Participate in internship opportunities	Career Center	Chs. 4
Personal Activities	■ Learn about and practice proper interview/ professional etiquette	Career Center/ Library	Ch. 8
	■ Continue honing written and oral communication skills	Faculty	All Chs.
	■ Exercise solid decision-making/problem-solving and critical-thinking skills	Resident Advisor Faculty	Ch. 6
	■ Manage time effectively	Faculty	Ch. 6
	■ Begin developing a professional wardrobe	Career Center	Ch. 8

SENIOR YEAR		COLLEGE RESOURCES	CAREER ADVENTURE
Academic Activities	■ If attending graduate school, apply in fall term	Grad/Professional Academic Advisor	Ch. 7
	■ Strengthen GPA	Faculty	All Chs.
Campus Community	■ Continue to offer leadership in clubs and student organizations	Student Activities	Chs. 4 & 10
	■ Mentor underclass leaders	Student Activities	Ch. 5
Networking Activities	■ Ask faculty, professional contacts, alumni to act as references	Faculty Academic Advisor	Ch. 5
	■ Interview former graduates who are employed in a field of interest	Career Center	Ch. 5
	■ Continue your Career Adventure Facebook page	Online Community/ CA Café	All Chs.
	■ Create a LinkedIn profile with a professional picture	Online	Ch. 5

SENIOR YEAR		COLLEGE RESOURCES	CAREER ADVENTURE
Career Activities	■ Polish your resume, job-search letters, and interview skills	Career Center	Chs. 7 & 8
	■ Have your resume critiqued by a career professional	Career Center	Ch. 7
	■ Conduct your full-time job search in the fall term	Career Center	Ch. 9
	■ Attend job, career, and graduate school fairs	Career Center	Chs. 5 & 8
	■ Send thank-you notes to anyone who has assisted you	Career Center	Ch. 7
Personal Activities	■ Adopt professional behavior	Career Center	Chs. 9 & 10
	■ Continue to expand your career wardrobe	Career Center	Ch. 8
	■ Budget for job search, travel, relocation	Career Center	
	■ Engage techniques for stress management, exercise, and healthy living	Academic Advisor	Ch. 6
	■ Celebrate your successes with those who have assisted you	Career Center	Ch. 10

BREAKTHROUGH
To better results

Give your students what they need to succeed.

As an instructor, you want to help your students succeed in college. As a mentor, you want to make sure students reach their professional objectives. We share these goals, and we're committed to partnering with educators to ensure that each individual student succeeds—in college and beyond.

Simply put, Pearson creates technologies, content, and services that help students break through to better results. When a goal as important as education is at stake, no obstacle should be allowed to stand in the way.

The following pages detail some of our products and services designed to help your students succeed. These include:

- Pearson Course Redesign

- MyFoundationsLab for Student Success

- MyStudentSuccessLab

- CourseConnect™

- Custom Services

- Resources for Students

- Professional Development for Instructors

Pearson Course Redesign

Collect, measure, and interpret data to support efficacy.

Rethink the way you deliver instruction.

Pearson has successfully partnered with colleges and universities engaged in course redesign for over 10 years through workshops, Faculty Advisor programs, and online conferences. Here's how to get started!

- Visit our course redesign site at **www.pearsoncourseredesign.com** for information on getting started, a list of Pearson-sponsored course redesign events, and recordings of past course redesign events.

- Request to connect with a Faculty Advisor, a fellow instructor who is an expert in course redesign, by visiting **www.mystudentsuccesslab.com/community**.

- Join our Course Redesign Community at **www.community.pearson.com/courseredesign** and connect with colleagues around the country who are participating in course redesign projects.

Don't forget to measure the results of your course redesign!

Examples of data you may want to collect include:

- Improvement of homework grades, test averages, and pass rates over past semesters

- Correlation between time spent in an online product and final average in the course

- Success rate in the next level of the course

- Retention rate (i.e., percentage of students who drop, fail, or withdraw)

Need support for data collection and interpretation?

Ask your local Pearson representative how to connect with a member of Pearson's Efficacy Team.

MyFoundationsLab for Student Success

Prepare your students for college-level work in basic skills.

MyFoundationsLab®

Built on the success of MyMathLab, MyReadingLab, and MyWritingLab, **MyFoundationsLab** is a comprehensive online mastery-based resource for assessing and remediating college- and career-readiness skills in mathematics, reading, and writing. The system offers a rich environment of pre-built and customized assessments, personalized learning plans, and highly interactive activities that enable students to master skills at their own pace. Ideal for learners of various levels and ages, including those in placement test prep or transitional programs, MyFoundationsLab facilitates the skill development students need in order to be successful in college-level courses and careers.

New! MyFoundationsLab for Student Success

In response to market demand for more "non-cognitive" skills, Pearson now offers **MyFoundationsLab for Student Success**, which combines rich mathematics, reading, and writing content with the 19+ MyStudentSuccessLab modules that support ongoing personal and professional development. To see a complete list of content, visit **www.mystudentsuccesslab.com/mfl**.

If you're affiliated with boot camp programs, student orientation, a testing center, or simply interested in a self-paced, pre-course solution that helps students better prepare for college-level work in basic skills, contact your Pearson representative for more information.

"Students like learning at their own pace; they can go as fast or as slow as they need. MyFoundationsLab facilitates this structure; it's more driven by mastery learning, not by what the teacher says a student should be doing."

—Jennifer McLearen, Instructor,
Piedmont Virginia Community College

Data from January 2007 through June 2008 offers solid evidence of the success of MyFoundationsLab:

91% of students who retested in reading improved at least one course level

70% of students who retested in writing improved at least one course level

43% of students who retested in math improved at least one course level

MyStudentSuccessLab

Help students start strong and finish stronger.

MyStudentSuccessLab™

MyStudentSuccessLab helps students acquire the skills they need for ongoing personal and professional development. It is a learning-outcomes-based technology that helps students advance their knowledge and build critical skills for success. MyStudentSuccessLab's peer-led video interviews, interactive practice exercises, and activities foster the acquisition of academic, life, and professionalism skills.

Students have access to:

- Pre- and Post-Full Course Diagnostic Assessments linked to key learning objectives

- Pre- and Post-Tests dedicated to individual topics in the Learning Path

- An overview of objectives to build vocabulary and repetition

- Videos on key issues that are "by students, for students," conveniently organized by topic

- Practice exercises to improve class prep and learning

- Graded activities to build critical-thinking and problem-solving skills

- Student resources, including Finish Strong 24/7 YouTube videos, professionalism tools, research aids, writing help, and GPA, savings, budgeting, and retirement calculators

- Student Inventories designed to increase self-awareness, including Golden Personality and Thinking Styles

Students utilizing MyStudentSuccessLab may purchase Pearson texts in a number of cost-saving formats—including eTexts, loose-leaf Books à la Carte editions, and more. Contact your Pearson representative for more information.

Topics and features include:

- College Transition
- Communication
- Critical Thinking
- Financial Literacy
- Goal Setting
- Information Literacy
- Interviewing
- Job Search Strategies
- Learning Preferences
- Listening and Taking Notes in Class
- Majors/Careers and Resumes
- Memory and Studying
- Problem Solving
- Reading and Annotating
- Self-Management Skills at Work
- Stress Management
- Teamwork
- Test Taking
- Time Management
- Workplace Communication
- Workplace Etiquette

Assessment

Beyond the Pre- and Post-Full Course Diagnostic Assessments and Pre- and Post-Tests within each module, additional learning-outcome-based tests can be created using a secure testing engine, and may be printed or delivered online. These tests can be customized to accommodate specific teaching needs by editing individual questions or entire tests.

Reporting

Measurement matters—and is ongoing in nature. MyStudentSuccessLab lets you determine what data you need, set up your course accordingly, and collect data via reports. The high quality and volume of test questions allows for data comparison and measurement.

MyLabsPlus service is a teaching and learning environment that offers enhanced reporting features and analysis. With powerful administrative tools and dedicated support, MyLabsPlus offers an advanced suite of management resources for MyStudentSuccessLab.

Content and Functionality Training

Organized by topic, the **Instructor Implementation Guide** provides grading rubrics, suggestions for video use, and more to save time on course prep. Our **User Guide** and "**How do I…**" YouTube **videos** indicate how to use MyStudentSuccessLab, and show scenarios from getting started to utilizing the Gradebook.

Peer Support

The **Student Success Community** site is a place for you to connect with other educators to exchange ideas and advice on courses, content, and MyStudentSuccessLab. The site is filled with timely articles, discussions, video posts, and more. Join, share, and be inspired!
www.mystudentsuccesscommunity.com

The **Faculty Advisor Network** is Pearson's peer-to-peer mentoring program in which experienced MyStudentSuccessLab users share their best practices and expertise. Our Faculty Advisors are experienced in one-on-one phone and email coaching, webinars, presentations, and live training sessions. Contact your Pearson representative to connect with a Faculty Advisor or learn more about the Faculty Advisor Network.

Integration and Compliance

You can integrate our digital solutions with your learning management system in a variety of ways. For more information, or if documentation is needed for ADA compliance, contact your local Pearson representative.

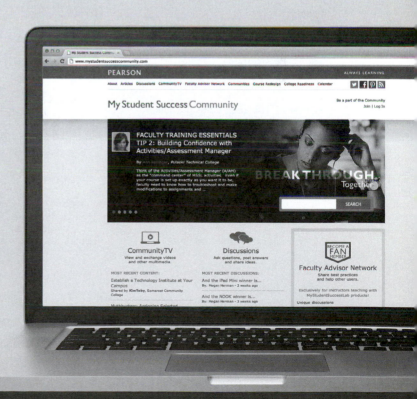

CourseConnect™
Trust that your online course is the best in its class.

Designed by subject matter experts and credentialed instructional designers, **CourseConnect** offers award-winning customizable online courses that help students build skills for ongoing personal and professional development.

CourseConnect uses topic-based, interactive modules that follow a consistent learning path—from introduction, to presentation, to activity, to review. Its built-in tools—including user-specific pacing charts, personalized study guides, and interactive exercises—provide a student-centric learning experience that minimizes distractions and helps students stay on track and complete the course successfully. Features such as relevant video, audio, and activities, personalized (or editable) syllabi, discussion forum topics and questions, assignments, and quizzes are all easily accessible. CourseConnect is available in a variety of learning management systems and accommodates various term lengths as well as self-paced study. And, our compact textbook editions align to CourseConnect course outcomes.

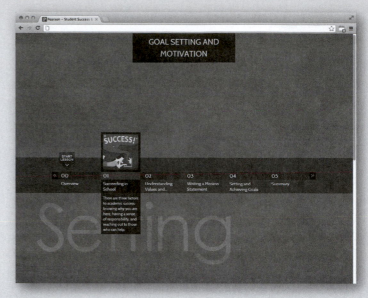

Choose from the following three course outlines ("Lesson Plans")

Student Success

- Goal Setting, Values, and Motivation
- Time Management
- Financial Literacy
- Creative Thinking, Critical Thinking, and Problem Solving
- Learning Preferences
- Listening and Note-Taking in Class
- Reading and Annotating
- Studying, Memory, and Test-Taking
- Communicating and Teamwork
- Information Literacy
- Staying Balanced: Stress Management
- Career Exploration

Career Success

- Planning Your Career Search
- Knowing Yourself: Explore the Right Career Path
- Knowing the Market: Find Your Career Match
- Preparing Yourself: Gain Skills and Experience Now
- Networking
- Targeting Your Search: Locate Positions, Ready Yourself
- Building a Portfolio: Your Resume and Beyond
- Preparing for Your Interview
- Giving a Great Interview
- Negotiating Job Offers, Ensuring Future Success

Professional Success

- Introducing Professionalism
- Workplace Goal Setting
- Workplace Ethics and Your Career
- Workplace Time Management
- Interpersonal Skills at Work
- Workplace Conflict Management
- Workplace Communications: Email and Presentations
- Effective Workplace Meetings
- Workplace Teams
- Customer Focus and You
- Understanding Human Resources
- Managing Career Growth and Change

Custom Services
Personalize instruction to best facilitate learning.

As the industry leader in custom publishing, we are committed to meeting your instructional needs by offering flexible and creative choices for course materials that will maximize learning and student engagement.

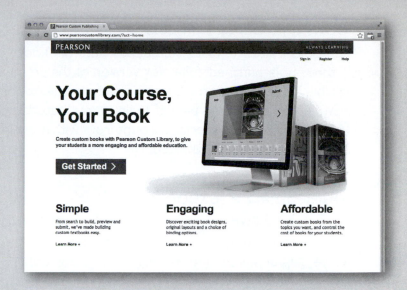

Pearson Custom Library

Using our online book-building system, create a custom book by selecting content from our course-specific collections that consist of chapters from Pearson Student Success and Career Development titles and carefully selected, copyright-cleared, third-party content and pedagogy. www.pearsoncustomlibrary.com

Custom Publications

In partnership with your Custom Field Editor, modify, adapt, and combine existing Pearson books by choosing content from across the curriculum and organizing it around your learning outcomes. As an alternative, you can work with your Editor to develop your original material and create a textbook that meets your course goals.

Custom Technology Solutions

Work with Pearson's trained professionals, in a truly consultative process, to create engaging learning solutions. From interactive learning tools, to eTexts, to custom websites and portals, we'll help you simplify your life as an instructor.

Online Education

Pearson offers online course content for online classes and hybrid courses. This online content can also be used to enhance traditional classroom courses. Our award-winning CourseConnect includes a fully developed syllabus, media-rich lecture presentations, audio lectures, a wide variety of assessments, discussion board questions, and a strong instructor resource package.

For more information on custom Student Success services, please visit **www.pearsonlearningsolutions.com** or call **800-777-6872**.

Resources for Students

Help students save and succeed throughout their college experience.

Books à la Carte Editions

The Books à la Carte (a.k.a. "Student Value" or "Loose Leaf") edition is a three-hole-punched, full-color version of the premium text that's available at 35% less than the traditional bound textbook. Students using MyStudentSuccessLab as part of their course materials can purchase a Books à la Carte edition at a special discount from within the MyLab course where "Click here to order" is denoted.

CourseSmart eTexbooks

CourseSmart eTextbooks offer a convenient, affordable alternative to printed texts. Students can save up to 50% off the price of a traditional text, and receive helpful search, note-taking, and printing tools.

Programs and Services

As the world's leading learning company, Pearson has pledged to help students succeed in college and reach their educational and career aspirations. We're so dedicated to this goal that we've created a unique set of programs and services that we call **Pearson Students**. Through this program, we offer undergraduate students opportunities to learn from, and interact with, each other and Pearson professionals through social media platforms, internships, part-time jobs, leadership endeavors, events, and awards. To learn more about our Pearson Students programs and meet our Pearson Students, visit **www.pearsonstudents.com**.

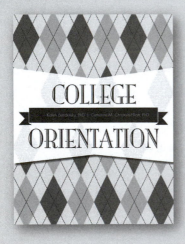

Orientation to College

In Bendersky's *College Orientation,* students learn how to adapt to college life and stay on track towards a degree—all while learning behaviors that promote achievement after graduation. This reference tool is written from an insider's point of view and has a distinct focus on promoting appropriate college conduct. It covers topics that help students navigate college while learning how to apply this knowledge in the workplace.

Help with Online Classes

Barrett's *Power Up: A Practical Student's Guide to Online Learning, 2/e* serves as a textbook for students of all backgrounds who are new to online learning, and as a reference for instructors who are also novices in the area or who need insight into the perspective of such students.

Effective Communication with Professors

In Ellen Bremen's *Say This, NOT That to Your Professor*, an award-winning, tenured communication professor takes students "inside the faculty mind," and guides them to manage their classroom experience with confidence. This book aims to facilitate improved relationships with professors, better grades, and an amazing college experience.

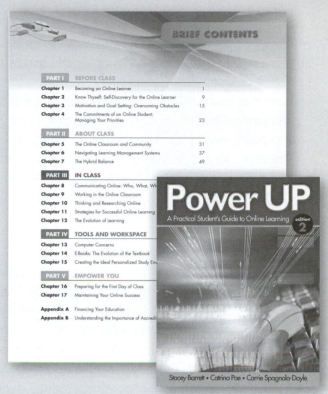

Power UP
A Practical Student's Guide to Online Learning   edition 2

Stacey Barrett • Catrina Poe • Carrie Spagnola-Doyle

Expert Advice

Our consumer-flavored *IDentity* series booklets are written by national subject-matter experts, such as personal finance specialist, author, and TV personality, Farnoosh Torabi. The authors of this series offer strategies and activities on topics such as careers, college success, financial literacy, financial responsibility, and more.

Quick Tips for Success

Our *Success Tips* series provides one-page "quick tips" on six topics essential to college or career success. The *Success Tips* series includes MyStudentSuccessLab, Time Management, Resources All Around You, Now You're Thinking, Maintaining Your Financial Sanity, and Building Your Professional Image. The *Success Tips for Professionalism* series includes Create Your Personal Brand, Civility Paves the Way Toward Success, Succeeding in Your Diverse World, Building Your Professional Image, Get Things Done with Virtual Teams, and Get Ready for Workplace Success.

Professional Development for Instructors

Augment your teaching with engaging resources.

Foster Ownership

Student dynamics have changed, so how are you helping students take ownership of their education? Megan Stone's *Ownership* series offers online courses for instructors, and printed booklets for students, on four key areas of professional development: accountability, critical thinking, effective planning, and study strategies. The instructor courses, in our CourseConnect online format, include teaching methods, activities, coaching tips, assessments, animations, and video. Online courses and printed booklets are available together or separately.

Promote Active Learning

Infuse student success into any program with our *Engaging Activities* series. Written and compiled by National Student Success Institute (NSSI®) co-founders Amy Baldwin, Steve Piscitelli, and Robert Sherfield, the material provides educators strategies, procedural information, and activities they can use with students immediately. Amy, Steve, and Robb developed these practical booklets as indispensable, hands-on resources for educators who want to empower teachers, professional development coordinators, coaches, and administrators to actively engage their classes.

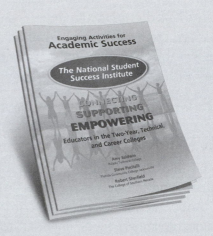

Address Diverse Populations

Support various student populations that require specific strategies to succeed. Choose from an array of booklets that align with the needs of adult learners, digital learners, first-generation learners, international learners, English language learners, student athletes, and more.

Create Consistency

Instructional resources lend a common foundation for support. We offer **online Instructor's Manuals** that provide a framework of ideas and suggestions for online and in-class activities and journal writing assignments. We also offer comprehensive **online PowerPoint presentations** that can be used by instructors for class presentations, and by students to preview lecture material and review concepts within each chapter.

Self-Assessment

The only place to start the career adventure is with *you*. Knowing as much as possible about yourself is critical to the decisions you make in the future. This is your chance to discover and appreciate the things that make you a unique individual.

The adventure begins by examining different areas of your life and experiences, with the goal of making any fuzzy and vague aspects more real and concrete. These components of who you are will gain meaning as you learn to relate them to your everyday life and translate them into possible career choices. Self-assessment reveals who you are more clearly. Then you can connect with a career that brings you meaning and fulfillment.

LEARNING ABOUT YOURSELF

PART ONE

Creating Your Dream 1

To start, let's dream a bit . . .

Your dreams, fantasies, hopes, or whatever you wish to call them, are essential elements in career decision making. You may have met people who say, "I've wanted to be a nurse (teacher, doctor, writer, and so on) ever since I was a child and here I am, and I love every minute of it." Sometimes it's that simple. Some lucky people have a dream or a vision of what they want to be. They pursue it and make it happen.

Think back for a minute about the dreams you had as a child. What did you see yourself doing as an adult? What did you dream about?

Jot down the idea(s) that you recall. How does it feel to think back to a time when anything seemed possible—a time before other responsibilities and obstacles may have eclipsed your dreams and made them unrealistic?

Do those dreams still appeal to you? Do they hold the same promise and excitement that they did when you were younger? Are they still possible as career choices? Or have you lost interest in the career that at one time seemed like the right one? Have you changed? Has the career you dreamt of changed?

WHO ARE YOU? WHO WOULD YOU LIKE TO BE?

A few years ago I worked with Jack, a young man who was struggling to decide whether to attend college or to find a job after high school. Jack had many interests and could not zero in on one specific career area. Finally I asked him just to imagine what he would do if he could do *anything at all*. He kind of snorted and said, "That's easy. I'd like to be a baseball player for the New York Yankees." His natural response revealed that he enjoyed athletics and competition. Now we had to identify some options that might utilize those strengths in the unglamorous world of everyday life. "Well," I ventured, "if you couldn't do that, then what else do you think you might like?" He said, "I could play football for the New England Patriots."

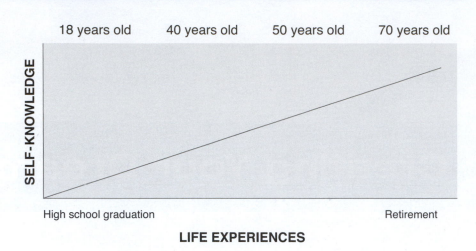

EXHIBIT 1.1   18-year-old's work life span.

Jack's dreams were understandable but probably unrealistic. He was focused on an idealized vision of himself, which made it hard for him to translate that vision into real-life terms.

Dreams allow us to see all the possibilities that exist within us. They give us insights into our true selves and what we want to be. Although it is enjoyable to imagine ourselves as superheroes, using our unique gifts to bring ourselves and others fulfillment, it is perhaps more important to identify realistic goals that encompass at least a *piece* of the dream. If you can't be Tom Brady, perhaps you can coach or perform in another athletic setting and still find satisfaction. You might discover that being a recreation manager or a trainer for a professional team would satisfy some aspects of your dream.

Exhibit 1.1 shows that at age 18, with luck, you can look forward to a career that may extend to the ripe old age of 70, allowing you over fifty years to get in touch with your true self. Inherent in that process is having time to make choices, rethink those choices, and possibly change them to achieve more satisfying outcomes—living and learning. Today an added dimension—the rapid rate of change in our culture—ensures that you will be challenged to reinvent yourself in new ways and in new professions to keep up with competition in the labor force. The trick is to keep your eye on the dream while learning and working with it so that it reflects your evolving identity.

I have also worked with people in their forties or fifties. People in this age range can expect to work for twenty to thirty more years. Older workers also have an advantage over 18-year-olds. They have lived long enough to have developed a sense of themselves, which helps them understand their needs, interests, and goals if they wish to seek a new career. In many cases, they have faced challenges in the course of their careers that have tested them and helped them acquire qualities of adaptability and resilience, which will serve them as they navigate the next transition.

Sometimes, however, their insight may be clouded. Many people who look for new careers later in life have often spent a great deal of time putting other people's needs first. Single parents, homemakers, adults with dependents, and people who were raised to be model children frequently struggle to discern what they want and how they feel, because they are unaccustomed to putting their *own* feelings first.

It may be difficult for you, too, to put aside the needs of those you love for the moment, but it is crucial, at least for the initial phase of the career decision-making process, that you allow yourself to be as free as possible to consider every option and every dream. Throughout the book, you will have ample opportunity to identify obstacles and to develop strategies for overcoming them. For now, your primary task is to look honestly at your needs and hopes and translate those into goals that will help you find meaning and fulfillment.

One final word. Now is not the time to start tallying your limitations and numbering the obstacles. Psychologists tell us that the ability to cope with and succeed in achieving our goals is fostered by resilience founded in hardiness. Hardiness is a perspective which is comprised by three qualities:

- *Commitment*—a belief that the things that you are involved in have meaning and value;
- *Control*—a belief that, of all the factors that influence the outcomes in your life, you have the greatest power in shaping those outcomes;
- *Challenge*—a belief that, even if problems or obstacles prevent the smooth progress toward a goal, you are capable of overcoming the obstacles and learning from the experiences so that you can be prepared for whatever life holds.

These qualities can be nurtured by supportive guidance and encouragement to persevere no matter what. The very fact that you have chosen to examine the issues related to careers and your own growth shows you are committed to engaging in your future in a meaningful, significant way. According to the most recent research in this area, successful career choice is more feasible when you approach the tasks associated with career decision making with hardy perspectives and can-do motivation. This will be your starting point as you move toward your goals, adapting as circumstances require you to respond to an increasingly unstable career landscape. The course you have selected will help you develop the abilities necessary to survive and move toward growth and success.

Take a Closer Look 1.1

CAREER ADVENTURE CAFÉ: A NEW CONCEPT FOR CAREER SUCCESS

This edition of *The Career Adventure* suggests a new approach to achieving your goal, one that is founded on working together with a group that is facing the same challenges and has the goal of making career decisions. From among your own group of friends and associates or from the people who are walking this path with you in your class, come together with them in the Career Adventure Café, or the CA Café. This will be the group you turn to, work with, and, in turn, support as you move toward your goals. So, now, stand up and look around and see who would like to join you in the CA Café. Once you have formed, stand by for further instructions. More to follow.

Facebook It

If you don't already have a Facebook page, now is the time to start one. Better yet, start a Facebook page that showcases your Career Adventure. Or have your CA Café start its own Facebook page. The page might reflect each stage, from self-assessment to job search. Use it to archive documents, pictures, notes, and thoughts and to ask friends, network contacts, and mentors to weigh in. Be creative with the space. Schedule CA Café events and keep each other motivated. This is the start of a new chapter, and it deserves to be documented and shared so you can celebrate your successes and support each other through your challenges. Get started by coming up with a great name for your launch on your Career Adventure! Keep your Facebook posts career related and make sure you are not posting information that is highly personal or that may reflect badly during your search for a job.

Discovering Yourself 2

MOTIVATIONS, LIFE STAGES, AND VALUES

Very likely, you are in the middle of the lifelong process of discovering who you are—not the person your parents want you to be, not the person your spouse and close friends think you should be, not the person your kids expect you to be, but the person you *are*. Self-discovery is a complicated process with no simple formula. It is the first and most important step in determining your career goals.

The assessment model presented here begins a process that in many ways will be self-propelling. Once you begin, you may find that you need little prompting to continue. In this chapter you learn more about your *motivations*, *life stages*, and *values*. Chapter 3 explores your *abilities and skills*, *personality*, and *interests*.

Those of you who are younger may struggle a bit with some areas of self-assessment that you have not yet encountered. Those of you with broad life experience may be a bit overwhelmed as you sort through the various aspects of your life. Change always involves some discomfort and anxiety. These are only the starting points from which you will begin your self-exploration. So be patient with yourself.

MOTIVATIONS: WHAT DRIVES YOU?

Motivations are the forces that move you to form goals and strive to achieve them. You may have heard high achievers referred to as being "on fire" or a "fast burner," images that depict someone consumed by the passion to reach a goal. Motivations are the "fire" or fuel that drives you forward.

Clearly, not all of us are motivated with the same amount of drive or by the same things. Some of us struggle just to get up in the morning, while others drive themselves to the brink. Much of what motivates us originates in where we are psychologically and culturally.

EXHIBIT 2.1	Maslow's Hierarchy of Needs.

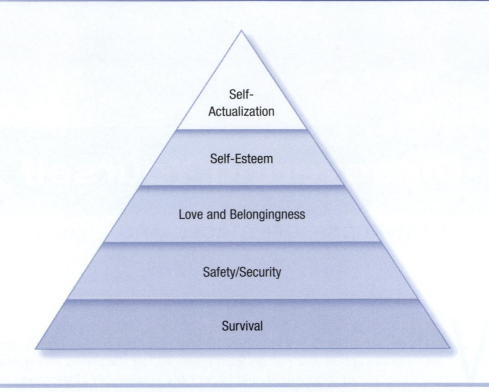

Source: Maslow, A. H., Frager, R., MOTIVATION AND PERSONALITY, 3/E, © 1987. Adapted by permission of Pearson Education, Upper Saddle River, New Jersey.

Abraham Maslow, a noted psychologist, developed a model that describes how needs influence motivations. Maslow's "Hierarchy of Needs" has been used for the past 40 years to explain what moves people and gives their actions meaning. The model is shown in Exhibit 2.1.

Maslow suggested that human nature requires us to have our needs met in a pattern resembling a "climb" up a pyramid to a peak. To advance to the higher levels of need, you must first satisfy the needs at the base.

Think of it this way: You are one of the first inhabitants of a scarcely populated region of Earth.* As a primitive human you depend on a few basic skills and tools, passed on through your tribe. These skills and tools represent the accumulated knowledge of your group and as such are all that stands between you and . . . well, let's not dwell on that. Through a series of misadventures, you become separated from your tribe and are forced to survive on your own until you can get back to the safety of the group.

Every day of this separation is a challenge to find enough food to eat and to keep your body healthy while living in the harsh elements. You find a cave, cozy and dry, a real stroke of luck. You manage to find plants and a few edible bugs for nourishment. You have food, clothing, and shelter—you have met the needs of Maslow's most basic level, Survival.

You hear a noise outside the cave. Fortunately, you know how to make a fire, and the one at the mouth of your cave will keep unwelcome predators away. Your club is nearby and you feel quite secure. You have now reached the second level, Safety, or Security.

---

*My thanks to Felix Marshall for the inspiration for the caveman scenario.

Still, you miss your home. You can't help recalling your spouse and your children. You would gladly return to the warmth of the home you knew with them. You may be warm and safe in your own cave, but you are alone, missing the benefits of Maslow's level three, Love and Belongingness.

As you grieve the loss of your loving home, you hear someone calling to you in the rudimentary language of your tribe. You listen and then respond. Soon you are reunited with your friends and family, who valued you enough to send out a search party. A happy reunion follows, and you are able to satisfy fully your need for love and belongingness.

Your return to the group is an occasion for great celebration. It seems that the tribe greatly missed your presence and your valued skills while you were gone. They are delighted to hear the exciting tales of your harrowing adventure. You are a significant participant in the group and have assumed an important role in your community. This level, Self-Esteem, represents your need to value your own importance and ability and your need for the tribe to value you as well. According to Maslow, esteem needs are basic to your growth as a healthy human being.

Advancing to the highest level, Self-Actualization, requires being sensitive to our inner voice, which speaks within each of us. Self-actualization is the process of becoming everything that you are capable of and experiencing a sense of fulfillment and satisfaction with your choices in life. Only a small percentage of people reaches and sustains this level.

According to Maslow, to reach Self-Actualization, you must first proceed through the other levels. After all, it would be very difficult to experience contentment with your life choices if you had to focus primarily on seeking food to satisfy your hunger or shelter to keep you and your family safe.

It is common to be grappling with decisions and opportunities on different levels, especially when those decisions relate to your career. Many people simultaneously struggle with the challenges of preparing themselves for second careers and also supporting their families by remaining in jobs they've long since outgrown. They may be forced to cope with the frustrations of a job that is going nowhere for the short term; yet their efforts toward change elevate them to a higher level on Maslow's hierarchy, enhancing their self-esteem, expanding their vision of the future, and allowing them to exercise more control over their future.

Since Maslow's hierarchy was developed, several psychologists, including Maslow, have proposed additional motivational levels. Above self-esteem, theorists suggest levels known as "Need to Know and Understand" (devoted to intellectual growth) and "Aesthetic Needs" (devoted to the appreciation of beauty, order, and symmetry). Maslow poses an additional level above Self-Actualization, referred to as "Transcendence," a level that's identified as connecting to something beyond ego or helping others find growth. These additional levels identify motivations that speak to individual differences and help us identify more specifically what draws us to particular careers.

When working with my clients, one of my favorite approaches to coping with the ambiguity of working at different levels on Maslow's hierarchy is to refer to the movie *The Shawshank Redemption*. In that movie, the hero, Andy Dufresne, is imprisoned despite his innocence. He spends 30 years digging a tunnel, waiting for the right moment to make his escape. The movie's theme, "Fear can hold you prisoner. Hope can set you free," embodies the challenge of working at making changes in small ways that may not be readily apparent.

I encourage you to accept the challenge of hope in the same way. Imagine yourself in Andy's place, trapped but working a little every day to arrange your freedom. Although you may find yourself "caught" on the survival level of Maslow's hierarchy, working to keep food on the table, your ability to see yourself take control of your future by making small steps in a new direction places you at the Self-Esteem level at the same time. Just taking this class is a step in the right direction.

Exercise 2.1 helps you see where you are on Maslow's Hierarchy of Needs and how your place on it may influence the direction of your career path.

2.1 Take a Closer Look

MASLOW'S PYRAMID

Take a look at the updated model of Maslow's Hierarchy of Needs and fill in the spaces with one- or two-word descriptions of ways in which you perceive your needs might be met at each level.

Tran-
scendence

Self-Actualization

Aesthetic Needs

Need to Know & Understand

Esteem Needs

Belongingness & Love Needs

Safety Needs

Physiological Needs

Source: Maslow, A. H. Frager, R., MOTIVATION AND PERSONALITY, 3/E, © 1987. Adapted by permission of Pearson Education, Upper Saddle River, New Jersey.

Your Hierarchy of Needs

Which levels have you completed?

_____

_____

Which have you completed partially?

_____

_____

Are you comfortable with where you find yourself? Are you at the highest point on the pyramid that you have ever been?

_____

_____

Are you looking forward to advancing to the next level? Why or why not?

_____

_____

Are you "stuck" in your present level? Why or why not?

_____

_____

Can you get "unstuck"? Do you want to?

_____

_____

Think about what is motivating you right now to examine your life and where you are going. At which level do your motivations place you?

_____

_____

If you are struggling to move to another level, are there things you can learn from this struggle that you can use as you continue to grow?

_____

_____

Have you learned anything from the discussion of Maslow's hierarchy that relates to you and your motivations?

_____

_____

Discuss these questions with your group or with the class.

LIFE STAGES: WHERE DO YOU FIT?

For many years, prior to the advent of psychology as an acknowledged field of study, philosophers believed that there were only two life stages, childhood and adulthood. Even after theorists began to question this assumption, they still believed that adolescence was just a brief detour in the growth of humans and that growth essentially stopped when we physically reached adulthood. Now, on the basis of Erik Erikson's work and that of other psychologists, we realize that physical maturation is hardly the end of our growth as human beings. In fact, we continue to change and adapt throughout our lives.

There is still much to learn about each life stage, and psychological research is continually adding to our knowledge of adult growth. Exhibit 2.2 illustrates the most commonly recognized life stages and the experiences associated with them.

Much research still needs to be done concerning life stage development and how it translates to everyday living. We do know that each stage identified by Erikson presents different opportunities for growth through the events associated with that life stage.

EXHIBIT 2.2	Life stage development.
Birth to Age 12 Childhood	Cognitive and social development; period of value development; modeling according to gender.
Age 13 to 18 Adolescence	Beginning of identity formation; period of intense questioning and testing of real versus ideal.
Age 19 to 22 Independent Adulthood	Continuation of identity formation; attempts to establish independent life and perhaps an intimate relationship.
Age 23 to 28 Adult Identity	Establishment of external place in society, i.e., decisions concerning career, relationships, personal experiences.
Age 29 to 32 Questioning	Attempts to integrate life choices; possible questioning of prior decisions with subsequent changes.
Age 33 to 35 Settling	Seeking stability; acceptance of adult decisions with goal of "rational" growth.
Age 36 to 45 Life Meaning	Reassessment; realization of mortality may initiate "midlife crisis."
Age 46 to 60 Resolution/Renewal	Based on midlife transition, may hold renewed vitality and challenge or loss of vigor and resignation.
Age 61 to 85 Retirement	Depending on health, possible "bonus" career to be realized on own terms; sense of satisfaction with life choices or despair over unsatisfying outcomes.

Source: Maslow, A. H. Frager, R., MOTIVATION AND PERSONALITY, 3/E, © 1987. Adapted by permission of Pearson Education, Upper Saddle River, New Jersey.

While some events may be linked to particular life stages, people can also experience events typically associated with one life stage during another part of their lives. They may reencounter experiences they thought they had already dealt with conclusively. For example, you may assume the issue of finding a life partner is behind you when you marry. Then, suddenly, at 42 or 43, your loving spouse begins to seem like a stranger. You wonder what you might be missing in life by being tied down. Without knowing why, the issue is back in your life. You are reassessing your life, one of the growth experiences associated with that life stage. The resolution of your restless yearning depends on a range of issues related to you and your partner, your individual histories and temperaments, and how well you are able to work through conflicts in your relationship.

We are all faced with similar trade-offs throughout our lives. Seldom do our decisions yield clear-cut outcomes, satisfaction guaranteed. The truly important issues are frequently ones that we visit more than once. In our increasingly open culture, we have many opportunities to revisit past choices and make responsible decisions.

Understanding the process of life-stage development makes one fact dramatically clear: We all go through periods of growth and change. The inevitability of our growth makes finding a career that offers satisfaction and meaning a compelling goal. I have known people who shrink from the prospect of four years of college because it seems like too long a time commitment with little assurance that the outcomes will be worth the effort. Pointing out that they will be four years older with or without the benefit of college education, so it might be worthwhile to invest their time and effort in something that will pay off, gives them a new perspective. Your future will be grounded on the foundation of learning and growth that builds from here. That foundation will offer stability as you encounter the ongoing waves of change and challenge that take place in all careers.

In her book, *The Defining Decade*, Dr. Meg Jay has explored the notion of defining yourself through the career selections you make that create what she refers to as *identity capital*. Identity capital is the value acquired from a first position that lays a foundation for you to convey who you are in ways that go beyond a resume. These may be positions that do not offer the conventional rewards of large salaries or advantaged connections but which allow you to act in roles that expose you to unique challenges and tasks that demonstrate an intrepidity not found in the more prosaic jobs most people find themselves in. These exceptional starts—like volunteering for the Peace Corps or Teach for America—test you and give you the chance to prove yourself through a crucible experience that offers transformation along with adventure. These situations set you up for a career distinguished by risk, commitment, perseverance, and success.

The right career can bring you a lifetime of fulfillment and growth. You have an outlet for using your unique talents, developing yourself through challenge and competition, learning to steady yourself through the trials of adult life, and reaping the rewards of doing a job to the best of your ability.

In Exercise 2.2, you will look at the life stages you have experienced, the events associated with them, and the opportunities that you may encounter in the future.

Take a Closer Look   2.2

YOUR CURRENT LIFE STAGE

Age _____   *Life Stage* _____

Review Exhibit 2.2. Find your life stage based on your age. Read the brief description corresponding to your age. Does the description reflect the way you see your current life stage?

_____

_____

If not, can you think of what circumstances in your life may have influenced your situation?

_____

_____

What do you hope to accomplish during this life stage?

_____

_____

As you consider the life stages you have experienced, how have you seen yourself facing life's challenges—with great calm and resolve, or do you find yourself becoming more easily discouraged if things don't go well? What do you think this means?

_____

_____

Discuss your reactions with your group or the class.

VALUES: HOW WELL DO YOU KNOW YOURSELF?

Values are the things that we consider important. They represent needs that ideally become more clear and firm as we mature and learn more about who we are. As these values "crystallize" they inform our behavior and help us set goals. Values are shaped by our families, friends, churches, schools, textbooks, the media, social networks, and the whole range of our life experience. As we go through life, we encounter a variety of people and events, viewing them through the perspective of our values and their meaning to us.

While we may have only a small number of internalized values influencing us, they compete with each other to shape our actions through a complex structure of inter-relationships. Let's say, for instance, that you value altruism, a concern for the well-being of others. You also value independence and autonomy. Your inclination toward altruistic careers might encourage you toward social work or counseling. Unfortunately, the salaries of social workers may not be sufficient to accommodate the competing value of independence. The decision is more complex if you have a need for prosperity. Only when values are prioritized can their competing influences be organized in a coherent pattern, a pattern that facilitates self-understanding and decision making.

Are the values that we are most in touch with today the ones that we are bound to follow for the rest of our lives? Much research indicates that while our attitudes and interests may change as a result of life experiences, our values remain relatively stable. We change and are influenced by life experiences, but our basis for understanding and evaluating our world is fairly consistent over time.

Think of your own life. While you probably do not prize the same things you did as a high school senior, your life is still a reflection of the core values to which you were exposed growing up. You've probably moved beyond the youthful idealism of your teen-age years to a more mature view of the world and your place in it. Experiences gained through school, work, marriage, parenting, or any number of roles in the community can influence your perspective and give you a broader view of life without changing your values.

Let's look at an example to better understand the nature of values. You would like to own your own home, a result of your strong value for self-reliance. Owning your home is important and desirable. You begin to look for a house and soon find one that is suitable. You buy it and, now that you own your home, you no longer continue looking for a home. You now invest your energy in maintaining and enhancing your new home. Your basic value of self-reliance realized through home ownership has not changed but, as a result of your new experiences and growth, your actions have. You may indeed outgrow the house and look for another. Your value remains and you adjust it to meet the changing needs it reflects.

The same process may be influencing your present search for a new career. Perhaps your decision to look seriously at your career direction is a result of maturity and growth while still reflecting your deeper, unchanged values. Sometimes you may feel strongly about a value in the abstract, e.g., "equal job opportunities for all," but find yourself struggling with how those values are manifest in reality. You may feel that affirmative action initiatives are an excellent way to create opportunities for groups of people who have been closed out in the past—until just such a program results in a job rejection or demotion. In that case, it is a real test either to hold on to your original value or to question your belief.

Other situations may bring values into direct conflict. While you may look the part of the perfect corporate employee, your ability to relate with your "friends on the block" when you leave the office may make you feel as though you are living a double life. Do you keep your life divided, juggling your views to fit the situation you are in, or do you find ways to harmonize your life? More threatening would be the situation in which one or the other side of your life demands your total commitment. While it is unlikely that would ever happen, your value for loyalty to friends and community may come in conflict with your value to succeed financially. Being able to resolve the tensions between those values will influence the direction of your life and career.

Our values ripple through *every* aspect of our lives to a greater or lesser extent. When we talk about jobs and the satisfaction we feel with our career choices, we can focus on a smaller, more manageable number of characteristics. We can begin to assess how our values affect our job/career priorities. Knowing clearly what *your* values are will enhance your ability to choose a gratifying career.

Exercise 2.3 gives you an opportunity to recognize your values as they relate to work and career and to prioritize their influence on your decision.

Take a Closer Look   2.3

DISTINGUISHING YOUR VALUES

How much do you know about your values and the way they might influence your career and job choices?

Look at the list of values that follows. These values describe a wide variety of attributes associated with various work settings. Rate the degree of importance in choosing a career for yourself using the following scale.

1—Not important at all	3—Reasonably important
2—Somewhat important	4—Very important

_____ *Help society:* Do something to contribute to a better world

_____ *Help others:* Be involved in helping others in a direct way

_____ *Work with others:* Close working relationships with a group

_____ *Competition:* Pit my abilities against others with win/lose outcomes

_____ *Work under pressure:* Face situations with time constraints or where the quality of my work is judged critically

_____ *Power and authority:* Control work activities of others

_____ *Influence people:* Be in a position to change attitudes or opinions of others

_____ *Work alone:* Conduct work by myself, without contact with others

_____ *Knowledge:* Pursue knowledge, trust, and understanding

_____ *Personal growth:* Engage in work that offers me the opportunity to grow as a person

_____ *Creativity:* Engage in creative work, e.g., art, graphic design, photography, program planning, interior design, writing, composing, performing, and so on

_____ *Variety:* Have responsibilities that offer variety in content or setting

_____ *Stability and security:* Have a work situation that is predictable, with probability that I can keep my job

_____ *Recognition:* Be recognized for the quality of my work

_____ *Excitement:* Experience a high degree of excitement at work

_____ *Profit gain:* Have a strong possibility of earning large amounts of money

_____ *Location:* Work in a place near my home, with a short drive or bus ride

_____ *Fun:* Work in a setting where I am free to be playful, humorous, exuberant

_____ *Autonomy:* Have work responsibilities that allow me freedom to determine how and when the work is accomplished

_____ *Status:* Have a position that carries respect within the community

_____ *Advancement:* Have the opportunity to work hard and see rapid career advancement

_____ *Productive:* Produce tangibles, things I can see and touch

_____ *Aesthetic:* Create things that are beautiful and contribute to making the world more attractive

_____ *Achievement:* Experience a feeling of accomplishment for a job well done

_____ *Environment:* Work in a pleasant, clean, comfortable setting

_____ *Supervision:* Work as part of a team that is managed with fairness and appreciation

Now list the values you rated with a 4: very important.

_____

_____

Note the values you rated with a 3: reasonably important.

_____

_____

Do you see a pattern emerging? Can you see groupings that point to similar values in certain areas, or do some of your values reflect a possible conflict?

_____

_____

Take a look at the values you ranked with a 4. Ask yourself, "Is this important to me because *I* want it or because it will please others or win their respect and acceptance?"

_____

_____

Keep in mind that even if your values do not change, your priorities might as some needs are satisfied and others emerge. As you grow and change, continue to reassess and prioritize your values.

_____

_____

Discuss some of the new insights you may have discovered through this exercise at CA Café or with the class.

Self-understanding can be an important part of choosing a career path and setting career goals. Exercise 2.4 may help you begin the process, using some of the tools we have already examined.

Take a Closer Look   2.4

PULLING IT ALL TOGETHER

You have already begun to work to better understand yourself in the previous exercises. These questions will help you pull those impressions together.

What dreams did you start out with?

_____
_____

Where are you on Maslow's hierarchy?

_____
_____

What life stage are you in right now, and what issues related to that stage are you currently considering?

_____
_____
_____

What do you want to accomplish in this life stage?

_____
_____
_____

What three work values did you respond to most strongly?

_____
_____
_____

How has identifying some of the factors that are important to you affected your understanding of yourself? Your career decision?

_____
_____
_____

As a result of the first stage of your career adventure, you should have a good sense of the issues surrounding your motivations, the life stage you are in, the pressures associated with it, and information about your values concerning work and career. These areas of self-assessment all have a direct bearing on your career choice and will be considered again in later chapters.

A LOOK BACK

For now, it is important to realize that the unique combination of innate gifts and individual experiences with which you have been blessed are resources you will use to select a career and to find within yourself the courage and enthusiasm to make that choice a reality.

Career Adventure Café

Visit the CA Café (Have you decided on a name for your group?) and share the results of your self-assessment so far. This is the exciting part . . . finding out about the unique and amazing people you will be working with as you all move toward your goals. Keep each other motivated and learn more about the values, motivations, and life stages from among your group members. Here are some questions to get you started:

Are you all from the same age group and life stage, or do the members of your group have more varied representation?

_____

_____

_____

Where are your group members in their motivations? Do you share the same drives?

_____

_____

_____

Values is an area that might represent the greatest range of differences. What values do the people in your group identify as theirs?

_____

_____

_____

Facebook It

Has your self-assessment started you thinking about career options? How has the self-assessment experience been reflected among the members of your group? If you feel comfortable, share your self-assessment experience on your Facebook page.

Other Sources and Suggested Reading

Live the Life You Love in Ten Easy Step-By-Step Lessons by Barbara Sher
> A book that encourages creative approaches to getting in touch with your identity and finding the means for expressing yourself in your life and career.

Passion and Purpose: How to Identify and Leverage the Powerful Patterns That Shape Your Work/Life by Marlys Hanson, Merle E. Hanson, and Arthur F. Miller, Jr.
> This book offers a slightly different look at motivations and how they translate to the workplace.

What Color Is Your Parachute? 2012: A Practical Manual for Job-Hunters and Career-Changers by Richard Nelson Bolles
> A completely revamped version updated to reflect the changing career landscape.

Web Sites and Internet Resources

www.assessment.com
> An appraisal at this site suggests the links between motivations and occupations, with the additional feature of researching jobs. Further information is available for additional fees.

www.careerperfect.com
> This is a full-service site that includes a variety of self-assessment measures.

www.testingroom.com
> This site offers a preliminary values scale with an option to learn more for an additional fee.

Continuing Your Self-Discovery

SKILLS, PERSONALITY, AND INTERESTS

3

I n the previous chapter, you began the process of self-assessment. This chapter gives you an opportunity to expand your knowledge of yourself by looking at three additional issues: *abilities and skills*, *personality*, and *interests*.

These three areas are valuable sources of information for developing your career decision. You will enrich your insight into your needs and how they can be met through your career.

ABILITIES/SKILLS: WERE YOU BORN WITH THEM? CAN YOU LEARN THEM?

Abilities refer to those qualities that are part of you and the way that you relate to the world, intrinsic parts of who you are. An ability may be something as fundamental as understanding mathematics easily or it may be as intangible as facing a crisis calmly. Both of these are qualities that enable you to bring special talent to a particular situation.

The term *skills* is somewhat synonymous to abilities but has a more technical connotation. Generally, skills are those capabilities that can be acquired and developed through the exposure to and repetition of a task or learning process that may take place in a classroom or a lab, through training or study, or in a workplace. On the other hand, abilities are those talents or powers that are typically innate gifts and may be enhanced and developed to their maximum potential through study, training, or practice.

What are your unique talents and gifts? Your ability to identify and tap into both your inner capabilities and your skills will not only give you added confidence, but will also make you more marketable in the work world.

How can you identify and categorize career skills and abilities and match them up with career choices? The Department of Labor has a number of sources that explain how skills are related to career markets. The Employment and Training Administration (ETA) site, CareerOneStop, as well as the O*NET (which are presented more fully in Chapter 4) describe specific categories that will help you evaluate your skills and abilities and explore how they may be relevant to further career development.

The skills listed in Exhibit 3.1, which are found at the O*NET site (www.onetcenter .org/skills), are grouped according to broad categories. The listed skills are based on research by the Department of Labor which identified new and emerging occupations of the twenty-first century. As you survey the categories, you may immediately see areas in which you consistently possess high-level skills. You may have become aware of these through school, athletic events, hobbies, leisure activities, or other situations apart from paid employment. Your task now is to focus on what you have learned in the past and what your talents are now. You will identify settings for applying those talents in a later section.

Before you review those skills though, check out what the Department of Labor identifies as abilities under "Worker Characteristics" (www.onetcenter.org/content .html/1.A#cm_1.A). These are capabilities that were formerly considered skills but have now been defined by the Department of Labor as individual attributes which influence performance in a work setting. They inform your understanding of who you are as you approach career decisions and should be factored in as you assess what you bring to the next step in your life.

EXHIBIT 3.1	O*NET categories and skills.

Basic Skills

○ **Active Learning**   Understanding the implications of new information for both current and future problem solving and decision making.

○ **Active Listening**   Giving full attention to what other people are saying, taking time to understand the points being made, asking questions as appropriate, and not interrupting at inappropriate times.

○ **Critical Thinking**   Using logic and reasoning to identify the strengths and weaknesses of alternative solutions, conclusions or approaches to problems.

○ **Learning Strategies**   Selecting and using training/instructional methods and procedures appropriate for the situation when learning or teaching new things.

○ **Mathematics**   Using mathematics to solve problems.

○ **Monitoring**   Monitoring/Assessing performance of yourself, other individuals, or organizations to make improvements or take corrective action.

○ **Reading Comprehension**   Understanding written sentences and paragraphs in work-related documents.

○ **Science**   Using scientific rules and methods to solve problems.

○ **Speaking**   Talking to others to convey information effectively.

○ **Writing**   Communicating effectively in writing as appropriate for the needs of the audience.

Social Skills

○ **Coordination**   Adjusting actions in relation to others' actions.

○ **Instructing**   Teaching others how to do something.

○ **Negotiation**   Bringing others together and trying to reconcile differences.

○ **Persuasion**   Persuading others to change their minds or behavior.

○ **Service Orientation**   Actively looking for ways to help people.

○ **Social Perceptiveness**   Being aware of others' reactions and understanding why they react as they do.

Complex Problem-Solving Skills

○ **Complex Problem Solving**   Identifying complex problems and reviewing related information to develop and evaluate options and implement solutions.

Technical Skills

○ **Equipment Maintenance**   Performing routine maintenance on equipment and determining when and what kind of maintenance is needed.

○ **Equipment Selection**   Determining the kind of tools and equipment needed to do a job.

○ **Installation**   Installing equipment, machines, wiring, or programs to meet specifications.

○ **Operation Monitoring**   Watching gauges, dials, or other indicators to make sure a machine is working properly.

○ **Operation and Control**   Controlling operations of equipment or systems.

○ **Operations Analysis**   Analyzing needs and product requirements to create a design.

○ **Programming**   Writing computer programs for various purposes.

○ **Quality Control Analysis**   Conducting tests and inspections of products, services, or processes to evaluate quality or performance.

○ **Repairing**   Repairing machines or systems using the needed tools.

○ **Technology Design**   Generating or adapting equipment and technology to serve user needs.

○ **Troubleshooting**   Determining causes of operating errors and deciding what to do about it.

System Skills

○ **Judgment and Decision Making**   Considering the relative costs and benefits of potential actions to choose the most appropriate one.

○ **Systems Analysis**   Determining how a system should work and how changes in conditions, operations, and the environment will affect outcomes.

○ **Systems Evaluation**   Identifying measures or indicators of system performance and the actions needed to improve or correct performance, relative to the goals of the system.

Resource Management Skills

○ **Management of Financial Resources**   Determining how money will be spent to get the work done, and accounting for these expenditures.

○ **Management of Material Resources**   Obtaining and seeing to the appropriate use of equipment, facilities, and materials needed to do certain work.

○ **Management of Personnel Resources**   Motivating, developing, and directing people as they work, identifying the best people for the job.

○ **Time Management**   Managing one's own time and the time of others.

Desktop Computer Skills

○ **Spreadsheets**   Using a computer application to enter, manipulate, and format text and numerical data; insert, delete, and manipulate cells, rows, and columns; and create and save worksheets, charts, and graphs.

○ **Presentations**   Using a computer application to create, manipulate, edit, and show virtual slide presentations.

○ **Internet**   Navigating the Internet to find information, including the ability to open and configure standard browsers; use searches, hypertext references, and transfer protocols; and send and retrieve electronic mail (e-mail).

○ **Navigation**   Using scroll bars, a mouse, and dialog boxes to work within the computer's operating system. Being able to access and switch between applications and files of interest.

○ **Word Processing**   Using a computer application to type text, insert pictures, format, edit, print, save, and retrieve word processing documents.

○ **Graphics**   Working with pictures in graphics programs or other applications, including creating simple graphics, manipulating their appearance, and inserting graphics into other programs.

○ **Databases**   Using a computer application to manage large amounts of information, including creating and editing simple databases, inputting data, retrieving specific records, and creating reports to communicate the information.

Source: National Center for O*NET Development. Skills Search. *O*NET OnLine*. Retrieved May 5, 2013, from http://www .onetonline.org/skills. No protection is claimed in original US government works.

Take a Closer Look   3.1

ACKNOWLEDGE YOUR ABILITIES, VALUE YOUR SKILLS

Look at the categories and skills in Exhibit 3.1. Do you see any areas that you recognize in which you excel or possess a high level of capability? List them here.

_____

_____

How do you know you have these skills? Describe the setting in which you were able to demonstrate your ability.

_____

_____

Describe a specific incident associated with your demonstrated capability in which others recognized your skills.

_____

_____

What were the outcomes—tangible or intangible—of your having used that ability?

_____

_____

Describe your feelings while you were performing this skill and afterward.

_____

_____

Are you aware of any skills and abilities you possess that are not listed? (Did you visit "Abilities" at http://www.onetonline.org/skills?)

_____

_____

Discuss your reactions at the CA Café or with the class.

Exercise 3.1 is designed to assist you in determining what types of skills and abilities you possess and how those skills might be instrumental in choosing satisfying work.

TRANSFERABLE SKILLS

Understanding your abilities and skills is vital to discovering who you are and what you have to offer, but this knowledge may not always determine your specific career path. Sometimes we may find the things at which we are best have not yet found a market in the world of work. Just ask any homemaker. Among your innate talents may lay the seed of your career.

Many of your skills, whether rudimentary or highly developed, are transferable. *Transferable skills* are those that can be used in a variety of careers and work settings. If you have a particular ability that gives you a great deal of satisfaction, whether it's rocking your baby to sleep or sketching in your notebook while your teacher is lecturing, it may be the key to a career in which you can apply that capability.

Transferable skills are different from job-specific skills, or *work content skills*. Work content skills are skills directly related to a unique job description, such as operating a bulldozer, editing digital media, or conducting lab tests.

Identifying your transferable skills can help you develop alternative career options. These skills are an especially valuable asset for career changers who have many talents but are seeking new ways and new settings in which to use them. Your transferable skills are often those you have used successfully during activities that you enjoyed. Using these skills may have given you a strong sense of satisfaction and should be highly valued as you consider the next step.

Exercise 3.2 will help you identify your transferable skills.

3.2   Take a Closer Look

YOUR TRANSFERABLE SKILLS

Of all the skills we enjoy using, choosing ones that are transferable can help us envision ourselves in different work settings and can suggest career choices to explore further. You will identify your transferable skills by focusing on achievements or peak experiences that gave you a sense of satisfaction and fulfillment.

In the following space, list five achievements that you think were peak experiences, ones that allowed you to use your skills with good results. Note the details of your achievement, delineating the specifics of the event or task so that your notes resemble a job description. For example, rather than "Responded to a customer complaint," you might write "Greeted the customer, listened attentively to the complaint, asked questions to determine the exact nature of the problem, discussed possible remedies, contacted department, gathered information, resolved customer problem." After describing the event or events, list the skills that were necessary to achieve the results. For the aforementioned episode, you might write down skills such as listening, remaining calm, negotiating, interpreting information, enlisting cooperation, and investigating and organizing resources. If necessary, review the list of skills in the prior section to help you identify those skills most critical to each of your specific achievements. The most important factor is that anything counts, whether you used a skill at work, school, home, or as part of a hobby. Your skills can be a valuable part of your career plan, so include everything that comes to mind!

Achievement Event #1

_____

_____

Facts pertaining to event

_____

_____

Skills used to achieve results

_____

_____

Achievement Event #2

_____

_____

Facts pertaining to event

_____

_____

Skills used to achieve results

_____

_____

Achievement Event #3

_____

_____

Facts pertaining to event

_____

_____

Skills used to achieve results

_____

_____

Achievement Event #4

_____

_____

Facts pertaining to event

_____

_____

Skills used to achieve results

_____

_____

Achievement Event #5

_____

_____

Facts pertaining to event

_____

_____

_____

Skills used to achieve results

_____

_____

_____

Do you see a pattern of skills emerging? Discuss your reactions at the CA Café or with the class.

ARE YOU WORKPLACE COMPETENT?

In April 1992, the Secretary of Labor's Commission on Achieving Necessary Skills (SCANS) released a report about the skills that will be necessary for the workplace of the future, "Workplace 2000." This report updated the notion of work-place requirements which had been in place since the 1960s and highlighted the increasing influence of technology and globalization on economic competition. The SCANS skills linked workplace productivity to economic well-being and growth, showcasing how productivity was directly related to workers' skill level.

In less than 20 years, the SCANS report, while informative, has been eclipsed by the new reality of our current workplace requirements. Increasing specialization has evolved a model for skills in the workplace that now offers career decision makers a more specific framework for deciding how to prepare for a rewarding career. The Employment and Training Administration CareerOneStop site (http://www .careeronestop.org/CompetencyModel/pyramid.aspx) showcases the Competency Model that reflects the increasingly focused approach to skill-building. Exhibit 3.2 depicts the model's building block approach to identifying the skills required based on particular workplace settings and requirements.

The model offers a comprehensive understanding of the foundational skills on which workplace productivity is based, but proceeds from that base to the skills that can be acquired through formal education and practical work experience. It then iden-tifies the specific capabilities necessary in particular industries. This is a sophisticated model. Developed in a partnership with industry through the initiative of the White House and The Aspen Institute, it takes into consideration not only the raw ability an employee brings to a job, but also the worker's willingness to acquire whatever skills the job demands to remain competitive within the industry, whether on a regional, national, or global scale.

We are all in a new world in which any skill might be easily acquired by a com-petitor across the street or on the other side of the world. This new world demands both superior skills and a commitment to continued learning and growth. It is a world that demands organizations possess the most current technology and have the leadership and vision to identify the competencies necessary to thrive, and that those leaders select only the most qualified people to join the organization. The competencies and skills cited in Exhibit 3.1 form the foundation necessary to revi-talize our economy. As we have seen, they haven't been implemented exclusively in the United States.

Workers have found that they need the competencies and skills identified in the Competency Model to land a good job. Managers in organizations now require employees

The building blocks model for workplace competencies.

EXHIBIT 3.2

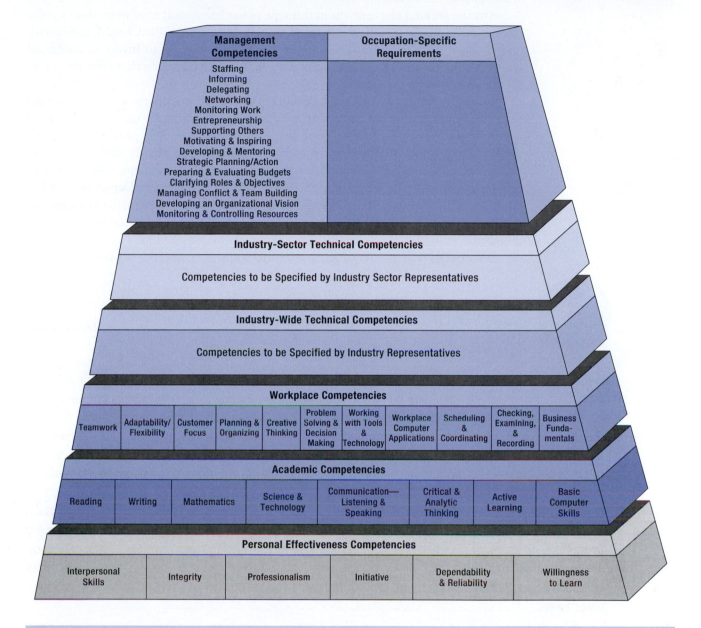

Source: Department of Labor/Education and Training Administration (DOL/ETA), retrieved 6 May 2013, http://www.careeronestop.org/CompetencyModel/pyramid .aspx. No protection is claimed in original US government works.

to work in teams, to assess critically their production systems, and to find the most efficient and cost-effective ways of accomplishing their work.

I observed this managerial approach first hand on a visit to an automotive component plant. Every aspect of the production environment was constantly critiqued and explored for possible improvement. The managers' attention to continuous improvement was evident down to the detail of the traffic lanes used by forklifts in the plant area. In most American plants, these lanes are marked by parallel solid yellow lines. In this plant, the lines were marked by two lines of parallel yellow dots. The plant engineer explained that the use of dots to mark the lanes saves time and paint and accomplishes the same purpose.

Anyone seeking employment in this type of workplace will need more than a pulse to perform the work. Companies demand employees who are skilled, bright, motivated, and engaged in their work. Competency and the motivation to invest in continual learning will become increasingly important in competing for jobs that offer the greatest opportunities for growth.

Research supports the necessity of skill development, not only as a means to secure rewarding employment but to steadily increase productivity and wage growth. Richard Murnane and Frank Levy in their book *Teaching the New Basic Skills* provide convincing evidence that, in addition to basic proficiency in reading and math, skills in problem solving, communication, teamwork, and computer literacy contribute substantially to finding jobs that offer solid income and growth. More significantly, Department of Labor reports cite investments in education and training as critical elements in increasing productivity and building a base of intellectual capital that supports continuing wage growth.

Exercise 3.3 will give you a glimpse of how you will fit into the workplace.

3.3   Take a Closer Look

ON-THE-JOB KNOW-HOW

Review the competencies in Exhibit 3.2 and at the CareerOneStop Web site. Now recall your achievements, prior work experiences, and current educational situation, going through each competency and skill to see how you rate. Rank your level of competency and skill by circling the number below that you think best reflects your level, 1 representing little or no skill and 10 representing maximum achievable skill. Try to be as candid and honest as possible. This is part of finding out what you need to do to find your place in the world of work. It will help you know what you need to do to be competitive. Remember, *where* you acquired the skills is irrelevant here, just whether you have them.

Rate your competencies at the foundations of Personal Effectiveness, Academic, and Workplace levels on this chart. To review the definition of each competency, go to http://www.careeronestop.org /CompetencyModel/pyramid.aspx and click on the cell in the pyramid representing the competency. Unless you are already able to identify a specific industry in which you have an interest, don't worry about the industry-specific competencies yet. That will be something to consider as you get closer to a particular career focus.

Industry Competencies

NO SKILL									MAXIMUM SKILL
PERSONAL EFFECTIVENESS COMPETENCIES									
Integrity	1	2	3	4	5	6	7	8	9	10
Interpersonal Skills	1	2	3	4	5	6	7	8	9	10
Professionalism	1	2	3	4	5	6	7	8	9	10
Initiative	1	2	3	4	5	6	7	8	9	10
Dependability & Reliability	1	2	3	4	5	6	7	8	9	10
Willingness to Learn	1	2	3	4	5	6	7	8	9	10

ACADEMIC COMPETENCIES

Reading	1	2	3	4	5	6	7	8	9	10
Writing	1	2	3	4	5	6	7	8	9	10
Mathematics	1	2	3	4	5	6	7	8	9	10
Science & Technology	1	2	3	4	5	6	7	8	9	10
Communication: Listening & Speaking	1	2	3	4	5	6	7	8	9	10
Critical & Analytical Thinking	1	2	3	4	5	6	7	8	9	10
Active Learning	1	2	3	4	5	6	7	8	9	10
Basic Computer Skills	1	2	3	4	5	6	7	8	9	10

WORKPLACE COMPETENCIES

Teamwork	1	2	3	4	5	6	7	8	9	10
Adaptability & Flexibility	1	2	3	4	5	6	7	8	9	10
Customer Focus	1	2	3	4	5	6	7	8	9	10
Planning & Organizing	1	2	3	4	5	6	7	8	9	10
Creative Thinking	1	2	3	4	5	6	7	8	9	10
Problem Solving & Decision Making	1	2	3	4	5	6	7	8	9	10
Working with Tools & Technology	1	2	3	4	5	6	7	8	9	10
Workplace Computer Applications	1	2	3	4	5	6	7	8	9	10
Scheduling & Coordinating	1	2	3	4	5	6	7	8	9	10
Checking, Examining, & Recording	1	2	3	4	5	6	7	8	9	10
Business Fundamentals	1	2	3	4	5	6	7	8	9	10

How do you rate? Do you see areas in which you might improve your competency or skill level?

_____

_____

How can you improve your skills in the areas where you see weaknesses?

_____

_____

Discuss your responses with the CA Café group or with the class.

WHAT MAKES YOUR PERSONALITY UNIQUE?

A particularly interesting area of self-assessment is personality or temperament. Your personality is composed of all your individual qualities. Your attitudes, behaviors, activities, and emotional reactions come together in your personality. Your personality reflects the way you view and respond to the world and the way you show the world who you are.

Ask any parent who has more than one child—they will repeat what psychologists know: *Everyone* is born with a distinct personality. Even identical twins, who share the same genetic makeup, take in and respond to their world differently. This uniqueness among individuals is a subject of endless fascination and study. Geneticists are beginning to trace some attitudes and behaviors to specific genes, a process that may reduce personality assessment to something resembling statistical analysis. For now, however, we rely on the work of psychologists to help us view how personality influences our lives.

Personality, however, is just one of many variables in career decision making. People with very different personalities may be drawn to the same career and people of a similar personality type may find themselves at opposite ends of the career spectrum. There are quiet, introspective salespeople and outgoing, gregarious accountants. Personality is only one dimension that influences career choice.

Have you ever been involved in a conversation in which someone says, "Oh, she's a typical teacher (banker, engineer, politician)"? Sometimes people make assumptions about someone's personality on the basis of their profession and vice versa. Some professions call to mind extreme, stereotypical traits. In the following section, remember that personality is only one factor to consider in your career choice. Keep all possibilities open. These exercises are meant to be guides to give you insight into yourself.

Jung's Psychological Types

An early pioneer in the area of personality development was C. G. Jung, a contemporary of Sigmund Freud. Jung developed a theory of psychological types in conjunction with an overall theory of personality development. Jung's typology led to the creation of a highly useful model for understanding personality.

Briefly, Jung's typology consists of these categories:

four attitudes

- Extroversion (E) or Introversion (I)
- Judging (J) or Perceiving (P)*

and four functions

- iNtuitive (N) or Sensing (S)
- Feeling (F) or Thinking (T)

Each of the categories listed describes how people adapt and experience the world. By examining each one we can learn more about personality development and its influence.

Extroversion (E)/Introversion (I)

The category of extroversion/introversion in Jung's typology refers to the mode through which a person relates to the world.

If your preference is for *Introversion*, your orientation is primarily focused on your inner world, an interesting, richly textured, but very private space. You might exhibit traits associated with quiet, reflective, or deliberate behavior.

If your preference is for *Extroversion*, your orientation is directed toward the outer world of people and things, usually displayed through outgoing, warm, candid behavior.

The attitudes described are best understood within the context of the following psychological functions. Extroversion and introversion influence how each function operates in our personality.

iNtuitive (N)/Sensing (S)

This function relates to the way a person takes in information. If your dominant way of gathering information allows you to handle several different things at once, see the "big picture," and work easily with generalities, but you find it difficult to manage details, your typology would likely be labeled *iNtuitive*.

If you are more comfortable with specifics and prefer tangible results and literal interpretations, then you are probably a *Sensing* person.

Feeling (F)/Thinking (T)

Whether you are a *Feeling* or *Thinking* person relates to how you prefer to make decisions.

Feeling persons are sensitive to others' feelings and consider them important; they are rewarded by interacting with others and value getting along well with people.

Thinking persons are able to remain calm in a crisis, prefer level-headed objectivity to soft-hearted subjectivity, and are noted for their logical viewpoint.

Judging (J)/Perceiving (P)

The last category was originally termed "rational" and "irrational" by Jung. The current terms, judging and perceiving, are not meant to be interpreted literally. Jung's original "rational" component, now dubbed *Judging*, referred to a reflective, linear response that leads to a particular judgment with little tolerance for ambiguity.

The "irrational" component was related to the *Perceiving* function and referred to an ability to perceive intangibles and function well despite disorganization and ambiguity. These two attitudes correspond to the way we subjectively evaluate things.

Exercise 3.4 may help you focus on some of your personality traits.

Several highly respected personality tests have become quite popular in recent years as tools to help people discern their personality type and some of the characteristics associated with those types. It is important to remember, however, that such tests are not intended to be predictors of behavior any more than a crystal ball would be. They are only tools in the overall process of growth and self-examination. Both the Myers-Briggs Type Indicator® (MBTI) and the Keirsey Temperament Sorter are based on Jung's psychological types. Both tests can enhance your insight into who you are and help in your self-assessment.

Take a Closer Look   3.4

IDENTIFYING YOUR TYPE

Let's examine each of Jung's eight categories separately to see which might describe you and your preferences. Place a check next to the phrases under each category that most accurately describe your style or preference. Mark down your "gut" reaction, trying not to read too much into each statement.

EXTROVERSION

- ○ Prefer fast pace
- ○ Enjoy variety
- ○ Enjoy interacting with people
- ○ High energy
- ○ Open, self-disclosing
- ○ Will talk with anyone about anything

_____ Total

_____ Category preference (E or I)

INTROVERSION

- ○ Prefer planned activities
- ○ Do one thing at a time until each task is completed
- ○ Work in a setting with a low activity level
- ○ Need to get away by yourself sometimes
- ○ Enjoy working on things "in your head"
- ○ Prefer to weigh all factors before deciding

_____ Total

INTUITIVE

- ○ Prefer "big picture"
- ○ Enjoy many things at once
- ○ Seek new challenges
- ○ Give weight to intangible factors
- ○ Impatient with literal interpretations
- ○ Resistant to detail work

_____ Total

_____ Category preference (N or S)

SENSING

- ○ More comfortable with specifics
- ○ Prefer working with details
- ○ Uncomfortable with unfamiliar challenges
- ○ Strict adherence to accuracy
- ○ Resistant to "gut-level" responses
- ○ Prefer literal interpretations

_____ Total

FEELING

- ○ Sensitive
- ○ Value others' feelings
- ○ Enjoy interacting with people
- ○ Work at relationships
- ○ Subjective
- ○ Capable of feeling deeply

_____ Total

_____ Category preference (F or T)

THINKING

- ○ Orderly
- ○ Enjoy working with numbers
- ○ Not easily influenced by others' feelings
- ○ Focused
- ○ Calm under stress
- ○ Objective

_____ Total

JUDGING

- ○ Prefer step-by-step planning
- ○ Uncomfortable with ambiguity
- ○ Motivated to reach closure
- ○ Decisive
- ○ Organized, linear
- ○ Unrelenting in pursuit of goal

_____ Total

_____ Category preference (J or P)

PERCEIVING

- ○ Comfortable with open-ended situations
- ○ Tolerant
- ○ Sensitive to intangibles
- ○ Able to function despite disorganization
- ○ Hesitant to exclude options
- ○ Aware of full implications of issues

_____ Total

Note the letter from each category that shows your personality preference and indicate each preference below.

Your code

____	____	____	____
E or I	*N or S*	*F or T*	*J or P*

Based on your responses to the checklist, you will come up with one of the four-letter personality codes listed in Exhibit 3.3.

You may wish to take either the MBTI or the Keirsey Temperament Sorter if you are interested in a more thorough assessment instrument. The MBTI is available only from someone who is certified to administer that instrument. The Keirsey Temperament Sorter can be found in the book *Please Understand Me* by David Keirsey and Marilyn Bates and through the Internet Web site. (See "Web Sites" at the end of the chapter.) Your instructor may be able to furnish more information regarding access to and interpretation of these instruments.

The MBTI applies a developed body of knowledge that correlates the four-letter code with career selection. The person administering the MBTI should be able to assist you in exploring further how the code can be interpreted as it relates to your career selection.

If you take the MBTI or the Keirsey instrument, share the results at the CA Café or with the class and describe your feelings about learning your personality type. Do the results match what you chose for yourself, or were you surprised?

Fitting the Pieces Together

It may be possible to understand each of the categories and the various characteristics, but it is a bit more challenging to discern how the various aspects of your personality are integrated to form a particular personality type. Keirsey and Bates have devised extended profiles for each of the 16 four-letter types derived from Jung's theories. The profiles in *Please Understand Me* are summarized in Exhibit 3.4 and should offer a way of gaining insight into your unique view of the world.

Reflect on your personality type using Exercise 3.5.

Four-letter personality codes.	**EXHIBIT 3.3**

ISTJ	ISFJ	INFJ	INTJ
ISTP	ISFP	INFP	INTP
ESTP	ESFP	ENFP	ENTP
ESTJ	ESFJ	ENFJ	ENTJ

| EXHIBIT 3.4 | Your four-letter personality type. |

ENFJ	ENFJs are the charismatic leaders who prize cooperation and value their interpersonal relationships over everything. Tolerant, empathetic, and highly intuitive, they are drawn to careers in counseling, teaching, ministry, the media, and performing.
INFJ	An exceptional sense of intuition contributes to the complexity of INFJs. Their need to give of themselves makes them exceptional therapists and ministers. Caring, creative, and visionary, they also find satisfaction in writing and teaching.
ENFP	*Intense, emotional,* and *authentic* are several words that describe ENFPs. Their enthusiastic approach to any task can be a powerful influence on others. They love being creative but become restless when bogged down with routine details. Careers in sales, politics, advertising, and writing are suitable outlets for their talents.
INFP	INFPs are the dedicated idealists, capable of deep commitment to a cause or a person. Sensitive and understanding, they prefer harmony and can handle complicated situations but may bridle if forced into a stifling routine. Architecture, psychiatry, college teaching, or missionary work would appeal to INFPs.
ENTJ	The ENTJs of the world are the leaders who take charge, provide structure, and drive a group forward. They are impatient with things that don't contribute to achieving the goal, whether they are structures that impede progress, illogical approaches, or people's feelings. Dedicated to their goals, ENTJs usually choose management and leadership positions in a variety of fields.
INTJ	Confident and decisive, INTJs are the creative pragmatists who are continually looking for new and better ways to accomplish something. Highly intuitive, they can become lost in the challenge of developing an innovative approach to a problem. Scientific research and engineering are fields that offer an outlet for their abilities.
ENTP	The sensitive and intuitive ENTPs are the problem solvers who can bring others along by using charm and enthusiasm. They enjoy improvising and innovating but only if the solutions work in the real world. This style can be awkward because ENTPs are not known for their attention to advance preparation. Nonconformists at times, they can be excellent teachers because they are always looking for new ways to get their point across.
INTP	Logical and literal with strong powers of concentration, INTPs are thinkers. They value intellectual pursuits but their curiosity can lead them in a dozen directions if they are not focused and directed. They prize logical thinking and can be abrupt if they see flaws in the logic of others. They are drawn quite naturally to scholarly and academic pursuits such as mathematics, philosophy, science, and teaching.
ESTJ	ESTJs are the responsible organizers. Rules, order, punctuality, and practicality are important to ESTJs, who believe those principles should be important to everyone else as well. Realistic, direct, and focused, they often work in management positions and are extremely dedicated to upholding duty and tradition.
ISTJ	*Reliable, patient,* and *dependable* are the words that best describe ISTJs. Despite the pressures they might experience, they have a quiet, conservative, practical demeanor. They are stable and able to perform consistently with details. ISTJs usually avoid risk taking. Careers suitable for this type include accountants, auditors, or tax examiners.
ESFJ	ESFJs are focused on the needs of other people and on maintaining harmonious relationships. They care about others' feelings and thoughts and are noted for their loyalty. Careers in administration, teaching, supervising, and coaching are excellent outlets for this type.

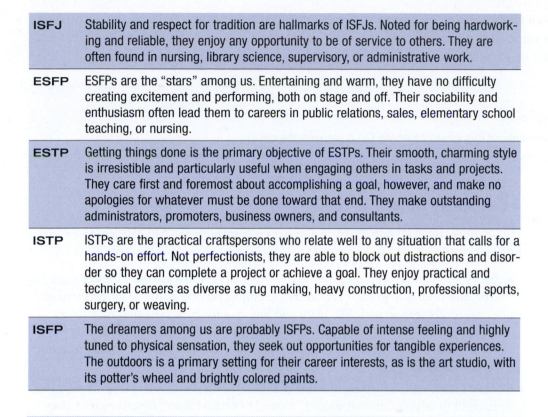

ISFJ	Stability and respect for tradition are hallmarks of ISFJs. Noted for being hardworking and reliable, they enjoy any opportunity to be of service to others. They are often found in nursing, library science, supervisory, or administrative work.
ESFP	ESFPs are the "stars" among us. Entertaining and warm, they have no difficulty creating excitement and performing, both on stage and off. Their sociability and enthusiasm often lead them to careers in public relations, sales, elementary school teaching, or nursing.
ESTP	Getting things done is the primary objective of ESTPs. Their smooth, charming style is irresistible and particularly useful when engaging others in tasks and projects. They care first and foremost about accomplishing a goal, however, and make no apologies for whatever must be done toward that end. They make outstanding administrators, promoters, business owners, and consultants.
ISTP	ISTPs are the practical craftspersons who relate well to any situation that calls for a hands-on effort. Not perfectionists, they are able to block out distractions and disorder so they can complete a project or achieve a goal. They enjoy practical and technical careers as diverse as rug making, heavy construction, professional sports, surgery, or weaving.
ISFP	The dreamers among us are probably ISFPs. Capable of intense feeling and highly tuned to physical sensation, they seek out opportunities for tangible experiences. The outdoors is a primary setting for their career interests, as is the art studio, with its potter's wheel and brightly colored paints.

Take a Closer Look   3.5

A GLIMPSE IN THE MIRROR

Now that you have learned a bit about your possible personality type and some of its characteristics, reflect briefly on how you see yourself.

From the previous exercise on personality type, what did you find your psychological type might be?

Your Four-Letter Personality Code

On these lines, note some key words from the text that are associated with your personality type.

_____

_____

Do these key words represent traits that you feel are true of you?

_____

_____

Look at the other descriptions, especially for those personality types that have letters in common with your own. Do any of the key words describing other personality types remind you of yourself? Note those key words here.

_____

_____

_____

Learning more about some of the characteristics associated with personality types has probably given you a better sense of some career areas that might appeal to you and bring you satisfaction. List some of your career ideas here.

_____

_____

Discuss the results of this exercise at the CA Café with the class.

A Cautionary Note

Please note several important issues when considering the categories or types just described:

- Everyone is gifted with each of the traits mentioned to a greater or lesser degree. The mix is unique to each person. For example, no one is always extroverted or consistently introverted. We adapt and incorporate behaviors that may lie on different ends of the continuum. The categories simply allow us to identify better the areas in which we feel most comfortable, and they, in turn, influence our responses and actions.

- There is no right or wrong attitude or function, no good or bad trait or response. Each of us enjoys our own special "recipe" of attitudes and functions that combine to form how we meet the world and how the world meets us. There is no right or wrong way to be you. In fact, Jung's definition of true maturity involves the ability to learn who you are and accept the gifts and richness of your attributes, rather than try to figure out how you can change yourself to be something you are not.

- The codes described here are helpful tools in understanding a person's overall orientation but do not fully represent all the complexities that make up an individual's personality. No human being can be reduced to or explained by a set of letters. Nonetheless, we continue to use any means available to understand better what it means to be human.

- The career possibilities suggested here are necessarily a limited list of jobs. Don't be discouraged if a career option you may be considering isn't listed or conflicts with your personality type. The options suggested are designed to help you focus your career decision making; they are not life sentences to limit and control you. Trust your inner voice and follow its wisdom.

How Personalities Complement One Another

Part of Jung's definition of maturity included accepting yourself for the special person you are. Jung also suggested that it is important to our growth to accept other people and their different ways of being.

David Keirsey and Marilyn Bates, the developers of the Keirsey Temperament Sorter, have studied personality and its influence on relationships in depth. Keirsey and Bates's model breaks down personality types from the original four-letter codes to two-letter codes that are associated with particular temperaments. Exhibit 3.5 shows the two-letter temperament codes and the corresponding four-letter codes.

Two-letter temperament codes. **EXHIBIT 3.5**

NT	SP	SJ	NF
INTP	ISTP	ISFJ	INFJ
ENTP	ESTP	ESFJ	ENFJ
INTJ	ISFP	ISTJ	INFP
ENTJ	ESFP	ESTJ	ENFP

Each of the two-letter codes in this model is associated with specific temperament traits, as noted in Exhibit 3.6. These traits describe the behaviors and attitudes associated with the people we might work with, be friends with, or choose as mates. Using Exhibit 3.6, see if you can pick out yourself, from either your code or the description. Then pick out those of your friends and acquaintances.

Now that you have an idea of Keirsey's temperament codes, try Exercise 3.6 to see how you react to the personality differences you encounter.

Keirsey's temperament types and traits. **EXHIBIT 3.6**

NTs:	About 5–7% of the population	Competent
	Want to understand ideas	Self-critical
	Never satisfied with results	Driven, seek knowledge
SPs:	About 35–40% of the population	Artists and performers
	Impulsive, enjoy a crisis	Highly changeable
	Add "electricity" in any setting	Dislike deadlines
SJs:	40–45% of the population	Prefer orderly setting
	Responsible and aware of duty	Rule/law-oriented
	Drawn to education, churches, hospitals as job settings	
NFs:	8–10% of the population	Seek meaning in life
	Very articulate and influential	Often drawn to writing
	Strive for self-actualization	Spiritual

3.6   Take a Closer Look

LOVE-HATE BETWEEN TYPES*

If you have taken the MBTI or the Keirsey Temperament Sorter, then you know your four- and two-letter codes. If not, try to determine which group you might be most comfortable in from the brief descriptions offered earlier.

Now divide up your class or group by two-letter types, with NFs and SPs in one group and SJs and NTs in the other. Once you are divided into groups, discuss the following question in your group. Have one member keep track of your responses.

What traits do you most dislike in the people in the other group?

_____

_____

_____

Have one of the people in your group read your responses aloud to the main group.

Now consider this question: What traits do you most like in the people in the other group?

_____

_____

_____

Again, share your impressions with the main group.

Surprised? Yes, for all the "strangeness" represented by the other personalities we encounter, we have to admit that they do have a lot to offer as well. Every group needs its creative, impulsive energy source along with dedicated, orderly producers. The beauty of the mix is in the balance it offers us. While there certainly are more SPs and SJs, the NFs and NTs make up in spirit and influence for what they lack in numbers. (It would almost seem to have been planned that way, but then I'm an NF and I see the "hidden" meaning in everything.)

Discuss your feelings about your type and the opposites as you view them now at the CA Café group or with the class.

*This exercise is adapted from the work done by Dr. Bruce Taylor, Janet Kalven, and Dr. Larry S. Rosen, based on Keirsey and Bates's _Please Understand Me._

WHAT DO YOU ENJOY DOING?

Regardless of your age, you probably know what kinds of activities and subjects draw you in and cause you to be excited and passionate. Or perhaps, if you are a bit more subdued in your responses, you might refer to certain things that make you feel comfortable and at ease with yourself. These activities or areas are commonly known as your interests.

Interests can be powerful predictors of career suitability. You may find careers that match your values, fit your motivations, and correspond well with your life stage; but if your interests lie in other areas, then you may be dissatisfied with your choice. Typically, if you are strongly attracted to a certain career field, you may decide to pursue it despite a host of potential obstacles. Just take a trip to Hollywood and you will find hundreds, even thousands, of people whose interest in the entertainment industry outweighs other considerations. They will endure daily rejection, substandard living conditions, and years of uncertainty in hopes of being one of the chosen few who becomes a star.

John L. Holland has also explored the issue of interests and their relation to career choice. Holland's theories suggest that in our society most people fit into one of six personality types, largely determined by their interests. He further found that career choice was often a reflection of personality type. If you can identify your personality type by interests, then you can match your type with career choices that would complement your personality type.

People seek situations in which they can use their skills and express themselves in positive ways. Frequently, people of like personality are drawn to the same vocation. Tracing these "links" will open up a series of career possibilities that you can explore through using library and Internet resources. (We examine these resources in depth in the next chapter.)

If you have had a variety of life experiences, you may find the process of identifying your interests and preferences much simpler than someone who is younger or has not had different opportunities. Your knowledge about yourself and the world of work will be reflected in your interests and preferences. Young people with less exposure to a broad range of experiences may find this a bit challenging. Identifying your interests is an important step to self-understanding. The six personality types identified by Holland in Exhibit 3.7 may help you identify your interests.

If you are able to discern your personality type, usually identified by one dominant type and influenced to a lesser extent by one or two others, then you can start matching

---

Holland's personality types.   **EXHIBIT 3.7**

REALISTIC

People in this category usually prefer physical tasks, athletics, and outdoor activities; they enjoy working with their hands and using utensils and machines.

INVESTIGATIVE

People in this category are usually quiet, inquisitive, or analytical and may be observant and enjoy academic and scientific pursuits.

ENTERPRISING

People in this category usually enjoy persuading or influencing others; they may seek leadership or management situations; they are comfortable organizing to achieve group goals; they prefer working with people.

ARTISTIC

People in this category usually prefer situations in which they can be creative and artistic; they may be flamboyant and imaginative, enjoying settings that are free of structure; some are visionary and independent.

CONVENTIONAL

People in this category usually prefer structure and order; they are comfortable with details of any variety—facts, numbers, any kind of data; and they find satisfaction in bringing situations to closure.

SOCIAL

People in this category usually gravitate to other people, regardless of the setting; they may have strong verbal and written communication skills and a special attraction to the helping professions.

your interests with those of people working in particular professions. Use Exercise 3.7 to look at your interests.

A number of vocational interest tests similar to Exercise 3.7 are available today. Your responses are used as a basis for developing possible career options. Holland's

3.7   Take a Closer Look

ASSESSING YOUR INTERESTS

Take a look at the following interest areas and the related occupational titles. Based on your preferences, write out the possible occupational choices that are related to your interests.

INTEREST AREAS	RELATED OCCUPATIONS
ARTISTIC	
Creative activities Endeavors requiring imagination and innovation	Art, Music, Dance, Fine Arts, Theatre, Design, Commercial Art, Advertising, Writing, Sketching, Composing, Acting
SOCIAL	
Helping activities Activities that offer outlets for idealistic action Teaching, leading groups	Education, Counseling, Human Services, Work, Political Science, Health Care, Law Enforcement
CONVENTIONAL	
Methodical activities Activities requiring efficiency and systematic skills Following defined procedures and routines	Accounting, Business Management, Computer Systems, Clerical and Administrative Services
ENTERPRISING	
Managerial activities Endeavors requiring high energy and self-confidence Planning projects, selling, promoting, and supervising	Management, Business and Hospital Administration, Purchasing, Human Resources, Public Administration, Retailing
REALISTIC	
Tangible activities Activities requiring operation and use of tools Working outdoors, tinkering with machines, sports	Architecture, Automotive, Engineering, Drafting and Design, Quality Control, Engineering, Graphics Production
INVESTIGATIVE	
Problem-solving activities involving independent, intellectual tasks using natural curiosity and scientific methods to solve problems	Sciences, Medicine, Research, Laboratory Procedure and Analysis, Computer Programming and Systems Analysis

My interests are in:

_____

Occupational areas:

_____

Self-Directed Search: A Guide to Educational and Vocational Planning (SDS), the Career Assessment Inventory (CAI), and the Strong Interest Inventory (SII) are among the most widely recognized instruments. Each of these tests is based on Holland's personality codes and offers a more comprehensive list of related career options. Holland's Self-Directed Search also includes measurement instruments for assessing leisure and educational interests. These tests are usually available through your college career counselor, who will assist you in interpreting the results.

Along with pencil-and-paper instruments, most colleges offer interactive computerized tools which provide access to self-assessment instruments. These programs provide self- and career-exploration exercises. DISCOVER and SIGI[3] are two options frequently used by career counselors to help students research their values, interests, and experiences. These automatically cross-reference your findings with possible occupational areas. We will look at these and other computer-based resources in more detail in Chapter 4.

Ask your instructor if it is possible to obtain one of these interest inventories, e.g., SII, CAI, or SDS. After you've had a chance to take the test(s), share with the CA Café group how you feel about the results. Do the results match what you might have chosen for yourself, or were you surprised?

Keep in mind that your interests are subject to change. Just as your priorities may shift as you grow, which then affects the influence of your values, so too can your interests shift and adapt. The results of any instrument you take now are a "snapshot" at this point in your development.

Take a Closer Look   3.8

PULLING IT ALL TOGETHER

By now, you can probably see more clearly how looking at the different aspects of who you are can help you discover possible career directions. While the process can certainly include a more intuitive approach, it may help to set forth specifically the key factors that have been explored in this chapter, namely:

What skills did you identify as most important to you and your growth?

_____

_____

What transferable skills did you identify?

_____

_____

How did you rate in "Industry Competencies"?

_____

_____

What were your two-letter and four-letter personality types?

_____

_____

What are some of the traits and characteristics associated with your personality type?

_____

_____

On the basis of your responses to the interest exercise, what was your interest area?

_____

_____

What are the occupational areas related to your interests?

_____

_____

Based on the information available to you in the college catalog, what majors relate to your interests and occupational areas?

_____

_____

If you were able to complete a personality or interest instrument, what occupational choices or college majors did you discover?

_____

_____

Did your process of self-assessment confirm the possibilities that you had considered or did it suggest careers that you had not considered before?

_____

_____

Careers to be explored:

_____

_____

_____

_____

A LOOK BACK

Your career adventure is taking you further along the path of insight into what a career might offer you. In this chapter, you examined your abilities, skills, personality, and interests. You explored those that are most rewarding to you and identified those that might be important in the workplace. You developed a better understanding of your personality type and some of its characteristics. You also began to assess your interests and those activities and settings that appeal to you. Additionally, you probably have a clearer understanding of how those aspects of your personality relate to possible career choices.

If you are feeling frustrated and somewhat confused at this point, don't worry. Those feelings may be a sign that some of the assumptions you have held are in flux. You may be facing the reality of the work world for the first time—a significant step in itself. Over time, your feelings will resolve themselves as you adjust to what lies ahead. Keep a positive attitude and you may find things will fall into place very soon.

On the other hand, if you're feeling sure of yourself because you got just the results you had expected, be prepared. You never know what you may encounter as you continue your career adventure. That's what makes this process exciting. Keep an open mind.

Career Adventure Café

Visit the CA Café and share the results of this phase of your self-assessment. You are moving through the first part of your adventure and ready to begin the next phase. Find out from the rest of your group what they learned about themselves. Share your insights and see if what you have come to know about yourself is reflected in the reactions of your group members. Here are some questions to get you started:

When you think about the skills and competencies that are now important in the workplace, where do each of you stand? Are you prepared personally, academically, practically? What competencies will you be focusing on as you consider your readiness for the world of work?

_____

What personality types are represented in your group?

_____

What career interests do the members of your group express? Do you share career interests with anyone in the group? How could you work together to support each others' career decisions?

_____

Facebook It

Where do you stand now that you have had a chance to look at different aspects of who you are? Has this process confirmed some of your expectations? Challenged them? What about your fellow group members? Has your self-assessment started your thinking about career options? Have you come up with a list of possible career options? If you feel comfortable, share what has happened on your Facebook page.

Other Sources and Suggested Reading

Discover (A Computerized Guidance System) by American College Testing Program
   This computerized career-planning program takes users through the spectrum of self-assessment and career-exploration issues in a user-friendly format.

Do What You Are: Discover the Perfect Career for You Through the Secrets of Personality Type by Paul D. Tieger and Barbara Barron-Tieger
   This book examines personality types and possible career choices that complement each.

Making Vocational Choices: A Theory of Careers by John L. Holland
   The Holland system of personality types and their relationship to career choice is explained in depth in this useful book.

The Pathfinder: How to Choose or Change Your Career for a Lifetime of Satisfaction and Success by Nicholas Lore

This book, written by the creator of the Rockport Institute, is a one-stop source for working through a comprehensive process for career decision making.

Personality Types: Jung's Model of Typology by Daryl Sharp

A basic guide to Jung's theory of psychological types.

Please Understand Me II by David Keirsey and Marilyn Bates

This book takes a closer look at personality types and their influence in the various aspects of life. The concepts are based on the personality theories of Carl Jung.

SIGI Plus (A Computerized Guidance System) by Educational Testing Service

This system offers many of the features necessary for self-assessment and career exploration as well as modules for local career market information.

Type Talk and *Type Talk at Work* by Otto Kroeger, with Janet M. Thuesen

Both of these books explore and expand on the Keirsey Temperament Sorter model and offer interesting insights on the impact of personality in contemporary work settings.

Web Sites and Internet Resources

www.keirsey.com

This site offers the Keirsey Temperament Sorter from which to derive Jung's four-letter code.

www.humanmetrics.com/cgi-win/JTypes2.asp

A quick test that provides the four-letter code based on Jung's typology.

www.onetcenter.org/CIP.html?p=3

The O*NET has an interest inventory, the O*NET® Interest Profiler™, which can give you insight into the types of careers that attract you.

Career Exploration

Being free to examine deeply who you are can be exciting and enlightening. Now it's time to explore aspects of the outside world. By this time you may have in mind a number of career possibilities that you identified through the self-assessment process. You are ready for your next step in your career adventure.

A key factor in your career decision will be your understanding of the current career market. As you make your career decision, it is important to consider a broad range of information and issues. Some issues relate to the basics of the position in which you have an interest—duties, salary, setting, and availability of openings. Other information crucial to this process relates to the general job market—the impact of technology on our way of doing work, trends in management and leadership, and the influence of globalization. As you weigh the information you retrieve against your priorities, you will be acquiring the discernment and critical-thinking skills that will serve you throughout your career.

As you gather information, the primary goal of this text is to help you focus on the place in the career spectrum where your unique talents can best be used and your individual needs can best be met. There are no more critical areas to your success in this book than those presented in this section.

LEARNING ABOUT THE WORLD OF WORK

PART TWO

Exploring the World of Work

At this point in your career adventure, you have the opportunity to explore the world of work. This part of your search is extremely important. As you plunge into the process of preparing for a career, you will make better decisions and be more competitive if you have a clear understanding of the career market. The current career landscape presents highly unstable terrain. The rapidity of change in contemporary culture proceeds at a pace that threatens to make information learned in freshman year less and less meaningful with each passing year, particularly if you are in a highly volatile technical field. Also, it is possible to choose a career and find that before you are fully trained for that career, the job you were hoping to land has been transferred to another country, another continent. Working overseas may be a pleasant benefit of your career, but only if you knew it was an option and chose it. Knowing how to assess the career landscape and navigate its hidden pitfalls or cul-de-sacs will help you find the most direct route to your career goal. Without this knowledge, you might experience entering the job market as if you were wandering in the wilderness without a map. You could survive, but your progress would be slow and possibly full of unpleasant, frustrating disappointments.

This phase of the career decision-making process will yield much valuable information and perhaps a few surprises. The information-gathering process will be an ongoing part of career planning throughout your life. You will continually use the skills that you develop as you investigate the job market, accept a position, change fields, and continue to grow in your career. Most important, you will be sharpening the critical-thinking skills you will rely on to evaluate career information essential to shaping your career choices.

When you attend school, especially an institution of higher education, your expectations for success are naturally raised. You envision a higher-paying, high-level job that matches your academic skills—you imagine you can do anything! That's okay, as long as your expectations are grounded in reality. For example, a student comes to me glowing with excitement and announces that she's decided to be a sculptor. Her next step is to find out who is hiring sculptors, how much they are paying per hour, and whether the first three years on the job are in Asia. If she finds that there is very little demand for sculptors and the potential starting income may be low, she may still wish to pursue her goal. People who pursue their dream career, wherever it leads, deserve applause. Being committed to a career goal is admirable, but knowing what lies ahead on your path is essential.

HOW CAN UNCLE SAM HELP?

In this chapter and those that follow, you will learn how to gather information about the world of work that will help you pursue your chosen career goal. We will look at a variety of tools and resources designed to assist you in the process. Some will be found in the library, others will be available through technology sources. In this section, we explore government data resources that provide you with a base of knowledge from which to broaden your search.

Department of Labor Resources

We dipped into the Department of Labor (DOL) site in Chapter 3 through the Bureau of Labor Statistics (BLS) site, the O*NET, and CareerOneStop. As you have seen, those sources are high-value repositories of current, up-to-date information related to understanding your interests, skills, and knowledge related to careers. Along with those, the DOL offers a number of publications, found in the reference section of the library, that provide valuable career data. These publications, such as the *Occupational Outlook Handbook* (OOH), are good sources of information about jobs, skills and settings of occupations, and labor market projections and trends. But you may find the DOL and BLS Web sites more convenient if you have online access. At these sites, you will find many of the same reference guides from the library available at the touch of the keyboard. These sites offer more current information because they are updated more frequently than the paper publications and, in some cases, may not have a corresponding publication as a library reference. The OOH online, the O*NET OnLine, and the CareerOneStop are three such resources that surpass those in the library in breadth of information and timeliness of data. Together they represent a comprehensive set of data resources for anyone seeking information about careers, occupations, wages, trends, labor markets, and job projections. Just as technology has influenced almost every area of our lives, it has become central to learning about jobs and career growth.

For almost 75 years, the Dictionary of Occupational Titles or DOT was the definitive document for cataloging jobs. While it is now generally accessed digitally, it is still considered an authoritative source for jobs and job descriptions. Listing almost 30,000 different jobs, it provides a standardized definition of positions and duties, and it groups positions according to occupational clusters and skills. The occupations described in the DOT are organized by numerical codes that match a job's skills and functions. While the DOT is the baseline resource for occupational definitions and classification, it has been eclipsed by the related data resources that are also available through the Internet. Appendix A features a sample page from the DOT.

A far more current and helpful resource that has replaced the DOT is the online database known as the O*NET, which we took a brief look at in the previous chapter. The O*NET offers detailed descriptions of thousands of occupations, highlighting aspects such as tasks, knowledge, skills, abilities, work activities, and context, and cross-references to the DOT and the Standard Occupational Classification (SOC) numbers. The SOC numbers group jobs into related classifications that allow you to scan whole classes of jobs based on related skills and settings. You can access the O*NET Online home page at http://www.onetonline.org. Click the Find Occupations tab to see various categories of occupations for you to explore. The job titles you explore there are linked to detailed descriptions of the positions. For a view of all that O*NET has to offer and to explore the whole site, go to http://www.onetcenter.org.

As your career search expands, information about the opportunities for growth and availability of jobs becomes more important. As a career counselor, I have had many students approach me with questions such as, "In which field will I be sure to get a job when I graduate?" or "Which job pays the most?" Salary and job availability are only two factors for you to consider in your career choice.

Wouldn't it be wonderful to own a crystal ball that could assure happiness and contentment? Students in the real world have to rely on more ordinary resources to help them assess the career market. The most readily available and comprehensive resource on job prospects is the previously mentioned *Occupational Outlook Handbook* (OOH). The OOH is updated every two years, and while still available in the reference section of your college or public library, it is more commonly accessed at the BLS Web site at www.bls.gov under the Publications tab (http://www.bls.gov/ooh). It profiles over 330 occupations and millions of jobs found within those occupations.

The information in the OOH ranges from the type of work found in particular jobs, the working conditions, employment statistics, training, qualifications, and advancement to earnings, outlook for future employment, and sources for additional information. Cross-references to O*NET SOC codes are available as well as references to other sites that offer relevant information. The current issue of the OOH offers projections on employment up to the year 2018. As you review the OOH, you may be tempted to view the data presented as the final authority on job availability. Although the information presented is helpful within the context of national trends, the specifics about the job outlook in your geographic area may differ or even run contrary to those cited in the OOH. The *Occupational Outlook Quarterly* (OOQ), a DOL publication also available at the BLS home page, updates occupational data and presents in-depth examinations of statistics on various careers during the interim between updates of the OOH. The OOQ often features more specific data on local career trends. Additionally, state bureaus of employment services may offer sites that focus on local and regional data.

The investment of time and money in training for a job is too significant not to consider the issue of job availability. Information on job outlook is a highlight of the OOH. The OOH features a chart of the fastest growing occupations between 2012 and 2020 at http://www.bls.gov/ooh/fastest-growing.htm. This chart shows that the positions in the service sector of the labor market will offer the largest number of openings. This continues the trends of recent years, which have seen real growth in service positions, particularly in technical fields and health care. Trades are showing new vibrancy, and despite the contraction of the labor force in manufacturing, the rise in costs associated with transportation has begun to make manufacturing in the United States a viable option, so we may see resurgence in that sector of the labor market. The take-away from this is to use the data available at these digital portals to inform your planning and decision-making.

As mentioned earlier, another DOL resource that is available only on the Internet is the CareerOneStop site (http://www.careeronestop.org). This is a full-service database that offers career information, a job bank, and links to local training/job-seeking resources. While this site is of more assistance to job seekers than career explorers, it is an excellent source of career data, and the job bank gives you a perspective on what is available out there, a crucial factor to consider in any career decision.

Exercise 4.1 will further familiarize you with the O*NET, the OOH, and other resources and will help you determine the outlook for the career you are exploring. Use the call-out box to guide you to the various sites to complete the exercise. Make additional copies as needed to accommodate all the job titles you are researching.

4.1   Take a Closer Look

FINDING YOUR WAY AROUND DEPARTMENT OF LABOR DATA

If you do not already have access to the Internet through your smart phone, tablet, or other computer resource, you can access these online resources through your college library, career center, or on-campus computer centers. Once logged on, take a look at the Web sites listed below. Go to each of the sites and review the data offered there. Then complete the exercise, thoroughly familiarizing yourself with the sites and the information each presents.

Department of Labor Career Web Sites

- **online.onetcenter.org:** This site is an up-to-date comprehensive resource on occupations.
- **www.bls.gov:** The Department of Labor's primary site for career data.
- **www.bls.gov/oco/home.htm:** The home page for the OOH.
- **www.bls.gov.opub/ooq/home.htm:** The *Occupational Outlook Quarterly* updates data found in the OOH.
- **www.careeronestop.org:** A site for job seekers and career planners surveying the career landscape.
- **www.oalj.dol.gov/libdot.htm:** You can view the DOT at this Web site.

In the following spaces, list on the left the occupations that you identified in your self-assessment from Chapter 2 and Chapter 3, especially those from the interest instruments, as ones you would like to explore further. Then start with the O*NET. Search the O*NET for the job title and explore the results. Click on "Summary" and "Details" reports and then try the "Custom" link to tailor the information to your interests and needs. The "CUSTOM" link allows you to rate the importance of specific factors in relation to the job title you are exploring. It also cross-references to the DOT code and to wages and salaries links. Also, jot down the information you have uncovered at this site in the blanks below. Note the SOC for future reference and record key facts of the positions you are researching, such as whether the position is highlighted as a "Green" job (one that is part of the trend to environmental and energy sensitive jobs) or is noted as having a "Bright Outlook" (representing a higher than average projected demand).

Career to Explore: _____ SOC Code Number: _____

Key Facts: _____

Kind of Work: _____

Skills: _____

Preparation Needed: _____

Other: _____

Career to Explore: _____ SOC Code Number: _____

Key Facts: _____

Kind of Work: _____

Skills:_____

Preparation Needed:_____

Other:_____

Career to Explore:_____ SOC Code Number:_____

Key Facts:_____

Kind of Work:_____

Skills:_____

Preparation Needed:_____

Other:_____

As you review the data, note the other job titles and descriptions for the positions listed following the one(s) you are researching. Do those sound interesting as well? Now go back and check the description of any new positions that may be related that drew your interest, noting key facts.

Related Job Title/O*NET SOC Code

_____

Related Job Title/O*NET SOC Code

_____

Related Job Title/O*NET SOC Code

_____

Does the information provided in the O*NET offer a better idea of how jobs are related by interest area?

_____

Are you aware of any related jobs or careers that you may not have considered before?

_____

Do the skill requirements of the positions you have researched indicate that you will need to acquire new skills or further training in order to perform the job duties?

_____

Did the information you found in the O*NET help you get a better idea of what occupational data is available? Were your expectations confirmed or were you surprised by some information? If you have had a number of different jobs, choose one and look it up on the O*NET. Does the description match what you recall doing?

_____

_____

Now go to the BLS home page (www.bls.gov) and click on the link to the OOH found under "Publications." Choose one of the job titles you identified in the exercise you just completed and search the site for the section that highlights labor market projections for your field. Answer the following questions on the basis of the information you gather.

How specific is the information related to your field? Does it mention the actual job title or a broad category of jobs?

_____

How does the information about the job compare to that found on the O*NET?

_____

Does the information cover national projections or regional?

_____

Are the projections specific (statistical, percentage of increase) or general (expected to grow, expected to decline)?

_____

Is this information helpful? If so, in what way?

_____

What else should you consider when researching a particular job's outlook for future growth?

_____

Where can you get additional information?

_____

If you wish, you can visit the CareerOneStop site and check the information about your career interests at the America's CareerInfoNet (www.careerinfonet.org) or the State Job Bank link (located on that page) to see about job availability for the careers you are exploring.

As you gather data about career possibilities, try to suspend your inclination to throw out any possibility that might present a challenge. Be sure that you have exhausted every possibility before you dismiss any options. Have faith in yourself and you will achieve your goal.

The exercise you have just completed helped you look beyond what might have seemed like your only choice. It is important to keep a positive, open view on what you are trying to achieve. Your goal is to find a full, rewarding career, not to fall into a trap from which you must later free yourself. Try to stay positive and flexible. It will help broaden your notion of what will work for you.

Discuss your new view of your career field in the CA Café or with the class.

INTERNET RESOURCES: CAREER DATABASE OR DATA DUMP?

As you can see, the Internet is an invaluable source of career data. It can also be a black hole of false starts, wild data chases, questionable fee-based services, and a time-sucking machine. One of the goals of this book is to offer you the best information, the best methods, and the best resources to accomplish your career goals. There are literally hundreds of sites on the Internet that offer career information. One Google search for the phrase "career planning" yielded over hundreds of millions of links, with several sites advertising services in the header. You can spend a great deal of time sifting through these sites looking for one or two that may provide you with useful information.

Be careful. Simply wading through these sites does not mean you are productively engaged in pursuing your career goal. Keep a focused eye on your goal and stick with sites sponsored by credible organizations and the links that they recommend. Sites that charge fees for testing or other services may be useful, but there are plenty of free sites that you should go to first. Take a look at the sites recommended in this book before you consider paying for information from a career-based Web site.

As mentioned above, a typical Internet search for career information will yield literally hundreds of millions of references. A few simple steps will make the time you spend online more productive.

1. *Use two or three search terms, clarifying with markers.*
   - Use *and* or a *plus sign* (+) to narrow your search (accountants AND treasury + Internal Revenue Service);
   - Use *or* or a *slash* (/) to broaden your search (college or university, college/ university);
   - Use *not* or a *minus sign* (–) to indicate a word that should not appear (cowboys NOT NFL, cowboys – NFL);
   - Use *near* when the words should be close to each other (cost NEAR accounting);
   - To limit to an exact phrase, put it in quotation marks; Career Information System without quotation marks gives over a million returns on Yahoo!; "Career Information System" gives over 175,000, still too many, but you get the picture.

2. *Use guidelines provided at the search engine sites to facilitate your search.* Each search engine has tips on the best way to gather data. Take a few minutes to familiarize yourself with the recommended shortcuts.

3. *Use sources that you can rely on.* Yahoo! and Google search engines offer directories, or online guides, on their home pages that are evaluated by human experts. These vertical portals, or "vertals," save time by linking you directly to the most useful sites when possible.

4. *Evaluate Internet resources before relying on the data found there.* Keep the following in mind when reviewing information found on the Internet:
   - Who is the author? Is the author the originator of the data? What are the author's credentials, background, education, and experience?
   - What organization supports the site? What is the relationship between the author and the site sponsor? Does the site sponsor monitor the information or is the author biased in favor of the sponsor?
   - Is the information current? Check the last date the site was updated, usually found at the bottom of the home page.
   - What is the purpose of the data? To inform? To persuade? To explain? To sell?
   - For which audience is the information intended?
   - How does the information offered compare to other sites as well as non-Internet sources?

America's Career Infonet (http://www.acinet.org) is a DOL CareerOneStop site. This site organizes information about jobs, employers, career planning, and job hunting in a colorful, interesting format that is user friendly and appealing. It is one of dozens that offer information you need about organizations, jobs, and careers.

Another site with a range of resources is The Riley Guide (http://www.rileyguide .com), a highly regarded source for a wide range of information on both the process and particulars of career planning and job seeking. This site is recommended for the information and the links it features. It even provides a basic tutorial for Web searching. As you research using sources like The Riley Guide to explore careers, you will have the chance to take the pulse of the job market by seeing what jobs are currently available.

Using the Internet to conduct your career exploration provides you with valuable information and allows you to become more skilled in the use of technology in making this transition. Take advantage of it. Use the sites in the Career Data Web Sites box below to get started exploring the Internet as a source for career information.

TO BLOG OR NOT TO BLOG?

As technology has become more accessible and usable by the average person, blogs have become a familiar source of information to people who surf the Internet. Blogs vary in origin and value and require thoughtful assessment. Some blogs fit the standard definition, that of a reverse chronological posting of journal entries that invite comment and dialogue. The subject matter can consist of a high-level exchange of data devoted to a specific area like political issues or foreign policy or the solitary musings of a technically adroit recluse with too much time on his or her hands.

Career blogs are available on the Internet. As with any source of data on the Internet, you need to be a critical consumer of what is presented. When evaluating a blog, check out the blogger's biography or the background of the organization that is posting the blog, if available, and review the postings to see if they correspond with the information you have encountered on sites you have found authentically reliable. Also, note how often the blog is updated. That will help inform your decision on how seriously to take the information found there.

Some blogs offer options to sign up for an RSS feed and Twitter updates. The RSS feed will send an email update to you whenever the site posts an update. Twitter is a microblog service that sends brief updates to followers. These are options that can keep you informed and alert you to issues in an immediate way that surpasses conventional means of communication. Blogs and tweets can connect you to funny, poignant personal portraits of the writer's experiences and insights or serve as helpful outlets to answer questions and offer support, but you may have to wade through a good bit of inane patter to get to the real "meat" of what you are seeking.

Career Data Web Sites

www.acinet.org/acinet	A site associated with the Department of Labor's CareerOneStop site.
www.rileyguide.com	A highly respected site offering comprehensive guidance on career planning and jobs.
www.jobweb.com	This is one of the best sites for college students and is produced by the National Association of Colleges and Employers (NACE). An added bonus is the app for your smart phone.
www.jobstar.org	The information here is most useful if you live in California, but everyone will find something of value here.
www.careerjournal.com	This *Wall Street Journal* site gives you a peek at the information executives use to make career choices.
www.careerpath.com	A division of CareerBuilder®, this is a great resource for undergraduate college students addressing a wide range of career decision topics.

Take a Closer Look   4.2

SEARCHING THE SITES

As some technical professionals see it, there are two types of people—those who use Google and those who use Yahoo! as their search engine. Both are valuable tools in any data-sorting process. Indeed, try them both in the following exercise. An additional option is to use a metasearch engine, such as Dogpile, Brainboost, ChunkIt!, or HotBot, that compiles the results from all the primary search engines including Google, Yahoo!, Bing, Ask.com, and several others.

Go to the Google (www.google.com) and/or Yahoo! (www.yahoo.com) search engine(s), and search using a job title in the career you are researching. If the title is more than one word, enclose it with quotation marks and see what the search yields. Note in the space below any Web sites your search revealed that are useful.

_____

Now select a career data site from the Career Data Web Site box in this chapter and go to that site. Click on the links there to access information that you believe will be helpful. Note the URL of the site(s) you visited below.

_____

What links did you click on? Did the search of the site present the information you were seeking?

_____

Did your search produce unexpected information or suggest further research options you hadn't considered?

_____

Has this brief tour of the Web sites given you a better understanding of the information available on the Internet and the process of career exploration?

_____

Discuss your experience and the results of your search at CA Café or with the class.

WHAT IS COMPUTER-ASSISTED CAREER GUIDANCE?

Just as you were able to acquire information about careers and trends from the Internet, there are a number of computerized systems that are valuable resources in making career decisions. Both as tools in self-assessment and as information databases for job information and educational institutions, these programs offer another way to approach career issues. While a session with a computer may never take the place of face-to-face counseling with a professional, many students can still benefit from using computers.

The computerized guidance systems that are currently available offer a variety of programs and modules from which to choose. The most popular programs are profiled briefly here.

Discover, Sigi³, Pinpoint

Discover, Sigi³, and Pinpoint are computerized career information systems that match students' self-assessment responses against occupations and then offer a complete database of information about the occupations. Although there are differences between the programs, they were all created with a strong foundation in career development theory and offer colorful and user-friendly programs. Updates provide multimedia enhancements with videos of professionals at work and background music. Most valuable is the depth and amount of information about careers and the world of work that is available at the touch of a button. Students can learn more about specific jobs, salaries, duties, outlook, and what professionals like and dislike about their jobs. Files related to financial aid, colleges, technical schools, and military programs are also available. An added benefit lies in each system's ability to store student information and responses, allowing the student to return to the program for long-term use. If your college offers any (or all) of these programs, access may be available by logging on from your computer with a password provided by the career center.

As with any tool that you use to make a career decision, digital resources can make the process more manageable. But, just as you have found with interest tests and personality exercises, they do not provide a magic answer that will lead you directly to the career of your dreams. They allow you access to a wealth of information and may assist you in gaining insight, but they will never completely replace the hard work necessary to make a career choice.

WHICH WAY TO YOUR COLLEGE CAREER CENTER?

One of the most valuable sources for current career information is your college career center. On some campuses it may be called career services or perhaps career counseling. Whatever its name, it is the best place to find many of the resources mentioned in this chapter as well as to obtain one-on-one career counseling. In addition, many career centers have corporate libraries that store up-to-date information about local and regional companies, their products, and the local economy. A few of the services that may be available from the career professionals at your college career center are listed below.

- Self-assessment tests for interests, personality, values
- Department of Labor publications
- Computer-assisted career guidance (i.e., Discover, Sigi³, Pinpoint)
- Information on occupations, careers, labor markets, corporations
- Workshops and seminars on career planning, resumé writing, interviewing, job seeking, on-campus interviewing
- Support services in diversity issues, job-seeking campaigns
- Orientation to use of the Internet in career development and job seeking
- Networking opportunities
- Resumé writing assistance and resumé posting services
- Job postings, on-campus interviews, job referrals
- Career fairs supported by employers

If your school is a member of the National Association of Colleges and Employers (NACE), you will find copies of their annual publication on job seeking. This free magazine for college students is published in several editions devoted to specific career areas, including health care, business, and science; also included are profiles about specific companies. In addition, a mobile app from NACE can provide you with much of the same information available in the NACE publications.

Most college career centers now have Web sites that describe the multitude of services they provide, some of which may also be accessible through the Internet. Access to self-assessment instruments, career data, employer information, career event schedules, career fair participation, and computerized guidance may all be available to you from your home, dorm room or even through your smart phone. But don't let that prevent you from accessing the many services available in the center. The professionals there are eager to support you in your career growth.

WHAT'S THE BIG PICTURE?

In the last section, we saw an indication of how information on job growth can be complex, multilayered, and contradictory. To have a solid understanding of a career, take the time to look at more than just the information related to a specific position. It is important to be informed on the job and the career as a whole as well as the labor market in which it exists. Be aware of the national and local economic and cultural trends that affect our society.

Social commentators contend that the rate of change in our society will be continuous rather than sporadic and proceed more rapidly than any of us might have considered possible. As major institutions struggle to meet the challenge that change presents, individuals will have to stretch their emotional, psychological, and physical resources to meet the new demands. Now more than ever, your understanding of how trends in our society and culture will affect your career is essential to your success and satisfaction in that field. Knowing what to expect places your decision in a context that will enable you to choose wisely and prepare yourself for what lies ahead.

Researchers have identified a number of trends that will have a lasting impact on the world of work. A compilation of a few noteworthy themes that are currently being played out in our workforce appears in the Trends in the Workplace box on the following pages. As you can see, our world will be undergoing dramatic change as the continuing influences of technology and global economics ripple through our lives. You will be part of that change. Being informed on these and other issues will provide you with an invaluable base from which to make decisions.

As you embark on your quest for a new career, you may find that the rapid rate of change is continually shifting the shape of the career you have chosen. You may need further training, and as some people have experienced, you may begin your training today only to learn that the positions you are seeking may be more readily available overseas, the result of organizations outsourcing positions offshore to reduce labor costs. If so, a number of factors have a strong influence on the success that college students achieve upon graduating. Your success will be determined in large part by:

- *your level of education*—education beyond high school will continue to offer greater opportunity for higher earnings over the life span.
- *what you study*—some fields of study will continue to enjoy growth and job availability.
- *how hard you work at school*—applying yourself to your studies will result in better job prospects after graduation.

- *what actual skills you develop*—your ability to demonstrate your value to an employer as soon after graduation as possible will make you a preferred candidate for employment.

- *the level of hands-on experience you've had*—any opportunities to become involved in hands-on work experience—even unpaid experience—help build your credibility for later employment. This includes co-op positions, internships, and volunteer and part-time jobs.

- *adaptability and resilience*—the more you are able to adjust to the changing demands of the career marketplace, the more you will find your career adventure taking you where you want to go, even if the route might not be the one you expected.

All these are variables that you control. Your ability to problem solve and engage thoughtfully in career issues rather than waiting for something to happen will determine your success. More important, knowing what you want, knowing what to expect, making your choice, and working hard have a greater impact than any external forces. You have the greatest influence over the outcomes in your career.

Trends in the Workplace

- The workforce will continue to reflect the increasing diversity of our society. The larger proportion of minority group members and women and the increase in the average age of our population will be a factor in the changing composition of the workforce. As baby boomers advance to retirement age, the impact will be realized in those careers that have the highest concentration of aging workers: education, public administration, management, transportation, and health services. Retirement either will be postponed to compensate for lack of income or will be followed by a second career reflecting the interests and drives of the individual.

- The end of mass produced, "dirty power," the development of driverless technology and robots for a wide range of applications will cause a shift in jobs from the old models to the new, customized applications made possible by micro technology. Even education, a field highly resistant to change, will see a shift associated with models that operate from OpenCourseware, which is free access to college-level education and modularized materials, like this book. While some jobs will be lost, energy, technology and services that meet specific user needs will provide jobs to those who have the education and skill.

- Workers will attempt to reintegrate home and work life. Companies and workers will find new ways to make work and home life compatible. On-site child care, job sharing, and working from home or telecommuting are examples of work arrangements that already benefit some corporations through increased worker loyalty and greater profitability while accommodating workers' needs. Look for more innovations as corporations attempt to take advantage of the flexibility offered by advances in technology to customize work situations.

- A greater number of jobs will be created in many small businesses rather than from the large business sector. New business start-ups will continue to offer the greatest opportunity for employment. Large businesses will continue to trim employees and contract for work in an effort to remain competitive and show profits. New business relationships will ensure economic survival by adding capabilities through new strategic alliances without adding cost or growth to the organization. Corporations will survive and thrive depending on how well they can integrate new technology features into their culture. Competition will come from unexpected places, as travel agents found when they realized that their greatest threat wasn't from the travel agency across the street but from the personal computer that their former clients could now use to book their own tours. Increasing scrutiny of

Continued

business practices, stemming from the corporate malfeasance which resulted in the Great Recession of 2008, will require organizations to monitor the ethics and behavior of managers and decision makers. Leaders will be pushed to show bottom-line results while maintaining full accountability for their fiduciary responsibilities to stakeholders.

- Competition from foreign countries will contribute to the continued realization of a global economy. Opportunities for growth in foreign markets will push the U.S. economy to open further while we struggle to keep up with scientific and technical competition from abroad. Corporate alliances across disciplines and national borders will rival political alliances, creating new power bases and new leadership roles. Globalization and technology are inextricably linked and will continue to change the way we interact. E-commerce, online education, and telecommuting—what we recognize as outsourcing, or the euphemism "right-sourcing"—will become increasingly common. The advantages customarily associated with U.S. citizenship and residency will diminish as information technologies reshape the way work and resources are distributed.

- Increasingly, the nature of work will demand a knowledge-based workforce. Jobs requiring little skill and training are disappearing. Even at the height of the Great Recession, those with college degrees had much lower unemployment rates than those with only a high-school diploma. Technology and the global economy have increased the need for further training after high school and made it a prerequisite to employment even in entry-level positions. Manufacturing, which had been shifting jobs to foreign venues, may find it economically feasible to keep jobs here based largely on transportation costs and the adjusted expectations of the labor force. College graduates from some disciplines will be in high demand. Engineering and information technology will continue to offer opportunities, but the continuing influence of globalization may take graduates from those areas halfway around the world. Others will find themselves facing diminished opportunities and underemployment as the amount of economic terrain that the U.S. economy controls evolves. Despite that, employees who generate ideas will be valued in the workplace of the future.

- Further change will take place in the relationship between employees and employers. The traditional career path of upward mobility through one organization to retirement is already a thing of the past. Outsourcing and contracting for portfolio or freelance and temporary employees who work on an as-needed basis will continue to provide challenges to individuals planning their careers and expecting it to conform to the conventions of the past. Corporations seeking to reduce overhead and save money will find a willing, competent, hungry workforce available overseas. Despite the cultural difficulties that may exist in transitioning to the new global economy, people who gather information from a variety of sources, assess the information with a critical eye, and remain adaptable and willing to "go with the flow" will be able to choose from a wide range of possible opportunities. In all organizations, "human capital," the organization's investment in its employees and their ability to innovate and respond quickly to market forces, will determine which organizations will survive. Employees will take responsibility for their careers, recognizing that performance and skill development are what count. Employers who are willing to respond by sharing profits and encouraging employee participation in the organization's success will create the synergy necessary to keep pace with the marketplace.

- Technology will allow employees to function in a work setting specially designed to suit their preferences, whether it's a specific temperature range, blinds automatically adjusting to the movement of the sun, or virtual travel to foreign shores. It will give employees the opportunity to visit with their children and observe them in day care on the other side of the city and make it possible to monitor the work site, and subordinates, on a 24-hour basis. Increasingly, feedback from your computer will enable employers to monitor employee behavior, health, and leisure activities. This "transparent workplace" will become more common and may create an environment in which privacy is increasingly rare.

4.3   Take a Closer Look

UNDERSTANDING WORKPLACE TRENDS

Take a look at the following Web sites:

Trends in the Workplace Web sites

- **www.wfs.org:** This is the Web site for the World Future Society.
- **www.shrm.org/trends:** The Society for Human Resource Management offers its take on future trends in the workplace.
- **www.epinet.org:** The Quarterly Wage and Employment Survey conducted by the Economics Policy Institute is available here, along with other useful information.
- **www.bls.gov:** The always reliable BLS home page.

Call up one of these Web sites and select one of the links that you think will offer you information about workplace trends.

What Web site did you go to? What page on the site did you visit? Is the information you sought specific to an occupation or career or generalized to economic or cultural trends?

_____
_____
_____

Check out other sites and note the results you found at each in the space below.

_____
_____
_____

Does the information you are finding here give you a better idea of what workplace trends may influence your job seeking when you begin your search?

_____
_____
_____

Has anything you learned from this search affected your view of your career decision?

_____
_____
_____

The "Other Sources and Suggested Reading" section at the end of the chapter cites other resources for workplace trend information.

Discuss the results of your workplace trend research in the CA Café or with the class.

TRYING OUT A CAREER

Buying a car is a decision that you have to live with for a long time. We all use various methods to come to a final decision on what car to buy. Some consumers trust the auto advertisements. Others might read consumer ratings or automotive magazines to find out more. They might talk to people who own the kind of car they're interested in. Almost everyone looks over the cars at a showroom, checking stickers just to see what the prices are. Usually, whether the car is new or used, they discuss with the salesperson the car's price. Even if contemplating an online purchase, they probably go to a car lot to see the model under consideration. Finally, after they've decided, signed the papers, and paid the money, the transaction is concluded.

"But wait," you say. "What about the test drive?" You're right. Few of us would be willing to purchase an automobile without first sitting in the driver's seat and driving the car ourselves. The test drive doesn't always guarantee that we will love the car, but it gives us a feel for the automobile that we cannot obtain from reading books and talking with people. Getting the feel of the car is one part of the information-gathering process we undertake before the final decision.

"Is This Right for Me?"

The process of career decision making is not unlike the process of selecting a car to purchase, with one important difference: Most career decision makers don't bother to "test drive" their career choice before they decide. Most of us are in too big a rush to jump into our professional lives and start building a career to stop and take the time to try one out.

There are several ways to try out a career. In this section, we examine a number of avenues to "test drive" your career before you actually make a choice. The possible ways of trying out a career that we cover are classroom study, community resources, part-time employment, and cooperative education/internship opportunities.

Classroom Study

Classroom study has already played a major role in getting you this far in your career adventure. During high school, you were probably beginning to understand how different academic disciplines relate to the world of work and how much or how little you enjoyed work in different areas.

Now you are ready to use your classroom experiences to determine further what career might be a good fit for you. This is particularly true if the field that you are considering is highly technical. Engineering, accounting, information systems, and health care are all fields that require classroom experiences in which you are immersed in the data and language of the discipline. If you are considering a career in systems analysis, then your study in the field of information systems will quickly tell you whether you would enjoy working in the field. If you are bored with the class's subject matter and alienated from the people who enjoy the class, you may be better off looking someplace else for your career.

Using classroom study as a barometer of interest works best when you think you may be more attracted by the image of a certain career than by the work itself. I once asked a young woman what she thought she might like to do, and she answered, "You know, all those women downtown who carry briefcases and go into the office buildings? That's what I want to do." She didn't need training to adopt that image. She did need

Take a Closer Look

SAMPLING CAREERS

Check through the college catalog and see if there are introductory classes with few prerequisites—you then have a chance to see what a particular discipline is like. Identify and list on a separate sheet any classes that you think could help you learn more about a particular field.

If you haven't done so already and you are interested in liberal arts as a major, you may wish to schedule an appointment with an advisor to learn about the kinds of careers in which graduates from that academic area eventually find jobs. Some networking with graduates, which will be presented in the next chapter, will also help you focus your direction academically.

Discuss the results of your catalog scan in the CA Café or with the class.

to learn more about herself and how to figure out if that image and the work that went with it would translate into a specific, satisfying career. Taking a few classes in business or accounting might have been enough to confirm her interest or to set her on a different path.

Community Resources

Opportunities to try out careers are available through a number of community agencies and organizations. United Way agencies, hospitals, government agencies, and service organizations all are possible sites where you might offer your energy and abilities in exchange for an introduction to the career of your interest. If you have an interest in health care, hospitals and long-term care facilities are eager for volunteers to interact with patients and assist health care professionals in providing service. If your skills or interests are in business areas, many agencies welcome accounting, marketing, and business majors who would like to try out their skills.

Take a Closer Look

LEARNING FROM YOUR COMMUNITY

Check with your local United Way agency or with the local department of human services to find out which organizations in your area have opportunities for you to volunteer your time and talents. Even if you are just handing out water at a 5K race, you will meet professionals who can play a role in informing your career exploration. The information and insight you gain from such an experience could help you make the right career decision now, rather than making a mistake later that could be costly in time and investment. List below the agencies that would be interested in your contribution:

_____

Discuss the different types of organizations that offer opportunities in the CA Café or with the class.

Take a Closer Look   4.6

ACQUIRING HANDS-ON EXPERIENCE

Check with the student services division of your college to see if there is an office on campus that arranges part-time employment for students. If so, look over its postings of available jobs. List below any that are related to your area of interest, even those that may not be an exact match but are perhaps in a related field.

_____

If no office on campus offers part-time job support, scan the want ads in the newspaper. See if part-time jobs are available in the area you hope to enter.

Discuss the results of your scan of the part-time market in the CA Café or with the class.

Part-Time Employment

A part-time job that brings you into the setting related to your career choice is one of the best ways to try out a career. Many aspects of part-time work parallel volunteer experience. In both situations you are working in the setting in which your career would take place and observing the type of work there. Part-time work also offers you the added benefit of income, which can be particularly important for enhancing your resume. One negative aspect of part-time work is the lack of flexibility typical of entry-level positions. If you have been hired to file and deliver mail, then you will have little opportunity to experience aspects of your career outside of those duties. You are employed not on your terms but on the terms of the employer, which are not geared to accommodate your individual need to understand a particular field or discipline on a broad level. Still, if your objective is to work someday in management for a Fortune 500 company, getting in anywhere, even the mail room, is a great way to start your career and learn more about how a large organization functions.

Cooperative Education/Internship Opportunities

The opportunity to participate in a cooperative education experience or internship is one of the best ways to try out a career. Since the first co-op program was instituted in 1906 at the University of Cincinnati, students have been using co-ops as a way of applying the theory they have learned in the classroom to the world of work and finding out at the same time if their career choice is the right one for them.

"Co-op job" refers to a job in a field related to your major that allows you to obtain academic credit that is applied toward your degree. While such credit may not be necessary to graduate, it does provide you with a work/learning experience that is otherwise unavailable. This differs from an internship, which is usually required by the school conferring the degree to qualify the student for graduation and does not include a salary.

The benefits associated with co-op education and internships can be summarized in three statements:

- You learn how the academic work to which you have been exposed relates to the world of work.

- You get a head start on your career by being exposed to the standards and expectations of the professional world. Such experience also establishes a platform from which to launch your own career.

- You have an opportunity to begin visualizing yourself as a professional by working as an associate and colleague with others who are established in the field.

In a co-op job, you are in the work environment as an extension of the learning environment. You earn credit toward your degree that is approved by the degree-granting institution. Your work must meet certain standards related to your major field of study or it will not be recognized by the college or university. That requirement ensures that your co-op job will offer you the opportunity to be involved in tasks and responsibilities that are substantial and integral to the work environment. Your time will be spent on meaningful work and you won't be exploited by the employer.

The easiest way to become involved in co-operative education is to find out if your college or university offers co-op and internship opportunities. Most institutions have some provision for granting credit for experiential learning.

4.7   Take a Closer Look

FINDING A SETTING TO HONE YOUR SKILLS

In order to learn more about how co-op education and internships work, find out if your school offers these programs. Make an appointment with an advisor in the co-op office and discuss the opportunities available through a co-op. Request assistance in talking with a typical co-op employer or co-op student. Using the referrals from the co-op advisor as well as the resources available to you through the library (directories, newspapers, professional journals, and so on), make a list of agencies, organizations, or companies that offer co-op jobs or intern opportunities.

ORGANIZATION	CONTACT	PHONE NUMBER/E-MAIL
_____	_____	_____

After compiling the list, choose one organization and contact the person responsible for co-op or intern positions. Discuss the types of opportunities the organization offers and the reasons for the organization's commitment to co-op education. Find out from your college co-op office what requirements you would have to meet to become a co-op student.

Discuss the results of your research and contact in the CA Café or with the class.

4.8   Take a Closer Look

PULLING IT ALL TOGETHER

Now that you've taken a look at specific careers, you have a base from which to make choices about your career. Use this exercise as a way to consolidate your information.

What careers did you find from the O*NET/OOH and Internet search that seem to offer you what you are seeking?

What does the OOH say about the field/job in which you are interested? The O*NET?

_____

What national trends recognized in the popular press are relevant or significant in terms of your career choice?

_____

List below one or two classes, volunteer settings, part-time jobs, or co-op/internship opportunities that might offer you the chance to try out a career.

Classes

_____

Volunteer Settings

_____

Part-time Jobs

_____

Co-op Jobs/Internships

_____

Discuss the results of your exploration up to now with the class or in the CA Café.

A LOOK BACK

At this point in your career adventure, you have acquired a great deal of knowledge about the different types of careers that appeal to you and could meet your needs. You are familiar with resources in the library and the Internet—like the O*NET and the OOH—that offer specific information about the duties, settings, skills, salaries, and outlook for a wide range of occupations. You are familiar with how these sources complement each other to offer information about how jobs and professions are related. You are becoming more aware of other Internet sources that may assist you in both career exploration and, later on, job seeking, and how your college career center offers services, information, and events that will keep you informed about local and national opportunities. You have begun to broaden your exploration to include learning about overall economic and social trends and their effect on the job market. Finally, you are aware now of how you can better understand career options through first-hand exposure to the subject matter, occupational setting, or actual job through study, volunteering, part-time jobs, or co-op or internship positions.

Career Adventure Café

Visit the CA Café and share the results of this phase of your career exploration. You have done your homework on the many resources that can inform your search and have developed solid information on occupations, salaries, career paths, and the requirements to move into those careers. Find out from the rest of your group what positions they are investigating and where they prefer to turn for information. Are there people in your group examining the same options you are considering? Share some of your findings and see what they have uncovered. Here are some questions to get you started:

What sources have the members of your group found to offer information that helps you understand the positions you are examining? Are some better than others? Do some seem to offer good information for some jobs but not others? Some types of information but not others?

_____

_____

What types of positions are the people in your group investigating? Do any of you share an interest in the same careers?

_____

_____

Do you see ways that you can support each other's movement toward your goals?

_____

_____

Facebook It

Whew! Has the whole world opened up to you? Is there more than you could have imagined to inform your planning? Share the options you are considering on your Facebook page. Post the information you have gathered—salary, projected growth, educational requirements . . . whatever you can find out. What about your fellow group members? Have they discovered occupations that might be of interest to you as well? Compare notes in the CA Café to find out what is going on with your fellow career adventurers.

Other Sources and Suggested Reading

The resources discussed in this chapter are the best place to develop a perspective on your chosen career field. In addition, your college or public library has numerous publications available from which you can obtain even more information. The resources listed are a few of those I have found most useful for students exploring their career choices.

The Guide for Occupational Exploration, 3rd ed. by J. Michael Farr, Laverne Ludden, and Laurence Shatkin

As a tool for expanding your vision of occupations and related careers, this resource is unsurpassed.

Best Jobs for the 21st Century by J. Michael Farr and Laurence Shatkin

Using expert analysis, this book is a good resource for future career trends.

American Salaries and Wages Survey, 11th ed. by Joyce Simkin

This book presents the salaries of thousands of occupations on both a national and local level.

Department of Labor Publications and Email Updates

The Department of Labor offers career information books through the United States Employment Service. These books focus on specific careers such as criminal justice, environmental protection, or health and medicine. These are useful for the extended examination of the occupations and are available wherever U.S. government publications are found.

In addition, you can subscribe to an email update service offered by the BLS at any page on the Bureau of Labor Statistics Web site (www.bls.gov/audience /students.htm). The box in the upper right-hand corner of the page allows you to input your email address to receive notices of changes in labor statistics, job postings, and other information related to the workplace and careers.

Encyclopedia of Careers and Vocational Guidance, 15th ed. by Ferguson Publishing

This is a comprehensive guide to careers and vocational information.

Book of Majors (College Board Book of Majors) by The College Board

Revised every year, this book is published by The College Board, an organization whose members are schools, colleges, and institutions of higher education. It is a source of information about the majors and credentials offered by over 5,700 member schools. It helps students better understand how to set goals and identify a field of study that is right for them.

Your Last Day of School by Eric Woodard

This book provides insight into internships as introduction to a career and as an advantage in competing for high value job options.

Web Sites and Internet Resources

Some of the most valuable information on the Internet is provided by the U.S. Department of Labor (DOL).

www.acinet.org

The Department of Labor presents this site, America's Career InfoNet. It offers a full range of career exploration data.

www.ajb.us

This DOL site, America's Job Bank, is a national job posting site.

www.careeronestop.org

This site is the "mothership" of Department of Labor Internet resources.

www.jobweb.org

The National Association of Colleges and Employers (NACE) provides everything you need for career exploration at this site. It also offers a mobile app for smart phones.

www.salary.com

Want to know the salary for an occupation in a particular city? Try this site for information on salaries and wages.

stats.bls.gov

You can navigate the entire BLS Web site from this home page.

www.usajobs.gov/studentjobs

A good site to visit to see the various openings and requirements of employment with the government.

Networking

5

ESTABLISHING CONTACTS AND SUPPORT

Think about the word *network*. Did the notion of wiring and computer links come to mind? At one time, the term network might have referenced a type of hardware we associate with electronic components. Now, however, we understand the meaning of the word to include a system of relationships that can have a dramatic effect on you and your career. Indeed, networking is a necessary part of establishing and maintaining a rewarding, meaningful career.

A network is a group of social and work acquaintances who know who you are and what you do or hope to do. It can include people from the most informal of settings, such as the woman who sits next to you at the ballpark, or formal business associates, such as the president of the company where you once worked. Both of these people are members of a club and may not even know it. It's the "Friends of You" (FOY) Club. Obviously, we are using the word "friends" in this case to refer to anyone who might be in a position to assist you in your career, including the frequently criticized but impossible to ignore social network groups like Facebook, Google+, and LinkedIn. Indeed, one of the goals of this text has been to activate the collaborative energy of your social network to inform or guide or celebrate your career planning experience through the creation of a Career Adventure Facebook page.

The members of the FOY Club may be familiar to you on a close or more distant basis. What is important to remember about your FOY Club is:

- *Your network is unique to you.* No one else has the exact same combination of relatives, acquaintances, and associates. Your FOY Club is a distinctive asset that is unique and valuable.

- *Your network can be expanded to meet your career needs.* It would be easy to limit your club membership only to those people whom you have met up to now. There are dozens of others—friends of "friends of you," if you will, who could play a role in your career growth. As a matter of fact, most job opportunities will be hiding among the people who may be one or two links away in your friendship network.

All you have to do is meet them . . . a task that can seem intimidating but is in fact easy. We will discuss how to do this in a later section.

■ *Your network will help you understand the local career market much better than any resource you can examine in a library or online.* Talking to people who are actually working in the field in which you are interested will provide you with a balanced insight into the job as well as an understanding of job availability, good places to work, and future trends in the field.

■ *Your network will help you to begin establishing yourself in your chosen career.* If you don't already know anyone who is working in a particular career that you are exploring, now is the time to meet these individuals. The people you meet now may be there later, when you are ready to enter the field, waiting to give you a welcome boost.

■ *Your network can be a means of visualizing yourself in your new profession.* As you meet with people at their places of work and talk with them, you will begin to imagine yourself actually performing the job just as you will learn the language of a new career. This initial phase of visualization in a profession will be a sustaining vision as you move toward your goal.

The process of invigorating your network so you can put it to work begins by organizing the members of your current network, the FOY Club.

IDENTIFYING YOUR EXISTING NETWORK

In my work with hundreds of students over the years, it has been gratifying to help them discover just how extensive their personal networks are. It is not uncommon for students to find that a family member or neighbor or previous classmate is working in a field in which they are interested. These connections are your most valuable asset in learning about your career goal. Exercise 5.1 helps you identify the range of your network by listing any friends and acquaintances who could tell you more about their careers.

5.1   Take a Closer Look

YOUR FOY CLUB

Think about your FOY Club, your circle of friends and acquaintances. Then look at the categories of people and jot down any names that come to mind. You may be surprised to learn how many people you can think of while doing this exercise. Be sure to include everyone who comes to mind, including people you might not have seen in years. If you are a member of a social network like Facebook—something you may have been doing as a part of your career adventure or something you have been using for a long time—now is a good time to fire it up to help you think of whom you should include in your career network.

Family members

_____

_____

Classmates/roommates

_____

_____

Coworkers

_____

_____

Former coworkers

_____

_____

Social club members

_____

_____

Neighbors

_____

_____

Sports team members/competitors

_____

_____

Social friends

_____

_____

Fellow volunteers

_____

_____

Former girl-/boyfriends

_____

_____

People from place of worship

_____

_____

Parents' friends and associates

_____

_____

People with the same hobby

_____

_____

Incidental acquaintances (e.g., transit stop companions, social network acquaintances, etc.)

_____

_____

Were you surprised by the number of people you could name? Granted, you may already know that many of the people on your list are working in jobs that hold no interest to you. More significant, did you find anyone in your circle of contacts who is working in the field you are investigating? If not, don't be concerned. You are about to enlarge the circle.

EXPANDING YOUR NETWORK

The best first step to expanding your network is to contact people with whom you are comfortable and familiar. After you have gathered leads and information from them, take the leap—reach out beyond the familiarity of your existing network to the larger career community.

To expand your network, start by identifying resources that you believe will yield names relevant to your field of interest. Keep a record of names, telephone numbers, and business addresses of people who work in your career area. Even if you don't know anyone in the career you're interested in, you may know *someone who knows someone* in that career.

As an example, take your friends on Facebook or Google+. Scan the people you have identified as 'friends' or who are in your group. As you scanned your social network, did you encounter anyone with whom you were friends but quite honestly you knew little about? That is hardly surprising since the temptation to 'friend' people, even those you may not have a firm acquaintance with, is hard to resist. As you examine the extent of your network, engage in this quick social experiment. Choose one friend. Note how many friends they have. Choose one of their friends that is not a friend of yours. Note how many friends they have. Now there may be the possibility of some friends that you will have in common, but there are far more acquaintances among the people to whom you are linked that do not overlap. They are one level removed from you, yes, but they are still now potentially members of your network. Granted, you cannot simply 'poke' them and expect a warm welcome. You will have to engage through the already existing network, but there are ways to orchestrate that as an option to increasing your range of acquaintances and even potentially career network 'friends.'

The same holds true for your network apart from the digital universe of Facebook or Google+ or LinkedIn. If you find that your present circle of contacts is limited, don't despair. There are other avenues by which to continue your exploration. The key to expanding your network lies in two directions. First, you can engage the members of your present network as "operatives" who can provide you with information and entrée to members of their network who then may become members of yours. Then, with confidence and resolve, you can expand your network to meet the people who may not be in your network now but who can introduce you to the career of your dreams.

One of the most effective methods of expanding your network is to become acquainted with the members of the professional organization associated with your area of interest. These groups usually meet monthly to discuss topics relevant to the profession and to network among themselves. Students are often able to arrange membership at a reduced fee. These meetings can provide a gold mine of information about the professions and available jobs. If you have zeroed in on a particular field that has a local professional organization, get in touch with the person in charge of new members and inquire about attending meetings or obtaining referrals. Most organizations are happy to work with someone who may later join the group.

Along with formal professional organizations, informal networking groups are a valuable resource for referrals and information. These groups are often more accessible than professional associations. You might find listings in your local newspaper under group meetings. If not, keep your ear to the ground when contacting new people and find out what you can about how *they* network. This is another route toward finding a group that will offer encouragement and support.

If you are undertaking a midlife career transition, then your professional network may already be quite extensive. Everyone with whom you have worked in prior positions is a member of your FOY Club. Even if they work in careers that don't interest you, they are another source of contacts and information. More significantly, if you were a valued member of your former associates' work group, you can ask them for advice, information, and recommendations. You need only to enlist them into your group.

Many colleges have lists of alumni who are available to assist students in their career investigations. These people are graduates who have settled in the geographic area near their alma mater. Check with the career services or alumni offices at your school to see if they offer this service to students. Alumni are an excellent resource for job market information and are usually glad to help, so feel free to approach them for a brief phone or in-person interview, even if you feel a little uncomfortable. Once you've done it, you'll find it gets easier and easier.

If by chance your school does not offer this service, it's time to start exploring companies and organizations. Resources such as Hoover's Business Directory (http://www.hoovers.com/100004996-1.html) by Dun & Bradstreet offer an array of information about organizations. You can search by organization, location, industry, or even by name. You will find information on the type of business these companies do, their addresses, phone numbers, perhaps a brief historical synopsis, or even the names of the organization's executives. The primary value of checking sources like Hoover's or other directories like it is to locate specific organizations that might employ people in your field of interest. Hoover's is available for a fee, so checking the reference section of the library first will offer you the most economical resource. You might also find names of possible network partners in the directories of professional organizations, chamber of commerce publications, or local newspaper articles highlighting companies.

Of course, for many careers, you need go only as far as your Web browser to find the names of many people who are working in a particular discipline. Medicine, law, accounting, publishing, and information technology are just a few of the areas in which professionals are listed under their area of expertise.

Internet contacts can assist you with information about professions and jobs through contact with blogs, listserv groups, bulletin boards, a Google or Yahoo! search, and online chat. While these contacts can yield a great deal of information, it is only as good as its source. It may be difficult to determine the validity of the contact you've made and, more significantly, something that holds true about a career in California may mean little if you live 3,000 miles away. Also, getting data from the Internet is an easy way to do research, but it may do nothing to help you meet people who could be helpful down the road. Of course, trying to meet network contacts through the Internet has its own pitfalls, such as being taken advantage of by unscrupulous individuals. Using the Web is no substitute for meeting people face-to-face.

We have already identified a source with great potential—your social networking sites. You may already be well-established online (Did your CA Café group or you start a Facebook site to track your career planning experience?) or on Facebook's business-oriented counterpart, LinkedIn. If so, now is a good time to look at those sources for possible untapped options for expanding your network. In particular, LinkedIn allows you to search companies. A quick search for Google in the Companies search option on my LinkedIn profile revealed 0 people at Google who were first-degree connections (someone in my circle), 86 second-degree connections (someone at Google who knows someone in my circle), and 38,823 employees at Google. The 86 people in my network (friends of someone I know) were showcased on the first page with an additional tab for fellow graduates from one of my colleges from which I've graduated. When I click on the first person from among the 86, I am linked to his profile page which tells me that 12 of my friends know this person. This would suggest that if the person I am viewing is in a position in which I am interested, I might be able to contact one of the 12 people that know him and get an interview to learn more about his position, the company, and his career.

The key factor in expanding your network is making contact with *the actual persons who are performing the work that interests you,* not the human resources office, the secretary, the receptionist, the operator, or "Steve47" from an online server. Once you actually talk with the person who can help you, you are much more likely to arrange a meeting with her.

Use Exercise 5.2 to compile a list of new network partners.

5.2   Take a Closer Look

DEVELOP CONTACTS

Using any resource available to you (newspaper articles, directories, yellow pages, Facebook, Google+, Yahoo!, LinkedIn), including your circle of friends and family, make a list of five companies or organizations in your area (or beyond) that might employ people in your field of interest.

COMPANIES/ORGANIZATIONS/PHONE NUMBERS

1. _____

   _____

2. _____

   _____

3. _____

   _____

4. _____

   _____

5. _____

   _____

Note the name of an organization and the phone number either in a hard copy directory or a digital archive. Head the entry about this organization with pertinent information like location, Web site, contact information, and anything else that you think is important to remember about this company (e.g., type of product, number of employees) that you may have picked up from your research. Exhibit 5.1 illustrates a typical company data archive and the type of information that might be pertinent. If you don't have a great deal of information to put down, that's all right. That will be the goal of your telephone conversation—to gather more information.

Ideally, you should be able to identify organizations and even people from online searches from whom you might gather good information. If you don't have the name of an individual, you might simply start with determining the area within the organization in which the jobs you are interested in might be found (e.g., engineering, marketing, accounting, public relations), call the main phone number and ask for the name of the manager of that department. Most operators will provide you that information; some may also give the extension or ask you if you want to be connected. For now, just get the name. (If you get a voice mail directory, simply select the option to talk to the operator.)

Some operators will explain that the company does not give out the information over the phone. If this happens, explain that you are a college student working on a project and your assignment requires you to contact a person in accounting, or marketing, or whatever. Then your request may get forwarded to human resources. Since you are not seeking a position at this time, just information, you may be able to get some names or tips from the human resources person. If not, simply offer your thanks and move on to the next company.

Once you have the name of the person in the department you are interested in, add it to the other information in your archive. You are now ready to expand your list of contacts through information networking.

Discuss how your actual inquiries were received when you drop into the CA Café or with the class as a whole.

Company archive.   **EXHIBIT 5.1**

Keeley Engineering, Inc.
3376 Industrial Parkway
Chicago, IL 60601
(312) 555-6255
www.keeleyengineering.com

Major product/service: Industrial engineering consulting

Areas of specialization:

Number of employees: 23

President:

Executive officers:

Engineering department manager/head:

Staff engineers:

Annual sales/receipts:

Additional information/comments:

Date of interview: _____   Time: _____

Contact: _____

INFORMATION NETWORKING

Information networking, the process of meeting face-to-face with a professional in the field you are researching, is one of the most valuable methods for gathering data about a career. This type of career research was popularized during the 1970s by Richard Nelson Bolles in his book *What Color Is Your Parachute?* and has become an integral part of any career or job search.

When contemplating information networking, the first question most people ask is "Whom will I interview?" As mentioned earlier, the easiest place to start is with your existing network, those contacts and acquaintances already in the FOY Club. They are your networking partners right now. With very little effort, you can enlist their help in your career exploration. Remember to use your social network to announce your need for information and contacts.

ARRANGING YOUR NETWORK MEETING

You have now reached the part of networking that typically causes the most anxiety: arranging network meetings. For many of you these may be your first business phone conversations. For others, this process may bring back memories of other business conversations that were less than pleasurable. Perhaps it's just the idea of calling someone with a request that makes you hesitate.

If you experience anxiety or hesitation, try to relax and take one step at a time. Remember, you are a college student completing an assignment. The community is a resource that supports your institution through taxes, donations, endowments, and a variety of other means. This is one of those other means. Students from your school return to the community after graduation and contribute to the organizations they join. It is in the best interest of the people with whom you will be talking to support you in your search. Based on something referred to as the Ben Franklin Effect, getting someone to do you a favor actually sparks an interest in your success on their part. This is characterized by the quote attributed to Franklin, "He that has once done you a kindness will be more ready to do you another than he whom you yourself have obliged." Feel free to ask for their insight and help. They undoubtedly have been helped by others before them . . . and you will do the same later, when you are a wizened veteran of your chosen career.

To start, try the following role-play exercise with someone in your class to get a feel for how it works.

5.3   Take a Closer Look

PRACTICE YOUR TELEPHONE STYLE

Once you obtain the name and number of the person with whom you would like to arrange an interview, you want to be concise, because her time is valuable. Get right to the point by using the telephone dialogue that follows. Practice the dialogue with a partner or make up one of your own to use with a new contact. Constructing your own dialogue will help you to sharpen and tailor your responses so that you will feel comfortable when you make your calls.

"ARRANGING THE MEETING" DIALOGUE

Operator: "Good morning, Acme Engineering."

You: "Good morning. May I please speak to Ms. Charlotte Ramsey?"

Operator:	"One moment, please."
Ms. Ramsey:	"Engineering, Charlotte Ramsey."
You:	"Hello, Ms. Ramsey. My name is John Black, and I am a student at Omega University here in Summitville. I am conducting research into engineering careers. I'm not looking for a job, just some information. I am wondering if you would have 15 or 20 minutes to chat with me at your convenience about your job and about engineering in general?"
Ms. Ramsey:	"I'm quite busy. I'm not really sure I can help you."
You:	"I'm sure that any information you can share will be very valuable to me, and I promise I won't take more time than you can spare. Perhaps I could come out and chat with you next week some time? Say Tuesday perhaps?"
Ms. Ramsey:	"Well, all right. Next Tuesday at 10:30 A.M. would be good. I can talk to you for a short time then."
You:	"Thank you, Ms. Ramsey. I look forward to meeting you."

How did the dialogue feel? Maybe a little stiff the first time, but you'll become more comfortable with it as you practice and use it. Vary the responses in your group to see how you might react under different circumstances. Role-play situations in which your contact is rude, rushed, distracted, resistant, evasive, or disorganized.

Discuss your practice experiences when you drop by the CA Café or with the class.

Now you are ready to make calls. Choose a time when you are sure to have a quiet space where you will be undisturbed. As a courtesy to the person you are contacting, avoid making calls on Monday, a particularly busy day for most people. When you are making the actual calls, suggest a date for the interview that is completely open for you so that your network partner does not have to rearrange her schedule to accommodate your needs. Once you have a date and time set, *write it down* in your archive for that company, program a reminder on your phone, and mark your calendar. Promptness is essential.

A word on voice mail: You may find that your call will be answered by voice mail. If you are uncomfortable with the idea of leaving your name and number, you may wish to keep trying until you reach the person. You may become quite frustrated since some people use voice mail as a way of screening calls. If this happens, leave a brief message stating your name, why you're calling, and when you will try to reach the person again. If you are still unsuccessful in contacting the person directly, you may then want to leave a number where you can be reached. Don't wait for him or her to call you, though. In the long run, it may be more productive for you to try reaching someone else who is more accessible.

While actually chatting with someone is preferred, another option is to acquire the person's email address and send a note. This is a less productive means to reach someone and offers less value since the likelihood that someone will extend themselves based on an email introduction is much less than a voice conversation. If you are truly determined to try email as a means to obtain an information interview, then start by stating you will be calling, the date and time, and that you are not seeking employment, just completing an assignment for school. That may ease the option of actually scheduling a meeting for both of you.

PREPARING FOR YOUR NETWORK MEETING

You have successfully arranged a meeting! It is time to do your homework and prepare yourself for the interview. The most important fact to remember is that this meeting is *not* a job interview. Meeting with contacts to inquire about their field is part of your ongoing career exploration, not a campaign to obtain a job. Think of your contact as a potential guide through unfamiliar territory—someone who will point out the pitfalls of your exploration as well as where to go for the best view. Focusing on this will free you and your network partner from the pressures associated with job seeking. In addition, your preparation for the interview includes two other areas—your appearance and the questions you will ask.

The simplest aspect of any network meeting is making sure that you dress appropriately. Typical campus attire would not be appropriate for this meeting. If you can, find out how people at the company dress. Respect your interviewer and take the time to conform to the dress code of the environment. Appropriate dress usually consists of a tie, jacket, and dress trousers for men, and a blouse, jacket, and skirt, a suit, or a simple dress for women. Also, make sure that your hair is combed neatly, nails trimmed, and shoes polished.

Ensure that you are on time for your meeting by "dry-running" your route to the organization the day before (remember to factor in rush hour traffic). On the day of the meeting, arrive at least five minutes early as a way of demonstrating your dependability and to give yourself time to relax in the lobby before the appointment.

The rest of your preparation should focus on making a list of questions to ask your new contact. You may have only 15 to 20 minutes, so it is best to ask clear, concise questions. Some examples follow.

- What drew you to this career?
- Describe your typical day on the job.
- What are the specific duties associated with your position?
- How did you obtain your present job?
- How would I prepare myself to enter this field?
- Where do you see this field going within the next 5 to 10 years?
- What do you like most about your job?
- What do you like least about your job?
- Who else would you recommend I speak with who knows about this field?

Any interview with a professional in the field you are exploring should include questions about that person's specific duties. After you have interviewed several contacts, you will see how people with the same job titles may perform very different jobs. Asking how the person got into her position will give you an idea of how career paths evolve.

The other questions you might ask focus on the type of preparation needed to enter the field and what might happen in the field in the future. If your allotted interview time is quite short, you might be limited to just these questions. You may find, however, that the person is willing to expand the interview beyond the time limit. Most people are quite generous with their time when they are discussing something they enjoy.

Be flexible enough that you can improvise, too, as the conversation progresses. Take advantage of any opportunity to pursue an area that interests you even if it deviates from your prepared set of questions. You can always get back to those.

Also, be prepared to discuss *your* interest in the career. Review in your mind how you came to choose this path—this will encourage a meaningful exchange. If you are in the middle of a career change and are comfortable sharing your experiences with your network partner, you will have an excellent opportunity to connect on a professional level. Your background and maturity can be a plus, but be careful not to talk negatively about a former employer or company.

The final question, "Who else would you recommend I speak with who knows about this field?" will provide you with another contact for your network, hence another avenue to explore and expand in your career network.

If you drew a picture of your network after meeting with a few contacts, you might find that it looks like a road map. In some respects it is a road map that intersects with you. As you interview more and more people, you may hear the same names repeated as "the people to know" in your field. If you have already met them, then pat yourself on the back. You have made valuable contacts and, if you were well prepared, you probably made a good impression. If you haven't made contact with one of these key people, you may want to do so. Such a meeting could prove valuable later on.

After you've had a chance to network with a few helpful new contacts and to digest the information you've gathered, take the opportunity to reflect on everything you've learned. Following are a few questions that may help you think through the data and inform your new perspective:

- Do the activities involved in the career you're researching sound interesting?
- Do the number of hours and schedule required to be successful seem reasonable?
- Does the preparation necessary to enter the field interest you?
- Does it appear that the field you are investigating will continue to offer job opportunities to new graduates ?
- Do you think that your preferences are reflected in the likes/dislikes of your contact?
- Would you be comfortable with the stress level associated with this career?
- What are the most valuable things you have learned about your career goal occupation?
- Did you learn things about the career that have changed your mind or do you feel more comfortable with your goal as a result of the network interviews?

FOLLOWING UP

After your network meeting, follow up with a thank-you letter or note, which brings your first encounter with that person to favorable closure. "Closure" doesn't necessarily mean that you will have no further contact with that person, however. Remember, she is a member of the FOY Club now. Also, make sure you express your gratitude to any person in your network who helped you make the contact that led to your interview.

If, as a result of your network meetings, you decide to make a commitment to enter that career, you may want to include that in your thank-you note. Exhibit 5.2 is an example of a short note expressing gratitude. If it is appropriate, mention that you hope to be able to call on this person in the future for advice and insight. As your study of the field continues, you may wish to write to those contacts you have made through the networking process to update them on your search and progress. These individuals may be key players in the realization of your professional goals.

EXHIBIT 5.2   Thank-you note.

Diana Mitchell

85 GREEN STREET ■ CHICAGO, IL 60601 ■ (312) 555-6742

March 23, 2013

Ms. Georgina Pavey
Keeley Engineering, Inc.
3376 Industrial Parkway
Chicago, IL 60601

Dear Ms. Pavey,

Thank you for the opportunity to meet with you last Tuesday to share your insights on industrial engineering. Our discussion was most helpful and has confirmed my interest in pursuing industrial engineering as my profession.

I will be continuing my studies toward my degree at the College of DuPage in the fall. Your informed perspective has been of great value to me. With your permission I would like to let you know of my progress.

Again, I deeply appreciate your time and consideration.

Sincerely,

Diana Mitchell

Diana Mitchell

FINDING MENTORS AND SPONSORS

Having a contact helps you to understand how a local career market has developed and what might be possible, but your contact may provide even greater benefits. Occasionally, you may encounter an individual who is willing to do more than just give information. A person who plays the role of mentor or sponsor can have a significant impact on your career. But finding someone to provide that support can be tricky.

The roles of mentor and sponsor have become a more visible reality in recent years. Mentors and sponsors have been around for years in an informal context, usually assisting young men through the transitions of their careers. When women began to enter the world of work, they found that they were frequently excluded from the relationships and informal settings such as the locker room at the country club, where mentoring commonly occurs. Therefore, women began actively to seek out individuals of either gender who could support them in their professional lives.

Some of the contacts were mentors, people who were experienced in their field, veterans of career wars, who could offer insight, encouragement, and a steadying influence on young people trying to succeed. Others became sponsors, individuals who were willing to promote actively a newcomer for opportunities within their organizations.

These alliances are certainly advantageous, but they are not without risk. Some young workers have been exploited by unscrupulous individuals. And some professionals have been victimized by young people pushing for a career boost. People on both sides of the relationship have experienced betrayal, scandal, and ethical blunders. That said, however, the advantages of having a mentor far outweigh the disadvantages.

The best opportunities to develop relationships of this type usually occur in actual work settings, where you can get to know someone well. In turn, that person will have the chance to see you at work and to establish a feeling of mutual respect and trust. Students who have had a cooperative work experience often encounter a coworker who will take the time to encourage them. The person who extends a helping hand might then become a source of continuing support.

Occasionally, prior to work experience, a person from your network may suggest that you keep in touch with them as you continue your academic work. If you are comfortable with the suggestion, you may find that this person may become a mentor or even a sponsor. If you are unsure, discuss the situation in detail with your college advisor, your parents, or your spouse. Make sure that all contacts with your potential mentor/sponsor take place in a professional setting and involve issues related to your career and training. If you become uncomfortable with any aspect of the relationship, you are not obligated to continue. Simply thank the person and end the association.

You may be wondering how mentors and sponsors benefit from their relationship with you. Many professionals enjoy the experience of nurturing fresh talent. In addition, the more successful they are in developing a corps of gifted new workers within the organization or within the field, the more their reputation in the company and the field is enhanced. If they are successful in establishing you as a hot new addition to the company, they have just added another loyal member to their own FOY Club. Keep that in mind. Networking never ends.

JOB SHADOWING

A different type of informational interview is known as *job shadowing*. This process involves an extended interview in which you accompany the professional whom you are visiting as he or she carries out the duties of a typical day's work. While this setup is not as commonly utilized as a network meeting, it is becoming recognized as a valuable career education tool. The most visible sign of this trend is Take Our Daughters and Sons to Work Day, when working men and women arrange for their children to observe them at their work settings. This effort is intended to raise the consciousness of young people about career possibilities and has led to the general acknowledgment that all young people need to know more about the career marketplace.

You can learn a great deal by actually "walking through" a day with someone—you get a front-row seat to their world of work. If it is possible for you to arrange this type of extended informational meeting, do so. It will be well worth your time. In some respects it resembles "test-driving" a career, referred to in Chapter 4.

While visiting any business organization, try to absorb as much as possible about the jobs employees perform. Observe the types of communication they are involved in, how they handle themselves in various situations, what is expected of them, how others respond to them, the tone and style of the organization, and the pace at which they conduct their duties. Paying attention to such details may tell you more about the job and the organization than the information you learn verbally.

You may discover as a result of networking or job shadowing that a career you thought you'd enjoy isn't right for you after all. It may not seem like it at the time, but that realization is a blessing. It is better to learn this now than to spend years preparing for a career that turns out to be a bad fit.

If you find after an interview that you are not as interested in a career, it may be the result of one of two things:

1. *You may be learning the true nature of the work for the first time, and you may realize that it isn't right for you.* If this is the case, regroup and take another look at the self-assessment and library research you did. See if there is anything in those two steps that led you down this cul-de-sac, and take steps to get back on track. You may have interpreted some of the results a bit rigidly, and now would be a good time to open yourself up to something else that interests you.

Testing and probing are part of making a choice. Changing your mind (or your major) is something most college students do, sometimes more than once. It is a normal and necessary part of finding a career that's right for you.

2. *You may have talked to the "wrong" people.* I require my students to talk to at least three people (college instructors excluded). Connecting with as many people as possible provides you with the broad view that you will need to consider all the aspects of a career. If you meet people who have nothing positive to say about their jobs, keep looking. Just because the job is not a good fit for them doesn't mean you won't love it.

Exercise 5.4 is designed to help you recap what you have learned so far from your networking experience.

Take a Closer Look

PULLING IT ALL TOGETHER

List all the contacts you have made who have provided you with helpful information about the career you are exploring. Then note the information that you found to be most helpful. Also, note anything that you found of special interest during your meetings.

Contact/Organization

_____

Helpful information

_____

_____

Observations

_____

_____

Contact/Organization

_____

Helpful information

_____

_____

Observations

_____

_____

Contact/Organization

_____

Helpful information

_____

_____

Observations

_____

_____

Were you able to develop other contacts for future reference from referrals during your meetings? If so, list them here.

_____

_____

Name/Organization/Phone Numbers

_____

_____

As a result of your meetings, have you begun to determine a possible career? If so, write it here.

_____

_____

If you are still undecided, have you narrowed your search to one or two possibilities? What are they?

_____

_____

Did you find from your meetings that the career you had an interest in is not a good fit for you?

_____

_____

If you answered yes to the previous question, are there related areas that interest you that you uncovered from networking, or will you need to look in another area?

_____

_____

Have any of your new contacts offered to act as a resource to you as you continue your career preparation?

_____

_____

Discuss the results of your networking experience at the CA Café or with the class.

A LOOK BACK

If you have followed the suggestions for doing this part of your career exploration, you will have developed a much better understanding of the career in which you have an interest. You have probed the boundaries of your existing network, including your social network, to identify people you might already know who would be a willing resource for you. You have learned more about the career area that interests you and the type of work involved in that occupation. You have begun to expand your network into areas that are directly related to your future career, or you have found from your meetings that the area you thought you'd enjoy actually might not be the right fit. You may even have initiated a professional association that could benefit you and your new network partner for many years.

Networking is a component of career development that is here to stay. If you have tried the approaches described here, you have already benefited from this process. Be prepared in the future for a call from someone like yourself who will be asking you to take some time to provide information and encouragement. Make sure you respond generously, just as your new friends have responded to you.

Career Adventure Café

Visit the CA Café and share the results of this phase of your career exploration. You have reached out to your circle of acquaintances and perhaps beyond to learn from people who know first-hand what the positions in the field you're exploring are like . . . the daily routines, the long-term possibilities, the good, the bad, the reasons someone might stay in a position for a whole career. If the members of your group have been busy exploring new contacts as well, you will have much to share. Here are some questions to get you started:

Who have you had the opportunity to meet and what were those meetings like? Did you find some interviews better than others? What about your CA Café group members? What information did you and your fellow group members find most helpful?

_____

_____

Did the information you learned confirm your interest in the career field you were exploring with networking? Did you find value in your interviews?

_____

_____

If you or your members didn't find what you needed, did you learn something someone in your group might benefit from?

_____

_____

Facebook It

If you have had a chance to try out your networking skills, share the experience on your Facebook page. Did you find out things about the occupation you are investigating that confirmed your interest, or were you surprised by something that made you change your mind? Was your network contact easy to talk to, or did you have to work hard to learn about their career story? Did the person you met with allow you to stay beyond the brief time you had requested? Check with your friends in the CA Café to see what their experiences were.

Other Sources and Suggested Reading

Networking for People Who Hate Networking by Devora Zack

If you are one of the numerous people for whom networking seems intimidating, this book offers the introverts among us a focus for gaining greater ease without making us feel like we must acquire traits that seem unnatural and false. A great book validating your natural way of interacting in the world, no matter what your preferences.

The Fine Art of Small Talk: How to Start a Conversation, Keep it Going, Build Networking Skills—and Leave a Positive Impression by Debra Fine

As a guide to those of us who would like to work on the elusive skills of social networking, this book provides actual techniques you can use to develop a new range of abilities in connecting with people you will use for the rest of your career.

Breakthrough Networking: Building Relationships that Last by Lillian D. Bjorseth

Recently updated, this book offers practical, hands-on networking approaches that focus on strengthening interpersonal skills.

The Networking Survival Guide: Practical Advice on How to Gain Confidence, Approach People, and Get the Success You Want by Diane Darling

A guide to networking with the people you know as the foundation for the network on which your career will continue to grow.

Web Sites and Internet Resources

www.careermag.com

This is a full-service career site with articles, job openings, and information on employers which now offers a mobile app.

www.mentornet.net

Although this site is focused on promoting underrepresented groups in engineering and science, it is a good example of how networking on the Internet can be accomplished. If you happen to meet the criteria for participation, you may wish to apply for a mentor to assist you in your career development.

www.quintcareers.com/networking.html

Quintessential Careers offers a comprehensive site that examines all issues of career development. The link to networking is a good place to learn more and offers additional links on the subject.

Decision Making and Goal Setting

6

Imagine yourself at a shoreline pointing your digital camera at a sailboat gliding across the water. Your first image is blurred, but as the autofocus works the image, you are able to see the boat more clearly. That process of watching the image become more clear is similar to what happens in the decision-making and goal-setting phase of your career adventure.

Now you are focusing in on just what your career choices are and determining the best way to achieve your career goals. Up until now, you have spent time gathering and interpreting information, some of it about you, some of it about the outside world. You have completed the necessary steps to make some choices about your career direction.

"But," you say, "I've made dozens of decisions just to get to this point in my career search. Don't all those decisions count?" Of course they do. You have made many important choices. These decisions were part of your self-discovery and your exploration of the career market. They set your direction up to this point by excluding options that didn't meet your needs and by including possibilities that kept you on your present course. Making these preliminary decisions has given you direction, stability, and momentum.

You are now ready to leave this phase of exploration and move to a new level of decision making, a level beyond information gathering. Decision making will help you organize your evolving thoughts and feelings about what you have learned in your experience and research and will help you develop meaningful career goals. The key word is *evolving*. This process is an evolution, a refining. You will now strive to establish goals that are achievable and that will set you on a definite path while still allowing you to be your own person.

In reality, you never stop exploring. You have selected a direction but you want to keep all avenues open as you learn more about your path. As physicist Richard Feynman said in Clark McKowen's *Thinking About Thinking*, "I can live with doubt and uncertainty and not knowing. I think it's much more interesting to live not knowing than to have answers which might be wrong."

You may change your mind many times before you find the career that fits you. That is part of the excitement and wonder of choosing. No one knows for sure if her decisions will lead to surefire success or even a sense of satisfaction. We do know that you can always change your mind. You are not required to live with unsatisfying choices.

DECISION-MAKING STYLES

People approach career decisions in much the same way that they approach other decisions in their lives. Some people prefer to analyze data and think things through while others "go with their gut," relying on how they feel about the issues.

Some of you may know people who never contemplate any purchase, even something as simple as shampoo, without consulting a consumer buying guide. Referring to outside resources and analyzing all the data about choices is one way of doing research on decision outcomes. Other people chart and graph every scintilla of information until all they know about a subject is down on paper. Only then can they make a choice. Another option is to take a sheet of paper, draw a line down the middle, write "Pro" above one column and "Con" above the other, and list factors related to a choice. These are all valid techniques for making decisions using the *cognitive approach*. People who are comfortable with this approach rely on reason and logic to determine their choices.

Other people prefer to make decisions based on feelings. Sure, they think about issues, but when all is said and done, facts may take on a secondary role. It may be that the facts are what produce the feelings. Others would claim that sensitivity to all the issues, implied and unspoken, actually enhances judgment since it factors in more than what's on paper. This approach, which is *intuitive*, is just as useful as the cognitive approach.

Ultimately you will need to think critically—to problem solve, to question the validity of the information you have, and, at the highest level, to examine your own assumptions to understand more fully whether they are meaningful as you change your view of the world. That will prepare you to recognize factors that are relevant and important to your decision, prioritize the ones that are most important, sort the options that meet your criteria, and set your goals.

Take a look at your track record on decisions you have made in the past. Did your decisions yield the results that you had hoped? Were you satisfied with the outcomes? If your answer is yes, then you may have a style of decision making that works for you. If you found that the results of your decisions have been disappointing, you may want to try some of the alternative techniques presented in this section.

You already have an idea about your decision-making style from completing the personality exercise in Chapter 3. As you may recall, the third letter in Jung's four-letter code represents how you prefer to make decisions. "T" people prefer logical, structured approaches and "F" people are the gut-level types. Both the cognitive and intuitive models are presented in this chapter. Try to determine if one fits you better than the other and how you might use both to make decisions.

DECISION-MAKING TECHNIQUES

So far in your career adventure, you have taken the following steps:

- *Self-assessment*—You started by looking at yourself—your motivations, life stage, values, interests, personality, and skills. From this base you began your career exploration, looking first at broad categories of occupations that interested you.

- *Career exploration*—You expanded your knowledge through research into jobs and careers that fell under the occupations to which you were initially drawn. You may have begun to do some actual decision making by discarding certain types of jobs and zeroing in on others that sounded right.

- *Networking*—You talked with people who were actually doing the work that interested you. This was your "reality check" to determine if your understanding of the job matched the real-world experience of others.

WHAT ARE YOUR PRIORITIES? WHAT ARE YOUR OPTIONS?

Now it's time to narrow your focus and set your goal. Think about what issues will carry the most weight in your decision to follow a particular career path. Setting priorities is critical to making your choice. Consider what is most important to you in a job in order to evaluate whether one career path is better for you than another. What do you believe about yourself and your career needs? By now you should have an idea of your priorities. You should also know from your research how the career options you are considering stack up. If the differences between your needs and the careers you are considering are dramatic, now is the time to find out. One way of evaluating alternatives is to set up a checklist that compares your career priorities with the career options you are considering. This point-by-point comparison helps you to see how a certain career choice might meet your needs.

Take a Closer Look   6.1

CAREER OPTION CHECKLIST

This checklist gives you a chance to compare your career priorities with your career options. The categories on the left represent some possible career priorities, needs, and preferences you may have identified through self-assessment and career exploration. The blanks at the end of the list are for priorities you may have identified as important that aren't mentioned in this list. As you review these priorities, in the center column, rate the importance of each issue in terms of your career needs: Use a number 10 to indicate items of highest priority and descending numbers to indicate items of lesser importance. The number 1 would thus indicate an item that is unimportant to you.

After you have rated each priority, use the column on the right to jot down any relevant information you obtained through career exploration about the career option you are considering. For example, if you've identified a salary range of $30,000 to $35,000 in your preferred geographical region, fill in that information. If you find you aren't sure how your career option stacks up against the priorities you have set, you may need to return to the resources or contacts you used in prior chapters for that information. If you are currently considering more than one career option, follow the same process, checking how your choices match your priorities and compare with each other.

Career Option _____

CAREER PRIORITIES	RATE (1–10)	RELEVANT INFORMATION
Salary range	_____	_____
Availability of jobs	_____	_____

Opportunity for advancement   _____   _____

Interesting work   _____   _____

Good benefits   _____   _____

Pleasant work atmosphere   _____   _____

Location of job   _____   _____

Job stability   _____   _____

Value to community   _____   _____

Variety of tasks/duties involved   _____   _____

Setting (indoor/outdoor, office, hospital, and so on)   _____   _____

Family friendly/flexibility   _____   _____

_____   _____   _____

_____   _____   _____

After completing this process for your career option, does the information you have assembled confirm your gut feelings about this career being a good choice for you?

_____

_____

If not, what else could you do to ensure that the option or options you are considering are appropriate?

_____

_____

Discuss the checklist exercise when you visit the CA Café or with the class.

WHAT ARE YOUR GOALS?

By this point, you have devoted a great deal of effort and time to your career exploration. You deserve to feel satisfied and excited about where you are going. Part of the excitement comes from knowing that you are already on your way simply because you have made a choice (or perhaps choices). You may face obstacles ahead, but your enthusiasm for your goals will sustain you through the rough spots. You are now ready to set forth your goals.

One way to maintain your enthusiasm is to make a commitment to a stated (long-term) goal and then develop a plan that will allow you to move toward that goal on a step-by-step basis (using short-term goals). Begin by establishing your *destination:* your long-term goal. Then look at the steps that lie between you and that end point.

Exercise 6.2 offers you a way to start moving toward your goal.

Take a Closer Look   6.2

YOUR LONG-TERM GOAL

State your career goal in a clear, specific way. To get started, fill in the Goal Commitment Statement.

My Career Goal

I, _____, will seek to enter the field of _____, with the intent of becoming a(n) _____. I will undertake and complete the training necessary to become a respected participant in this field and do whatever is necessary to maintain my commitment to my chosen discipline. I will review my progress toward my goal every six months and be prepared for unforeseen contingencies.

Signed _____   Date _____

WHAT'S NEXT?

What will it take for you to achieve your stated goal? Find out what stands between you and reaching what you have set out for yourself, and determine what you may need to do to keep your momentum going. I refer to this as fact finding.

Exercise 6.3 helps you think about what you need to do to achieve your goal.

Take a Closer Look   6.3

FACT FINDING

The process of achieving your goal is already under way. To be successful, you must anticipate what resources are necessary to meet the challenges ahead. Using the information that you developed from your self-assessment and career exploration, make a short list of the resources necessary to make your goal a reality. You may not be able to anticipate every obstacle you might encounter, but you will be much better prepared to overcome them if you marshal your resources now.

Further Information Needed (online or library research, networking):

Do you need to talk to anyone or do more research about your career goal? Do you know where training is available?

_____

_____

Further Training Needed (college, technical, experiential):

Do you need to contact specific institutions that specialize in the field you want to enter? Will you need to relocate?

_____

_____

Economic Needs (living expenses, tuition, care of dependents):

Will you need financial support to enter the career field? Are you eligible for financial aid? Will you have to take a paid job while preparing to enter the field?

_____

_____

Personal Support System (family, friends):

Are your parents or family aware of your career goals? Do they understand the reasons for your career choices? Do your friends support your goals?

_____

_____

Contacts Needed (college advisors, faculty members, placement personnel):

Whom do you need to talk with to find out how to be accepted in a program? Who can help you with financial aid? What about living arrangements? Do you know anyone who might help you get started in the career field through entry-level work?

_____

_____

Skills Needed (technical, verbal, written):

What skills do you need to acquire to accomplish your goals? Do you need to grow beyond the comfortable behaviors that have worked up to now? Will you need to adapt your behavior to fit in better in your new career?

_____

_____

Other Possible Resources (places to find employment):

Are there organizations in which you can find employment or volunteer work in areas related to your career field?

_____

_____

Some of the resources you listed may already be a part of your life. If not, obtaining the support you need to accomplish your goal will become part of your overall strategy, especially if you are considering a change that will take you into a different social and economic circle.

To complete your plan, make note of all the things you can think of that will move you toward accomplishing your goal. The list might include such things as arranging finances, changing housing location, talking with family and friends about your goal, or scheduling interviews with college administrators. The list might even include changes you would like to make in your own habits and behaviors that will make it easier to reach your goal. Come up with as many as you can think of and be as specific as possible. List them in the space on the next page.

STEPS TO THE GOAL

1. _____
2. _____
3. _____
4. _____
5. _____
6. _____

THE ONE-YEAR PLAN OF ACTION

You have set your long-term goal and identified the resources necessary to reach it. You are aware of the steps you must take to realize your goal. The final component in this process is developing your plan of action to accomplish your goals. This plan of action consists of accomplishing a series of short-term goals that will take you closer to accomplishing your long-term goal (use Exercise 6.4).

Determining short-term goals is a critical step toward your eventual goal of a rewarding career. We all know people who announce boldly that they've decided what to do with their lives. We might run into them six months later and find that they are no closer to their goal. They may still believe that they can reach their goal. They just don't know how to break the process down into manageable steps and accomplish them one by one. Deciding is only the first step. Making many small steps toward the goal is what actually gets you there. These short-term goals are the key to success. Map out those steps into a one-year plan of action—a road map to follow toward your goal. Your short-term goals then become the benchmarks by which you will measure your progress, build your momentum, and keep your focus. Include points during the year's plan when you step back, assess your progress, and fine-tune your direction.

Take a Closer Look 6.4

SETTING SHORT-TERM GOALS

Read the following statements. Complete the sentences with the information developed in the previous exercise. Some examples of statements you might use are offered. For instance:

"These are the things I can do within the next week to take me closer to my goal." Example: *Discuss my plans with my family and identify any changes we might have to make to help me reach my goal. Make an appointment to meet with a financial aid advisor to discuss grants and aid.*

_____

_____

"These are the things I can do within the next month to take me closer to my goal." *Register for classes in my major. Arrange for child care during class schedule.*

_____

_____

"These are the things I can do within the next six months to take me closer to my goal." *Meet with a career counselor to discuss opportunities for part-time employment in my field. Explore co-ops and internships.*

_____

_____

"These are the things I can do within the next year that will take me closer to my goal." *Join study group or campus club related to major. If none exists, start one.*

_____

_____

Discuss the results of the goal-setting exercise when you visit the CA Café or with the class.

CONSOLIDATING YOUR RESOURCES

Exercise 6.3 required you to think in a concrete way about the resources you will need to accomplish your goal. The list included a variety of items, both economic and personal. The people who will be involved in your journey are probably supportive and encouraging and will make an effort to help you on your way. In some cases, however, you may find that you are not getting the help you need—people don't understand or aren't concerned whether you succeed or not. In such cases, stay focused on yourself and your goal. Concentrate on using your skills to work effectively within the system and continue to reach out in a personal way to those people who can and will help you. Surviving and even flourishing in pursuit of your goal will require you to use all your energy and resources.

You may stumble upon some unanticipated obstacles in your path—people who are important to you may actively discourage you and express doubt about your choices. If your parents or spouse are uncomfortable with the career goal you have chosen, they may unwittingly make it much more difficult for you. If you announce that you are switching your major from premed to archaeology and that next semester you will be going on a dig in Tanzania, don't be surprised if your plan is met with less than enthusiastic support from your tuition-paying parents. They may be wondering just what is going on up at that college and if you are in touch with reality. In fact, your decision may be quite reasonable, and you can present the data you have gathered through self-assessment and career exploration. Your family usually just needs to know on what you are basing your decision.

If you find that even with convincing arguments, your family is still skeptical, try to remain positive. You can make it happen. Sometimes in life we have to go out on a skinny limb. We can't live in ways that meet everyone else's needs and expectations. If this happens to you, make sure you have your own "cheering section" to keep you focused on your goals. You can usually find recruits for this role among your professors and fellow students. Most important, be your own cheerleader—pat yourself on the back when things go well and give yourself a break when they seem to fall apart.

When you work through the process of career decision making, you are working on two levels. The first level is "decidedness," a process of being secure in your choices based on the information you gathered. You may not be sure of the outcome, but based on what you have already learned about yourself and the career marketplace, you are confident you are on the right track.

The second level is "decisiveness," a quality of being able to act on the choices you make. Your ability to "get the ball rolling" and move forward based on your knowledge is founded in confidence and security in yourself. Your self-confidence, in turn, is based on how you feel about yourself, that slippery subject of self-esteem.

If you find yourself hesitant without knowing why, it could be that you are lacking a key piece of information that may "seal the deal." If so, go back over the earlier information-gathering exercises and look for the key piece of data that may be missing. If the source of your hesitation is more elusive, you may be struggling with your ability to see yourself as successful in your new career and could benefit from a stronger belief in your ability to succeed. Now is the time to make an effort to build your self-esteem, if for no other reason than to get yourself to move from square one.

The process for building your self-esteem is presented in a gem of a book by Bonnie Golden and Kay Lesh, *Building Self-Esteem*. In their book, Golden and Lesh offer a structured process for reframing your view of yourself. The steps in Exhibit 6.1 are drawn from the approach presented in this book. If you are struggling with this step, however, don't rely on the information in the exhibit alone. The model offered by Golden and Lesh is the most productive I have encountered, and I have seen students flourish using their suggestions.

Steps in building self-esteem. **EXHIBIT 6.1**

1. **SELF-ACCEPTANCE** Accept yourself for the valuable, gifted person you are. Yes, you may make mistakes, as does everyone, but you are uniquely gifted with very real strengths that will allow you to grow and play a meaningful role in your life and the life of those around you.

2. **CHALLENGE YOUR IRRATIONAL BELIEFS** Refuse to accept ideas like "everyone must always like me all the time," or "I must be perfect or no one will like me," or "if someone is unhappy with me, I have to fix it." Unquestioning acceptance of these absolutes prevents you from enjoying life fully and focuses your energy in areas in which you may have no control or influence. Focus your energy in areas that will yield results and stop obsessing about things that can't be fixed.

3. **ALLOW YOURSELF TO TAKE CHANCES (RISKS)** Fear of failure forces you to live a narrow, constricted life. Taking chances and trying new things give you the opportunity to live a rich, full, interesting life.

4. **BE BRAVE ENOUGH TO BE WHO YOU REALLY ARE** By saying what you really think and letting others know where you stand, you allow the real you to come out authentically. Instead of being different people, one on the inside and the other the one the world sees, you can be just one person, the real you. The effort to bring yourself out balances your world and lets you live in harmony with yourself.

5. **DON'T TAKE YOURSELF TOO SERIOUSLY** If you try something and you fall flat on your face, pick yourself up and have a chuckle with everyone else. Everyone will love you for being able to let yourself be you and you will love yourself more by being gentle with yourself.

Career decision making is the heart of your career adventure. It requires courage, strength, and resolve. Now is the time to start developing the psychological "muscle" that will get you through the rough spots in life. Enjoy your chance to choose. You are exactly where you want to be.

DEALING WITH UNCERTAINTY: INFORMATION AND AFFIRMATIONS

Have you ever picked up a video controller and tried to play a game that you have never tried? Depending on who else might be playing, you may have felt overwhelmed by the setting, the action, and how to control your avatar or player. If you are fortunate, someone may have tried to assist you, but it may have felt disorienting to listen and translate instructions while competing or trying to keep your character alive.

Sometimes when you are experiencing the ups and downs that go with any career, you may feel like you are watching yourself stumble through a computer game, groping in unfamiliar terrain, knowing that any move you make may lead to a game-over message. In a sense, you are competing in a new world. You will have to make decisions without enough information or based on assumptions that you can't confirm. Checklists and goal setting help, but they can't eliminate all uncertainty and risk. Anxiety comes with uncertainty. If you are struggling with choosing, try to remain as flexible as possible. As the impact of global economic change and technology advances continue to influence the career marketplace, your path will be deeply dependent on two critical qualities:

- *Adaptability*—Be creative as you consider your capabilities and where they might be best valued. Seek new ways to use the skills you have mastered. Broaden your portfolio of skills and take advantage of new opportunities to learn.

- *Resilience*—There may be unexpected situations that seem to delay your progress or defer a desired outcome. Don't focus on your frustration. Use your problem-solving skills to make the changes that will overcome obstacles and create a new outcome, one that either continues on your path or creates a new way to get there. Never, never give up . . . persistence will pay off. That is your best insurance against the unpredictability of the future.

Keep in mind that you are well prepared and maintain a positive outlook. One way to maintain that positive outlook is through *affirmations*. Affirmations are statements you can use to give yourself a boost when you experience doubt and uncertainty. When you feel discouraged, try repeating some of these statements as a way to steady yourself during the rough spots.

"I make good decisions and I am happy with the results."

"If I don't like the outcome, I am smart enough to know how to change things."

"I always achieve my goals."

"I'm gifted and energetic and I believe in myself."

"I'm lucky to be here and the people I meet feel lucky to know me."

Say these affirmations over and over as many times a day as you need. You will be surprised at how the use of affirmative statements refocuses your energy in a positive way. Exercise 6.5 will help you develop your own affirmations.

Take a Closer Look   6.5

POSITIVE SELF-TALK

Everyone has had negative experiences that cause self-doubt. But our faith in our ability to accomplish our goals can be reinforced through affirmations. Repeating affirming statements is simply an acknowledgment of what you may already believe but may have come to doubt because of a bad experience.

Think about a situation that might make you feel uncomfortable, hesitant, or even fearful. Maybe it's entering a classroom full of new faces or completing a final test. Whatever it might be, imagine yourself experiencing that same difficult situation in a way that you never have before—as your ideal self— confident, self-assured, at ease.

How do you look in this fantasy? Describe yourself as you might look and feel.

_____

_____

Pick a few words that describe how you are in your fantasy. Then develop an affirmation using those words to describe yourself in a positive, encouraging way.

_____

_____

In the following space, write additional affirmations to encourage and support yourself.

_____

_____

_____

Repeat the affirmations, eyes closed, putting your trust in the words you have chosen. How do you feel now?

_____

_____

Discuss your responses to your affirmations when you drop into the CA Café or with the class.

One final word. Students sometimes ask me if the day will come when they won't have doubts about themselves and the choices they make. They are disappointed when they find that even the most competent and respected professionals have moments when they question themselves and wonder if they can pull it off. If you are truly growing and challenging yourself, there may be times when self-doubt will cause you to hesitate. Your challenge is to keep trying, keep getting better. You might have fears, but they needn't paralyze you. Facing your fears and doing your best is part of meeting the challenge to grow. You are working to achieve *long-term* goals. It's worth the risk.

6.6 Take a Closer Look

PULLING IT ALL TOGETHER

Read the following statements and complete them as honestly and realistically as you can.

The most important issues for me in any job/career are:

_____

_____

The options on my career option checklist were:

_____

_____

The most favorable options on my checklist were:

_____

_____

My career goal is:

_____

_____

My realistic and achievable plan of action and short-term goals are:

_____

_____

Discuss any reactions you have to this chapter in the CA Café or the class.

A LOOK BACK

This chapter has given you the tools you need to have a better, more focused view of where you are going. By now, you are able to set priorities and criteria for evaluating choices and can complete a career option checklist that helps you compare your options.

You have also been able to set long- and short-term goals. You have stated your goals with conviction and have developed a coherent plan of action that you can begin using right now to start on your new path. You have anticipated what lies ahead and you are affirming your belief in your ability to achieve your goals.

Does this mean you are finished with your career decision making? While you may have made a choice that will lay the foundation for your career for some time to come, you will probably refer back to and use many of these tools in the future. As you gain experience personally and professionally, you will continue to be presented with choices regarding your career. Have faith in your ability to make the right decision. Stay flexible and keep a positive focus. These attitudes will be crucial in helping you reach your goals.

Career Adventure Café

Visit the CA Café and share the results of this phase of your career process. Your adventure has brought you to a major milestone . . . the decision before you is the result of your investigation on two levels, the assessment of who you are and an exploration of the career market. At each step in this adventure, new information has emerged. Has that information confirmed the vision of what you hope to achieve? Has there been information that has made you adapt your vision to the reality of what lies ahead? Or have you discovered something that has made you rethink your original plan? What have the members of your group found in their investigations? Compare notes on where you are in the decision cycle and see what everyone else has developed to support their choices. Here are some questions to get you started:

Have the other members of your group decided what their career goal is or are they weighing more than one option?

_____

_____

If you are considering two options, what are the aspects that distinguish them and is there a way to determine which might be a better choice? What do the members of the group think about their options?

_____

_____

Is it necessary to be sure right now? What do the members of your group think?

_____

_____

Facebook It

Have you decided the career path on which you are going to embark? Have things begun to become more clear? Have you set your priorities and made some choices? Share those choices on your Facebook page and then see what your friends have decided when you drop by the CA Café.

Other Sources and Suggested Reading

Smart Choices: A Practical Guide to Making Better Decisions by John S. Hammond, Ralph L. Keeney, and Howard Raiffa

This is an excellent resource for a systematic, step-by-step, decision-making model.

Rational Choice in an Uncertain World by Reid Hastie and Robyn M. Dawes

This highly accessible book uses real-world examples to teach decision making as a skill that produces favorable outcomes.

Complete Confidence: The Handbook by Sheenah Hankin

An excellent resource to challenge you if you are caught in a loop that blocks your desire to make more productive choices.

Thinking Fast and Slow by Daniel Kahneman

This Nobel Prize winner describes the two different types of decision-making styles and how some decisions are worth the effort to think about slowly.

Web Sites and Internet Resources

www.byu.edu/ccc

This is a great decision-making site from Brigham Young University. Select the "Choosing a Major" option under "General Advisement" to begin.

www.dailyfeats.com

This is a digital goal-setting site that allows you to track your ongoing progress toward your goal. You can note each time you accomplish an objective that takes you closer to your goal. It is a great way to reinforce your commitment and encourage continuing movement forward.

www.mindtools.com

This site presents a wide variety of tools that address decision making and models for every perspective. Click on the "Toolkit" and then click on "Decision Making" in the drop-down menu.

The Job Campaign

You are now prepared to take the next step in your career adventure: organizing your job campaign. This phase of your career development will provide the tools for actually entering the job market—your resume, cover letter, interview preparation, and job marketing skills.

Any formula for success includes being ready for opportunities when they arise. You have prepared for your decision by doing research on yourself and on careers. You will continue to move toward your chosen career by gaining the technical and academic training you need to be a competent professional. It is time to focus on gaining the skills that will allow you to showcase your abilities when you are job hunting. This is an opportunity that might not happen for several years, or it could happen next week. You will be ready for the challenge of competing in an increasingly crowded and complex job market.

Your next task is to organize your research about yourself and careers into a portfolio that markets you successfully. You are entitled to succeed. The way you use your information and training will make the difference in whether you stand out as a shining star or get lost in the crowd.

ORGANIZING YOUR SEARCH

PART
THREE

Designing Your Resume and Cover Letters 7

What is the vision you created of the professional you would like to become? Entering the career market is your route to realize that vision. You can accomplish that only if you can effectively communicate to others what you see in yourself. The resume is the primary vehicle for introducing yourself to employers who can assist you in reaching your goal.

CONVEYING WHO YOU ARE

A resume is a business document created to help employers and candidates talk about possible employment. It is expected to reflect systematic organization characteristic of most business documents. The trick is, however, to conform to those expectations and still present yourself as an individual. Your resume should highlight the unique blend of skills and experiences that makes you the ideal candidate for a position, while still respecting the conventions and expectations of the work world. You control what information is included in your resume. A well-crafted resume emphasizes only those aspects of your background that make you a serious competitor for a job.

Make no mistake. This is a competition, and there will be situations in which you compete against other well-qualified candidates. Designing a resume that presents your abilities best will give you the necessary edge to be successful.

Various styles of resumes serve the needs of job seekers in different ways. Your challenge is to find a resume style with which you feel comfortable. Ideally, it will allow you to describe your background in ways that suit the various opportunities available to you and also to convey your abilities competitively and honestly. Once you decide which resume style works best for you, then you develop the content based on your background, taking into account the needs of the specific employer and the requirements of a particular job.

THERE'S NO SUCH THING AS A "SUREFIRE" RESUME

In any library or bookstore you will find a great number of resume manuals that advertise a set way to write resumes that "win" jobs—if you simply follow the formulas in the book. There are as many ways of writing resumes as there are resume writers and, so far, the "surefire," guaranteed-to-get-you-a-job resume has yet to be developed.

Only one resume will work best for you—the one you develop using information about your special combination of skills, abilities, training, education, experiences, and qualifications. Be conscious of the standard formats when developing your resume, but know that any one style prescribed by a book can never take into account all of your needs for a particular situation.

The reason that resume writing defies simplistic formulas is that resume *reading* is highly subjective. If you show your resume to ten different people, some may think it is perfect, some will suggest minor changes, and others may suggest substantial revisions. Depending on the current trends in business communication, any or all of them may be correct. People in charge of hiring are just like your well-meaning advisors. They apply their personal preferences and idiosyncrasies when evaluating resumes. Trying to predict how a particular employer will respond is nearly impossible.

The only logical way to create your resume is to identify and describe those aspects of your background that relate to the potential position and then select a style of resume that showcases you and your abilities to your best advantage. Next we will look at different styles of resumes and what each style offers job seekers.

RESUME STYLES

Almost all resume formats and variations can be categorized under one of three resume styles: chronological, functional, or achievement/accomplishment.

Chronological Resume

The resume style with which most people are familiar is the *chronological resume*. This resume focuses primarily on work experience and presents your background in *reverse* chronological order. This means that you list your most recent position first and your earliest job last.

Most employers prefer this resume style since the focus is on your work history, the factor they consider most relevant. The chronological style is appropriate if you are seeking employment in a field in which you have an established and successful track record. The emphasis on work experience presents your background in a way that helps the employer visualize you in that position. The format shows a natural progression, from the bottom of the page to the top, of increasing responsibility and growth, culminating with your professional summary or profile at the top, which should closely parallel the job for which you are applying. It is an ideal style for you if you have had a long career in one discipline and want to continue to work in that field. The chronological resume in Exhibit 7.1 illustrates how this style enhances the candidate's appropriateness for the job.

Emphasizing your work experience may work well if you have a strong background in the field in which you are applying, but this technique is less effective if you don't have much prior experience. For this reason, the principal drawback of chronological resumes is the focus on work experience. If your employment has been primarily in the food service industry, for example, there may be little that you can state to help an employer see you as a serious professional in another area. You may have an excellent

The chronological resume.   **EXHIBIT 7.1**

Julie Reese

315 Cedar Street	Business (319) 658-9341
Parnell, Iowa 52325	Cell (319) 367-1152
Residence (319) 439-6348	jreese@netlink.net

Profile:	Accounting professional with broad range of experiences; strong background in computer accounting applications
Professional Experience:	Basic Printing, Inc., Parnell, IA *Accounting Assistant,* 2011 to present Responsible for assisting controller in performance of accounting functions, including posting journal entries, general ledger, forecasting, and accounts payable/accounts receivable; some tax experience. ■ Specialized Skills: Microsoft Excel/Word, Windows 8 Hawkins' Lithography, Parnell, IA *Accounting Clerk,* 2008 to 2011 Responsible for posting to general ledger and journal entries.
Education:	University of Iowa, Iowa City, IA Graduated 2012, Bachelor of Science Major: Accounting GPA: 3.6
Special Achievements:	2011 Recipient, Parnell Jaycee's "Outstanding Young Woman" Scholarship; Dean's List, 2008–2012
Extracurricular Activities:	Member, Accounting Club, 2008–2012 University of Iowa Alumni Association

academic record, plenty of organizing experience from volunteer projects, and maybe even co-op experience. If you use a chronological resume that highlights your work at the fast-food franchise, you may project an image of yourself standing behind a counter, while the more relevant data is buried at the bottom of your resume.

Work experience unrelated to the job you currently seek is not totally irrelevant. Steady employment of any type speaks well of you as an applicant and, more important, identifies skills (e.g., customer service, managerial responsibility, performing under pressure) that could benefit future employers. You must learn to identify and describe those skills using the appropriate format. It is critical that your first presentation to a potential employer establish an image that matches the employer's needs and assumptions about the job the employer wishes to fill. The goal of your resume is to make the connection between yourself and the employer's vision of the skills needed to fill the job, as different as they might be from what you have done in the past. A chronological resume style might not always be the best style through which to accomplish this task.

Functional Resume

The *functional* (or *hybrid*) *resume* highlights the skills and abilities of the job seeker rather than the settings in which the person obtained those skills. This makes it an ideal resume for the midlife career changer or someone with limited work experience in the field. Exhibit 7.2 shows a sample functional resume.

The functional resume may seem to be the perfect resume format since it focuses on the skills relevant to the position you seek. While it is typically an excellent format for anyone trying to enter a career in which they have little experience, it is not the best style for the job seeker who has a strong work background. The functional style simply doesn't offer the proper forum to show the depth of skill and career maturity that comes from extended or relevant work experience. In addition, a list of your skills isn't a helpful sales tool if you have nothing in your background to establish how you obtained those skills. Related academic study is helpful, but most employers are skeptical that it can completely take the place of hands-on experience for developing a high level of proficiency in any field.

Achievement/Accomplishment Resume

The *achievement* or *accomplishment resume* uses many of the same elements of the previous styles with one important difference. It uses actual events from prior experiences and training as the method for conveying information about you. This type of resume provides the employer with the basics of your training and work life and also substantiates your skills through outlining your past accomplishments. Exhibit 7.3 illustrates one style of the accomplishment resume.

As noted in Exhibit 7.3, the achievements associated with the work Ray is performing support the image that he is attempting to convey—that of a motivated self-starter capable of making the sale.

Every employer is interested in two aspects of your background:

1. *What can you do?* This is the skill question. Effectively answering this lets the employer know what you are capable of contributing from the very start.

2. *What have you done?* This is the "prove it" question. You may have the skill, but that in itself may not be enough. Citing your achievements enhances your credibility. It is the most powerful and understated way of backing up what you claim to be able to do.

The functional resume.

EXHIBIT 7.2

David Muñoz

654 Walnut Drive
Aurora, CO 80012
Residence (303) 682-4330

Business (303) 365-5729
Cell (303) 348-2773
dmunoz@earthlink.net

Summary	Seasoned self-starter able to create opportunities and make the sale seeks a position in sales and marketing
Skills and Abilities	▪ Recognized abilities in all areas of market forecasting ▪ Knowledgeable in marketing aspects of product development ▪ Practiced in developing sales leads and creating interest ▪ Well-developed organizational skills ▪ Able to make the sale; strong closer
Education	University of Colorado, Boulder, CO Graduated 2013, Bachelor of Science Major: Business Administration/Marketing GPA: 3.4
Awards and Achievements	Dean's List, 2012, 2013 Member, National Honor Society
Work Experience	Steve's Place, Aurora, CO *Sales/customer service for clothing retailer,* 2011 to present Hale's Quick Stop Photos, Boulder, CO *Customer service and sales for photo development outlet,* 2009 to 2011
Extracurricular Activities	Volunteer, United Way, Special Funds Committee Member, National Marketing Association, Aurora Chapter

EXHIBIT 7.3   The achievement/accomplishment resume.

RAY GRANT

733 Elm Street   Business (919) 822-1562
Kinston, NC 28502   Cell (919) 635-4883
Residence (919) 843-7638   raygrant43@aol.com

SUMMARY OF QUALIFICATIONS	Skilled sales/customer service professional able to anticipate and respond to customer needs; technical sales orientation
EXPERIENCE	The Hershey Chocolate Company, Hershey, PA *Sales Representative,* July 2011 to present Responsible for service and expansion of major wholesale accounts in the Kinston area; coordinate corporate promotions and advertising campaign through wholesalers; negotiate ad rates and charges; monitor use of displays, product samples, pricing, distribution, and warehouse inventory.
ACCOMPLISHMENTS	■ Increased sales volume with two major grocery wholesalers by over 30 percent ■ Received Outstanding Quarterly Sales Representative Award three times in one year ■ Developed team approach to marketing product with local store managers
EDUCATION	East Carolina University, Greensboro, NC Graduated 2011, Bachelor of Arts Major: Liberal Arts/Communications GPA: 3.0
SPECIAL ACTIVITIES	Volunteer, Small Business Development Center, Kinston Office Assisted small business owners in various development activities, including creating employee handbooks and developing and presenting training.

The functional and chronological formats are good vehicles for describing your skills and history but do little to establish the dynamic image conveyed by the achievement resume. The latter type of resume is especially beneficial to people with an extensive experiential background who are facing particular career obstacles, such as job displacement through downsizing. Start building an achievement resume even if you don't expect to be laid off. Everyone, even individuals with standard sales or counter work experience, has accomplishments that can be quantified. In a later exercise we will generate ideas for listing accomplishments and achievements.

WHICH STYLE IS RIGHT FOR YOU?

The style of resume you choose is largely determined by the type of position for which you are applying. If the position is in a field in which you have a significant amount of experience, you may wish to use the chronological style. It will meet the employer's expectations and highlight your strengths in the field.

If you are trying to enter a new career or looking for your first job out of college, you may want to consider the functional style. This style shines a bright light where it belongs, on your ability to do the job, not on the places where you developed your ability.

If you can identify events in your life that you feel are noteworthy and will make you an appealing candidate for a position, then the achievement resume is probably the resume style for you.

As we proceed through the various phases of developing a resume, you will see how you can integrate elements of each format based on specific situations to give your resume a customized look. You can custom design your resume simply by shuffling the various components of the resume to suit the specific needs of the job you seek. Keep copies of all the resumes you create to respond to different opportunities. That will make customizing your resume to meet the specific requirements of the various jobs you compete for fast and easy.

When deciding which style of resume to use, ask yourself, "What are my strongest qualifications for the job?" Your answer, whether it relates to academic skill, technical training, or work experience, will help you determine which style will present you in the best light.

Once you have decided on a resume style, begin to focus on developing the content for your resume.

DEVELOPING CONTENT FOR YOUR RESUME

What information should you include in (or exclude from) your resume? Remember, you want to create a picture with words that lets the employer imagine you in the job for which you're applying. Think about the following two questions:

- What skills are needed to do the job for which I am applying?
- What experiences and training have I had that match those skills?

A critical factor in determining how many people see your resume is the choice of key words representing your skills. Those key words will be the flags that mark your resume for review because your skills match those the organization seeks. For example, if a company conducts a search based on the criteria of "B.S., engineering, mechanical, automotive," it first will be referred to the resumes of people who meet all criteria; next, to those that meet most but not all; and so on.

Key words that describe the parameters of the job to be filled may determine whose resume is read and whose remains in database limbo. Thus, depending upon the type of job you seek and the companies to which you apply, you may need to prepare yourself for a job search on two levels—one for people and one for electronic resources. Until now, the goal has always been to get someone to read your resume in order to get a shot at an interview. Now, with some firms your resume won't even be read unless it is developed with a clear understanding of the position you want. That requires some thoughtful work on the content of your resume.

If you are just beginning a new career, you probably will not have had any positions that relate directly to the job you're seeking. That's nothing to be discouraged about. All jobs can be broken down into specific tasks, regardless of their setting. Focus on the tasks that most closely parallel the tasks and skills necessary for the job you seek. For example, perhaps you have an extensive background in retailing and customer service but would like to work in human services. By focusing on certain aspects of customer service you can establish your qualifications in that field. Skills such as sensitivity to customer concerns, listening skills, and the ability to work under pressure contribute to your portfolio as a human services professional. Combine these skills with your academic background and you can begin to see that you have a strong foundation for a winning resume.

If you are unsure what key words might be most effective, scan the classified job ads for the type of position in which you have an interest. Make a note of the words that appear in the ads. These skills, the ones employers mention again and again, represent the key words that should appear in your resume as well.

The same process is equally effective for other disciplines. If your work experience has been in one area and you want to get started in another profession, focus on the skills that relate to your new job, regardless of their importance in your current role. It's what you are going to do with them that counts, not where you got them. If you already have paid experience in a field, you are halfway there. Use Exercise 7.1 as a way to find the parallels that will help you achieve your goal.

7.1   Take a Closer Look

FINDING PARALLEL SKILLS

In this exercise, you distill your prior experiences and skills into a summary that incorporates key words that match the job you are seeking. By now you have done the homework necessary to know which skills are important in the job to which you aspire. See if you can match your experiences (including jobs, internships, volunteer work, workshops, courses and laboratories, etc.) and the skills acquired through them to the skills needed in your future career.

SKILLS (KEY WORDS) REQUIRED IN THE JOB YOU WANT	RELATED SKILLS (KEY WORDS) YOU'VE DEVELOPED IN PRIOR JOBS AND OTHER EXPERIENCES
_____	_____
_____	_____
_____	_____
_____	_____
_____	_____

_____   _____

_____   _____

_____   _____

Keep in mind that even the most routine and basic jobs offer the opportunity to use and master skills that can become the building blocks for other positions. Try to find the parallel skills that intersect with job titles and categories. These skills will help you determine what to include in your resume. As you develop the components of your resume, reinforce your qualifications by including experiences and examples that reflect your skills as they relate to the position you want.

Discuss the results of this exercise when you drop in at the CA Café or with the class.

COMPONENTS OF A RESUME

The six basic components of a resume are the _identifiers_, the _summary_ or _profile_, _skills_, _employment history_ or _work experience_, _education_ or _training_, and _related information_. We examine each of these separate areas next.

Component 1: The Identifiers

The identifiers on your resume are those parts that tell the employer your name and how you can be reached. While these are the most straightforward parts of the resume, it is quite common for people to forget to include their phone numbers or overlook a typographical error in their names. Be sure to proofread your resume to ensure there are no errors. Neglecting even a small item in resume writing tells the employer a lot about your attention to detail and your ability to present yourself professionally.

A good rule to remember when seeking employment is that written responses are most often rejections, but phone calls are usually invitations to an interview. That's why your correct phone number is critical. When you include the phone numbers where you can be reached, be sure that anyone answering the telephone at those places knows who you are and that a potential employer might be calling. Even the most open-minded employer will be irritated by rude responses and loud background music. Make sure your outgoing voicemail message is professional and be sure to include your email address and cell phone number on your resume. It's also a good idea to use a standard ringback tone so that your presentation is professional at every point of contact.

Component 2: The Summary/Profile

The summary or profile component of a resume is a statement about your background and strengths as they relate to the position you seek. It usually goes at the beginning of the resume, immediately following the identifiers. This component evolved from the old "objective," a part of the resume that stated the job seeker's goal. The use of a summary or profile statement accomplishes the same thing by focusing attention on your ability to do the job.

This component can be a valuable part of your resume, but you must use it carefully. If your summary statement is vague or too general, you will not be providing useful information. I have personally seen hundreds of resumes that began with an all-purpose statement: "A strong performer able to use my skills and abilities in any setting." People who begin their resume with this type of statement would do better to exclude it altogether or to change it to a specific statement.

A well-crafted summary or profile statement ideally should do three things:

1. Communicate that you are a thoughtful, mature individual with a clear idea of who you are and what you are able to do.

2. Briefly summarize your primary skills as they parallel the position, draw the employer's interest in you as a potential employee, and encourage her to continue reading the rest of the resume.

3. Assert your goals and commitment to growth.

Developing a summary or profile that accomplishes all of these things is not an easy task. Ideally, your profile, and your entire resume, should be tailored for the specific job for which you are applying. That isn't always possible, however, especially if you are providing a resume to be distributed by a third party, such as the college career services office. In most cases, however, to be a competitive candidate for a position, your resume must correlate closely to the specific needs of the position, beginning with the summary. Once you have the summary or profile, the rest of your resume will fall into place.

Some profiles can be disarmingly simple. One of my students who was a union carpenter felt strongly that a two-word phrase, "Skilled carpenter," would accurately reflect who she was. The type of profession you are entering will often determine how you frame your statement.

Occasionally, students feel that a summary statement is limiting. They prefer to leave out specifics, hoping to increase their marketability in a broad range of positions. If you feel this way, you can try putting together a resume without a summary or profile, making sure that you don't fall into the trap of trying to be all things to all people. Stay focused and you may find that the resume can be just as effective.

Exercise 7.2 gives you ideas about developing a strong career summary statement.

7.2   Take a Closer Look

A PRACTICE SUMMARY STATEMENT

Your work on your summary or profile statement will continue throughout your career as you grow, develop your skills, and seek new goals. To get started, try the fill-in-the-blank format below.

"A(n) _____(a)_____ background in _____(b)_____ with ability in _____(c)_____ and _____(d)_____ ."

Doesn't look like much at this point. That's okay. It's your job to provide the specifics depending on your career goal, interests, and specialized experiences that fit the situation. Here's an example of a summary that might work using this format.

"A broad background in human resources development with ability to develop and implement programs."

Or:

"Specialized experience in elementary/preschool education with emphasis on special needs populations."

Each blank has a purpose. Blank (a) gives you the chance to present a positive description of your experience. Blank (b) offers the category of experience that your background falls under: accounting, education, business, engineering, management, sales, technology, health care, and so on. Blanks (c) and (d) allow you to focus your skills on specifics that spotlight your greatest strengths.

Now develop your own summary or profile using the parts of the format that you think work best for you. Review the following list of words to help you fill in the blanks.

BLANK (A)

strong	advanced	extensive
effective	proven	demonstrated
broad	outstanding	substantial

BLANK (B)

administration	customer service	education
human services	library services	programming
marketing	sales	engineering
business	management	retailing
accounting	graphics	technology
research	food service	health services

BLANKS (C) AND (D)

(These terms should be related directly to the job or field in which you are applying.)

implementing programs	initiating programs	developing programs
organizing	problem solving	troubleshooting
administering programs	design/layout	team building
taxes/cost accounting	counseling/referral	coding/debugging
programming/systems analysis	developing leads/closing	acute/critical care
server-side programming	database administration	construction

If the suggested model seems like too much, don't worry. Just take what you need to get started. For example:

"Recognized performer, able to provide full range of accounting support services."

"Chronic and long-term care specialist, familiar with needs of geriatric clients."

"Public relations expertise with specialized skills in copywriting and marketing development."

Any of these models or your own statement are fine as long as they set the right tone for the employer by briefly expressing your unique combinations of strengths and interests.

Discuss the results of this exercise when you drop into the CA Café or with the class.

Component 3: Skills

Sometimes students with little paid experience in their field find that resume writing is just one long, discouraging exercise. They've spent years preparing for their first job, but when they begin to summarize everything they've learned using conventional resume formats, their background looks insignificant, hardly representative of their hard work and preparation. If this is true for you, then you will have better results emphasizing your skills over your paid experience. A combination format that focuses on skills will allow you to flesh out your resume using experiences from a variety of sources: part-time jobs, co-op and intern experiences, volunteer work, lab work, classroom learning.

The growing reliance of digital scans to screen resumes increases the significance of the skills section of your resume. When a person doing hiring determines the parameters for a job and then performs a scan of resumes for key words, the computer will flag those resumes that meet the parameters, with those meeting the greatest number of parameters pulled first, those meeting fewer parameters pulled second, and so on. You can see how a thorough survey of your skills in a resume becomes critical.

The skills component of your resume is simply a series of statements that expand on the profile statement by describing in detail the abilities and qualifications that are suited to the position you seek. This section builds credibility for the statement with which you began the resume. Here are a few examples:

"Knowledgeable in all aspects of tax compliance accounting"

"Strong written and verbal communication skills"

"Skilled in network design and setup"

"Experienced in use of scientific methods and observation"

"Able to read blueprints"

"Capable in full range of administrative and clerical skills"

As you develop a broader, deeper knowledge of your chosen field, you can expand this part of your resume to reflect your increasing level of skill, citing specific buzzwords that not only identify you as a pro but also better flag your resume for electronic search. These skills deserve to be highlighted in a special section. You have worked to acquire them. Showcase them in a way that markets you effectively. Exercise 7.3 will help you develop skills statements.

7.3   Take a Closer Look

HIGHLIGHTING YOUR SKILLS

When developing your skill statements, keep in mind the exercises in Chapter 3 devoted to skills and abilities. Remember to focus on those parts of your skill portfolio that are relevant to the position you seek. Use the phrases below to start developing a few statements that communicate concisely your greatest strengths. Remember to incorporate key words associated with your skills.

"Knowledgeable in all areas devoted to _____."

"Strong background in _____."

"Able to _____."

"Exceptional _____ skills."

"Experienced in _____."

"Knowledgeable in use of the following (software, machines, and so on) _____"

Continue to develop statements that highlight your relevant skills. Focus on skills that are as specific as possible to the job for which you are applying. The more detail you can include, the better—you can include as many as five or six statements in this special section, more if you have strong credentials in a particular area.

Discuss the results of this exercise when you drop in at the CA Café or with the class.

Component 4: Employment History/Work Experience

Your employment history or work experience is a significant part of your resume. Most employers will not consider someone a viable candidate without some knowledge of that person's employment background. At some point during college, you should begin to look for opportunities to acquire hands-on experience in your field. Part-time jobs, volunteer work, and co-op/internship positions are all fruitful areas for you to begin your career and add to your resume. When you detail your experience, mention where you worked, your job title, and how long you worked in that position. Remember: If you are competing for the chance to interview alongside people who have qualifications as strong as yours, strive to showcase your experience in a format that best highlights your capabilities.

Your prior employment can be divided into two aspects:

- *Your routine duties*—These were the responsibilities you were expected to fulfill on a daily basis. The particulars might be cut-and-dried and may sound at times like your job description.

- *Your accomplishments*—These are the high points of your work or academic life that serve as the basis of the achievement resume. They usually reflect your unique combination of skills and abilities.

When describing routine duties, use phrases and action words that convey a dynamic image. Words such as "designed," "managed," "organized," "supervised," "wrote," and "created" work better at establishing an active image than do words like "was responsible for" or "acted as." The Boston College Career Center Web site offers a comprehensive list of action verbs by category (http://www.bc.edu/offices/careers/skills/resumes/verbs.html). Keep in mind that you should use present tense for your current position and past tense (-ed) for prior jobs.

You have to get the employer's attention quickly and keep it, so use short, concise paragraphs, without pronouns and modifiers that may bog down your description. Succinct phrases do not need to be complete sentences. Limit your paragraph on routine duties to no more than four lines. Accomplishments should include one brief statement highlighting the specific results you achieved.

In most cases, the experience component should include only jobs you have held within the last ten years. Emphasize jobs and skills that are relevant to the job you're seeking. Focus on skills so that digital scans will "grab" your resume in a key word search. If a job is not related to the field you're entering, omit or condense it. State only the basics, using one line to describe your duties. "Various customer-service-related duties" serves the purpose.

Look at the following example. The paragraph on routine duties is a concise overview of the person's responsibilities. The accomplishment statements tell the reader that the person was involved, responsible, and willing to go beyond what was expected to help the organization.

EXPERIENCE:

- KREMER'S SUPPLY, INC., Vestron, WA
- Mail Clerk, 12/02 to present

Responsibilities include sorting and delivering mail to all personnel in company of over 150 employees; organizing and distributing packages and priority mail; arranging for overnight shipment of priority packages; delivering messages for executive personnel.

ACCOMPLISHMENTS:

- Reorganized mail sorting system resulting in approximate savings of $800 annually
- Supervised mail room duties when mail room manager was absent

The figure of $800 savings noted in the first accomplishment was developed by estimating the average amount of time saved on a weekly basis and multiplying it by the hourly rate of the employee. When extrapolated, the annual savings might be $800. Estimates and approximations are legitimate methods for calculating quantifiable results of an accomplishment.

Exercise 7.4 will help you think about your experience profile and the accomplishments you have had in your jobs.

7.4   Take a Closer Look

SHOWCASING YOUR WORK EXPERIENCE

To describe your work experience, focus first on your routine duties and then on the accomplishments that resulted from applying your skills. Remember to emphasize the skills that relate to the job for which you are applying.

Experience:

Company name, city, state

_____

Title/dates of employment

_____

Duties:

_____

_____

Accomplishments:

_____

_____

If you are having trouble coming up with accomplishments, answer these questions:

Have you ever supervised anyone?

Have you ever worked as part of a team on a specific project?

Have you ever shown initiative, the drive to learn something new, or your ability to adapt to a new situation?

Have you ever demonstrated strong communication skills, your ability to act as a team player, or a strong commitment to principle or integrity?

Did you ever see a problem and suggest a solution that was adopted? Did it save time or money?

Did you ever improve an existing system or situation? Did the improvement save or increase funds?

Did you sell anything? Did you meet your goals? Did you exceed your goals?

Did you receive awards for your work, as an individual or part of a team?

Did the workload increase while you were on a job? Did you handle the increase successfully?

Develop a concise description of your experience at all the recent and relevant positions you have had.

Job A

_____

_____

Job B

_____

_____

Job C

_____

_____

Review the information you have compiled about your experiences and see if it reflects your current job goal and the skills that might be needed. If you see something that may detract from your relevant skills or aren't sure if the information applies, leave it out. Be brief and focused.

Discuss the results of this exercise when you drop in at the CA Café or with the class.

Component 5: Education/Training

When presenting your education, the key factor again is whether the training you have had is relevant to the stated objective. Anything—college, seminars, workshops, work, or military training—that is related to the objective is important to include in this component of your resume. The format to present this information is quite flexible, and this example is only one of many possibilities.

EDUCATION

Columbia University, New York, NY

Graduated 2004, Bachelor of Science

Major: Business Administration

GPA: 3.5, magna cum laude

The basics of this component are the name of the institution from which you received your education, the location, the year you graduated (or attended), the degree conferred, and major area of study. Include your grade point average only if you have achieved a GPA of 3.0 or above; a lower GPA does not "show" well on a resume.

If you have been fortunate enough to attend workshops or seminars related to your field, either on your own or through your job, include these under a subheading in this section of the resume. You can choose to group these experiences either chronologically, providing dates, or under subject headings. A title such as "Additional Training" or "Seminar Training" suffices to indicate the education subcategory.

Some of you may have prior educational experiences or classes from one or two years of college that you wish to include. Perhaps the time you spent involved in previous study fills a gap in your resume. Emphasize only the information you feel will help you. Note the institution; location; dates, if not too long ago; and the type of study in which you engaged. A statement such as "Various business courses" offers enough pertinent information for the prospective employer.

If training you received is not relevant to the goal of your job search, you risk hurting your chances for getting the job by including it. It is understandable that you would want to acknowledge your efforts; however, sometimes unrelated information can detract from the vision you are trying to create. For example, Paul was seeking a job in risk management and felt that his prior training in truck-driving school could be helpful. It was only after some discussion and several rejection letters that I was able to convince Paul that his history as a truck driver might be confusing and distracting to the conservative insurance executives who were considering him for a position. He removed the statement about his prior unrelated training from his resume; within a month he was offered a position with a large property management company.

Component 6: Related Information

The final component of your resume is a section on related information. This section can include any information that doesn't fall under another component and further supports your appropriateness for the job. Included in this area would be:

- awards or scholarships you may have received
- extracurricular activities
- licenses and certifications related to your career field
- memberships or offices held in professional organizations
- published works
- community involvement

As in all the previous components, keep the focus on the skills or abilities that directly relate to the employer's need and to your objective. You might well be proud of your hobbies and outside activities, but employers' reactions might be considerably less enthusiastic.

Now complete Exercise 7.5, listing some of the things that you might include in this component of your resume.

7.5   Take a Closer Look

THE WHOLE YOU

The related information component of the resume gives you the opportunity to broaden your image for an employer; however, choose carefully when providing these details. Fill in the categories that might be helpful in presenting yourself.

Professional Membership/Offices:

_____

_____

_____

Awards/Scholarships:

_____

_____

_____

Extracurricular Activities:

_____

_____

_____

Published Work:

_____

_____

_____

Volunteer/Community Work:

_____

_____

_____

If you have devoted a substantial amount of time to volunteer or community work that is related to your objective, you may want to include it under your experience component instead. Remember that no matter how committed you may be to a cause, you may scare off an employer who has a great job opening if you broadcast your political or social position in your resume. Be careful! Keep the focus on your skills and ability to do the job.

Generally, any mention of references is unnecessary. Instead, if you have a LinkedIn profile with details related to your academic or professional work, you can reference that with a line at the end of your resume such as "Professional recommendations, industry-specific advice, and extended list of affiliations available at http://www.linkedin.com/in/yournamehere" with the URL to your site. If you choose to do that, however, make sure your LinkedIn site is flawless and portrays you as the ideal candidate for the job for which you are applying.

APPEARANCE, FORMAT, AND ELECTRONIC DISTRIBUTION

This section considers the overall appearance of your resume. Most important, the resume must be readable. Your resume should be not only informative but also attractive and pleasing to the eye. Frame your resume with margins wide enough to present the document as if it were a picture to be admired. Although it is best to use only one or at most two of the more traditional typefaces, the use of uppercase, underlining, italics, and boldface can add to a resume's appeal. Use these functions conservatively and consistently. If you use all caps for job titles then don't use that style for the names of the companies. If you underline job titles then don't capitalize them, except as appropriate for capitalization of proper names. Experiment with different highlights and choose an attractive final format that emphasizes your marketability. Include enough white space—bunched-up information is difficult to read and unappealing to employers. Have you ever turned a page in one of your textbooks and groaned upon seeing that the entire page is one long paragraph? Employers feel the same way. Keep them interested by dividing up the information in a lively style.

Generally, a resume should be confined to one page, but you may need two pages to include all the relevant information. Don't hesitate to use a two-page format if your details fill both pages in a balanced way. Details lend credibility to your resume and this may be especially appropriate if you have a strong experiential background. Don't worry if you only come up with enough for one page, though. One strong page is better than two pages of "fluff."

Any word processing software can be used to create your resume. Additionally, there are resume software packages available that allow you to use formatting tools to create a resume and distribute it on the Internet. The final product can then be printed on a high-quality printer, emailed, or downloaded to a job seeking site for distribution to possible employers.

You may also have your resume reproduced at a copy service on its high-quality photocopiers. If the copier works correctly, the originals and the copies should be indistinguishable. Most of these shops also sell paper and matching envelopes suitable for resumes and cover letters. Choose conservative, basic colors such as white, ivory, buff, or light gray, and high-quality bond paper.

Store your resume on a flash drive or email it to yourself as a means of archiving it. Most colleges, libraries, and quick-print shops now offer resume services or personal computers with which you can update your stored resume. This allows you to distribute your resume electronically and makes revision an easy process. You can then tailor your resume to specific positions as they become available. When you save your resume, make sure you include your name. Databases are a graveyard for resumes saved as "resume.doc." Some colleges now offer an electronic resume database from which employers can access, scan, and select resumes. If this is true of your school, find out from the career services professional who administers the database what you need to do to effectively showcase your resume on that system.

Formatting your resume for Internet distribution may take a little more planning, but it's worth the effort, particularly if you are open to seeking employment outside of your community or region. Electronic format requires that the font you choose for your resume be readable when scanned electronically. The best fonts for this purpose are "nonproportional" fonts, which allocate the same amount of space to each letter. Examples are Courier and Prestige, the traditional "typewriter" fonts, or Times New Roman, Ariel, or Helvetica. You may also have to remove those features that make the paper resume visually pleasing: italics, underlining, boldface, tabs, brackets, and hard returns. These enhancements may distort your copy when transmitted electronically. As with the hard copy, keep the text open between sections and use wide margins. If possible, save your resume as a PDF file to help maintain the integrity of the formatting.

Your resume is a living document that should change as you grow and acquire new skills. Some people get lazy and assume that now that they have a resume they'll never again have to bother writing another. This may be your first resume but it won't be your last.

THE STEPS IN FINDING A JOB

Finding a job using traditional means is a step-by-step process. (This process may vary slightly if you use nontraditional job-search methods, such as being referred by a friend. [More about that in Chapter 9.])

The first step is crafting a well-written resume. After that, you are ready to start using it as your introduction to employers. The cover letter is the next step: It acts as your resume's escort in your presentation to an employer. The cover letter is just as important as the resume because you want to convince the employer to read your resume. Once an employer reads and is impressed by a resume, he will invite the applicant for an interview. From the interview comes the job offer.

Once you begin sending out your resume and cover letter, you can begin to determine the weaknesses in your job campaign. If your resume is reaching employers and yet you are not being invited to interview, then you may need to fine-tune your letter or your resume. If you are getting interviews but no offers, then you may want to evaluate your interview style and make the necessary adjustments. You will be able to see exactly where you need to focus your attention based on the real-world results of your efforts.

You have already met the first challenge of job seeking: writing your resume. The next step is to write a persuasive cover letter.

THE COVER LETTER

Your cover letter is a crucial step toward getting a job. You must write a letter that convinces the employer to review your resume, interview you, and then discuss employment with you. A well-written cover letter follows a logical progression in each of its paragraphs:

Paragraph 1: This is why I am writing to you. (newspaper ad, referral)

Paragraph 2: This is who I am and what we have in common.

Paragraph 3: Conclusion: We should get together.

If you follow this format and back it up with solid reasoning, you will increase your chance that the employer will clearly see your value as a serious candidate for the position. The cover letter in Exhibit 7.4 uses this traditional but effective approach. Each of the paragraphs in this letter contributes to the writer's goal of making a logical, persuasive presentation. In addition, the candidate takes every opportunity to refer to the attached resume, further encouraging the employer to read on and consider him as a serious candidate.

Tailoring a cover letter to the specifics of each job for which you apply is one way to ensure that you are doing everything you can to market yourself effectively. Each employer wants to feel that her job is the only one in which you are interested. Take advantage of this fact by paying careful attention to any job description. Address your letter to a specific person within the organization, rather than writing to "Human Resources Director." If you must send your letter to a blind address, then use the salutation "Dear Sir or Madam:" rather than "To Whom It May Concern." (Never use just "Dear Sir:"—it would rightly be interpreted as sexist.)

If you feel confident enough to pull it off, you might try incorporating a touch or two in your cover letter that is designed to catch the attention of the reader and demonstrate that you tailored the letter specifically for that organization. For instance, instead of starting your letter with the reason for sending your resume, try a bold statement assuring the reader you are the ideal candidate, such as "Here are the reasons I am convinced I could be the candidate you are seeking for the position of account representative." Then insert bulleted statements that highlight the relevant skills mentioned in the ad or job announcement.

Another technique that is an eye-catcher for someone who is willing to risk standing out is the addition of a postscript. The P.S. is something that will always get attention so it has to be well-crafted and specific. Do your homework and reference something that is relevant and current. For example,

"P.S. Your most recent project, the renovation of the old Palace Theater, is one in which I have a particular interest, having worked on rehabbing urban neighborhoods during my summer breaks."

EXHIBIT 7.4   Sample cover letter.

William R. Gooding

1463 49TH AVENUE NORTH, ST. PETERSBURG, FL 33703

Residence (727) 765-2231   Mobile (727) 344-5671

July 6, 2012

Ms. Barbara Burke
The Vaughan Group, Inc.
45 North Banks Street
St. Petersburg, FL 33705

Dear Ms. Burke,

I am writing in response to your ad for the position of entry-level account assistant which appeared in the St. Petersburg Times Web site on July 1.

As a recent graduate of the University of Southern Florida, my training and experience in market analysis, advertising design/copy writing, and client services are close parallels to the portfolio of skills you indicated you are seeking. My co-op position at Affiliated Accounts provided me with the real-world experience that will allow me to provide immediate support to the clients of The Vaughan Group. As you can see from my attached resume, my background is ideally suited to the needs of your firm.

I have attached my resume to help you evaluate my background and am available for an interview at your convenience. Please don't hesitate to contact me at (727) 344-5671 should you have any questions. I look forward to hearing from you.

Sincerely,

William R. Gooding

William R. Gooding

Attachment

Use these approaches with caution, however. Inserting items that break with traditional format work only if they include substance. Without solid information that showcases relevant background, the same things that get attention can work against you and come off as gimmicky and false.

Again, your cover letter is crucial. As with your resume, consider having one or more people read/edit/proofread your cover letter. You may miss errors or awkward statements that others may catch.

You will need a cover letter every time you send out your resume, so take the time now to come up with a format that you can fine-tune for specific jobs. Use the form provided in Exercise 7.6 to write your own persuasive cover letter.

Take a Closer Look   7.6

WRITING A PERSUASIVE COVER LETTER

Complete the form letter using the logical approach just described. Refer to the appendix for other examples of persuasive cover letters.

_____ Your Address

_____ City, State, Zip

_____ Date

_____ Name of Contact Person

_____ Organization Name

_____ Address

_____ City, State, Zip

Dear Mr./Ms. _____: (Salutation)

Paragraph 1: Why

_____

_____

Paragraph 2: Who you are and what the organization and you have in common

_____

_____

_____

_____

_____

_____

Closing paragraph: Logical conclusion—We should get together!

_____

_____

Sincerely,

_____

(Signature here)

Typed name

Enclosure

If it is a little awkward at first to write about yourself, that's okay. You'll get used to it. You aren't expected to be original or creative in cover letters. So feel free to get ideas from books or manuals with phrases that you think capture what you are trying to say. Just be sure that your letters don't sound "canned." If you use ideas from manuals, alter the language.

Discuss your reactions to all of the exercises when you drop in to the CA Café or with the class.

JOB APPLICATIONS

Many organizations may ask you to complete an application as part of your candidacy for a position. Your resume allows you the freedom to decide what aspects of your background to highlight and what to exclude, but the application process doesn't give you quite as much latitude. Applications are usually straightforward, fill-in-the-blank documents that would appear to dictate your responses. You may have little choice about revealing your prior positions, but you may consider it prudent to keep certain aspects of your life private.

Your name, address, and telephone numbers are standard requirements on any application. You will be asked to list prior positions, the organizations in which you have worked, the inclusive dates, and the responsibilities you held. Carry an index card with you or make a note in your cell phone that recaps this information so you can be sure of the dates of your former employment. If you are asked to state your reason for leaving a job, always relate your departure to an opportunity for growth or improvement. Avoid mentioning that you couldn't get along with an employer or a supervisor. If you are not a U.S. citizen but have applied for citizenship or have a Green Card, note that on the form. Some positions require that you be bondable, a term that refers to a type of insurance policy on employees that vouches for their performance. Unless you have had a criminal conviction, you should not have any trouble being bonded. Answer all questions simply and honestly.

It is possible that the application may ask questions that are illegal and probe areas of your life that are private in most states. Information related to your race, color, religion, sex, national origin, disability, age, or ancestry is protected by law. Attempts to elicit private information to exclude you from a job are illegal. Despite laws that prohibit these types of questions, you may find that employers continue to include these questions as part of the application process. Your answers may make the difference between an opportunity for an interview and no response. If full candor is going to jeopardize your chance at the job, then you must make a decision. If you feel that being straightforward with an employer will decrease your chance for a job, then leave that question blank. Never answer dishonestly. Leaving the answer open may not be the answer that the employer wants to see, but if your background makes you a strong candidate for the job, there is still a good chance that you will get an interview. Once you are in the interview, you always have an opportunity to overcome the interviewer's objections and sell yourself around negatives that come from those gray areas.

For example, the application Jenny is filling out asks her (illegally) if she has children and their ages. Jenny has two children but knows that this fact does not compromise her ability to do the job for which she is applying. She can respond in two ways. She can answer that she does have kids and that they are well provided for through her child care arrangements or she can leave the question blank. There are risks with either approach. It is up to you to decide which one works best for you if you find yourself in a similar situation.

The most difficult judgments concern people with disabilities and those who have had encounters with the criminal justice system. Despite laws that protect people with disabilities, most people are still not ready to leave their biases behind when evaluating people for employment. Any physical or mental impairment can incorrectly be assumed to represent increased costs to most employers. For this reason, if you have a disability but it is not apparent, do not indicate your disability on the application. You are being hired for your *ability* to do the job. Anything else is irrelevant. If your disability is apparent, then when you get to the interview, emphasize your skills, accomplishments, and ability to do the job.

Having a criminal record can pose another obstacle to employment. Most applications ask if you have ever been convicted. If you have, leave the spot blank on the application. The worst thing that can happen is that you won't get an interview. If you do get an interview and the subject comes up, you can then sell yourself by emphasizing that you have paid your dues and are now on the straight and narrow. You may be surprised to know how many people are hired who have made mistakes and are working to turn their lives around.

Some applications ask for references. Make sure that the people whose names and numbers you provide know you are using them as a reference and will speak favorably of you. Again, noting their names and contact information on your cell phone will help you.

CAREER PORTFOLIOS

In recent years, a new tool for marketing your skills has evolved—the electronic career portfolio. For students it offers a vehicle to organize and process experiences and a method for monitoring the acquisition of transferable skills. Although it is not required by most employers, it is a tool to prompt a structured, comprehensive compilation of your background.

What goes into an electronic career portfolio? It is more than a Facebook page, although that is a good place to start. In addition to that basic information, include the following:

- *An introduction*—This tells whoever is reviewing the portfolio your philosophy as it relates to yourself and the field you hope to enter.
- *Your career goals*—Your plan for the next two to five years.
- *Your resume*
- *Your skills*—The key skills areas that are related to your career. This should include anything that substantiates your skills (i.e., samples of written work, letters of recommendation related to specific skills, evaluations, etc).
- *Current projects*—A list of projects or activities in progress.
- *Certifications, degrees, and awards*
- *References*

Part of your portfolio package should include links to the organizations and activities in which you are involved.

- *Community activities*—Letters of appreciation, certificates, and brochures related to volunteer efforts.
- *Professional memberships*—Any memberships in professional organizations.
- *Academic plan of study*—The colleges/universities where you have studied and the relevant academic qualifications, including classes, projects, etc.
- *Faculty and employer biographies*—Brief background on influential faculty and people who have mentored your growth professionally.

Once you have accumulated this information, create an electronic file as a Word document or try a more elaborate file using Microsoft Publisher or Adobe Acrobat. As you expand your base of experience and gain new skills, add the documents associated with that growth to the portfolio. This portable "life story" is a powerful device that you can use as a repository cataloging your development as a professional and as documented testimony validating everything you claim to potential employers. You may decide to create a hard copy of your portfolio, which you can use to prompt the discussion that takes place during an interview. The portfolio gives you the option to show employers examples of their work, much as artists use a portfolio to show their artistic style.

While portfolios may not be a requirement for employment yet, they represent the next level of authentication that showcases you at your best. Consider the possibilities of organizing all your credentials in one place. Before you know it, you'll have your portfolio. Selected data from this file can be copied to a flash drive or on your tablet or even stored in a secure cloud application to be provided as an adjunct to your resume or interview process. Just like the resume, each CD is tailored for the specific opportunity you are seeking.

If you are a graphic or visual artist, another option has emerged recently that will offer optimal visibility. Pinterest is an online network for visual presentation that can showcase your skills, background, and projects in a format that is unsurpassed. Take a look at http://pinterest.com to see samples from artists presenting their talents with narrative resumes, video presentations, photo albums, pictures of art projects and graphics, woodcuts, prints . . . the entire range of artistic interpretation represented. This is only the beginning. As technology advances even more exciting and elaborate forms for presenting your talents will develop. The holographic introduction is just around the digital corner.

7.7   Take a Closer Look

PULLING IT ALL TOGETHER

Now that you have had a chance to work on the individual components that compose a resume, try pulling the components together to develop a solid integrated document.

Identifiers

_____

_____

_____

_____

Summary/Profile

_____

_____

_____

_____

Skills

_____

_____

_____

_____

Experience

Company/City

_____

Title/Dates

_____

Duties _____

_____

_____

Accomplishments _____

_____

Company/City _____

_____

Title/Dates _____

_____

Duties _____

_____

_____

Accomplishments _____

_____

Education

College/University _____

_____

Date of Graduation/Degree Awarded _____

_____

Major Area of Study/Emphasis _____ GPA [if over 3.0] _____

Other Training _____

_____

_____

_____

Related Information _____

_____

Memberships/Awards/Scholarships/Licenses/Volunteer Work, and so on _____

_____

_____

_____

Based on your career goal and the unique combination of skills and abilities that you possess, decide whether a chronological, a functional, or an achievement resume will work best for you.

- *Chronological*—Showcases work experience and continued growth in one field
- *Functional or hybrid*—Showcases skills; ideal for career changers, new job seekers
- *Achievement*—Aggressively showcases accomplishments as they relate to expected job skills

You may already have a good idea of how to lay out your resume. If not, use cut-and-paste to reposition the different components of the resume you have developed. Shuffle the components around, remove those that don't work, and see how different combinations sound and flow. This should help you decide which format and layout will work best for you. Open your laptop and start writing!

Discuss the results of your "shuffling" when you drop in at the CA Café or with the class.

A LOOK BACK

To review, you have found out that the resume is a unique document in which you determine what information to provide and how to present it. You can conform to the conventions of typical hiring practices and still present an image of competence and self-assurance.

You should now be able to decide which resume style will work best for you in different job-seeking situations and how to present the information you include. You also should be comfortable designing a document that will change and evolve as you mature, a document that is as appealing as it is informative. You also are able to take advantage of a variety of conventional and electronic means to circulate your resume.

You are now ready to write cover letters that do more than "cover" your resume. Your letters should be developed using facts that persuade the employer to act on your resume and offer you an interview. You are now prepared to distribute your resume online, as well as respond to inquiries on applications that could be awkward or ambiguous.

Finally, go over this checklist before you send out your resume:

○ Is my resume completely free of errors in spelling, punctuation, usage, and grammar?

○ Does my resume have enough attractive white space?

○ Is my use of type styles simple, conforming to the requirements of electronic scanning?

○ Is my resume one solid page of information?

○ If I have two pages, is the information meaningful or "filler"?

○ Does my resume flow and have a logical layout?

○ Do I use short phrases and action words?

○ Is the information focused only on the skills using key words needed for the job, excluding irrelevant or meaningless facts?

Career Adventure Café

Visit the CA Café and share the results of this phase of your job search process. Now you are accelerating your move to the real world by stating your job goal in written documents, which will open doors and take you to the next level. If you are still not 100 percent sure, don't panic. This is your opportunity to step out as the new version of yourself in your resume, testing versions until you get the one that works best for you. The members of your group will be your best resource in moving you through the resume-building process. They will let you know what works, what doesn't, and whether your resume conveys you at your best for your career goal. They will proofread it, catch your typos and grammar goofs, and help you polish it like a diamond. You will do the same for them. What kind of resume formats do you see among your group members? Do the various resumes 'work' for their goals? How about the cover letters . . . do they make you want to read the resumes they are presenting? Pass the resumes around in your digital space and see how yours compares. Give each other feedback that makes the resumes stronger. Here are some questions to get you started:

What do you think of the resumes and cover letters of your group members? What do they think of yours? Is it difficult to give feedback?

_____

_____

Are you able to offer each other feedback that makes the resumes of your group better?

_____

_____

Has anyone used the portfolio process to present their capabilities? How has the portfolio been received? How can you most effectively use one in your campaign? What do the members of your group think?

_____

_____

Facebook It

What was it like to put together your resume for the career you are launching? How did it feel to pick and choose the right combination of experience and education and format it in a style that reflects you? Share your experience on Facebook and see what everyone else is saying in the CA Café.

Other Sources and Suggested Reading

Purple Squirrel by Michael B. Junge
    If you are ready to stand out among the crowd of job seekers, this book offers a
    powerful model to make sure you get noticed.

Get the Interview Every Time: Fortune 500 Hiring Professionals' Tips for Writing Winning Resumes and Cover Letters by Brenda Greene

A concise, to-the-point guide on what major corporations seek, which is a good way to begin understanding the skills and experiences that are most valued.

e-Resumes: Everything You Need to Know About Using Electronic Resumes to Tap into Today's Hot Job Market by Pat Criscito

The process of using electronic resumes is presented along with various e-resume samples and three-dimensional Web resume design.

Best Keywords for Resumes, Cover Letters, and Interviews: Powerful Communication Tools for Success by Wendy Enelow

The significant role that keywords play in drawing attention to your resume is the focus of this book.

Killer Cover Letters and Resumes! The WetFeet Insider Guide by the WetFeet Staff

This is a good resource for tips on focusing your cover letter, with samples of letters that work.

Preparing and Managing Your Career Portfolio by David Brown

This book, available on Kindle, can be borrowed for free and provides a guide-book for planning and assembling a portfolio.

Electronic Portfolios: Practical Principles of Personal Information, Personal Knowledge and Personal Development by Simon Grant

A guide to current approaches in drawing the significant components of your background together in a powerful statement of capability, this book also uses the process to foster the reflection and decision making foundational to your career development experience.

Web Sites and Internet Resources

www.eresumes.com

A very well-developed site for electronic resume information.

www.jobweb.com/Resumes_Interviews

This site, offered by the National Association of Colleges and Employers, offers different approaches to resume writing and job seeking based on major field of study.

www.quintcareers.com/resres.html

This site, part of a full-service career Web page, covers everything from resume writing and distribution to tips on portfolios, and links to other resume sites.

www.pinterest.com/source/vizualresume.com

Pinterest, an online bulletin board that you can create a free account with just like Facebook, allows you to create a graphic display to describe qualities not easily captured in a resume.

Interviewing with Confidence

8

Probably the most intimidating aspect of anyone's career development is the prospect of interviewing for jobs. Job interviews present a unique challenge to job hunters. You are offering yourself as a candidate for employment and, as such, may have limited control over the circumstances of the interview. You may feel that you have to win the approval of the all-powerful interviewer and thereby influence him to offer you the job.

Your challenge is not to please the interviewer, however. A positive dialogue with the interviewer is only one of the goals in interviewing. The real challenge is in preparing yourself and performing during the interview so that your capabilities are clear to the interviewer. All of your preparation is about to pay off. You know about the prospective job and organization through your research and network interviews. You are familiar with the field. You have gained the technical and academic background you need to compete effectively. The only thing remaining is preparing yourself for the scrutiny that comes with the job interview.

Preparing for a job interview involves a rather complex set of dynamics, which can be broken down into specific parts.

PREPARING YOURSELF TO INTERVIEW

Getting ready for an interview can be divided into specific tasks:

- *Developing and sharpening your style*—A significant part of interviewing well is projecting a sense of personal power and confidence. This is accomplished through carefully assessing your appearance, poise, and presentation, everything from what you wear to the way you speak and move.

- *Knowing your field and your skills*—All the poise in the world will not make up for a lack of substance and competence. To be credible, you must convey the knowledge you have gained about the field and the job through education, experience, company research, and so on. Operate from a solid base of information.

■ *Understanding the rituals of the interview*—Everything about you is magnified and amplified during the interview process. You will be expected to respond in certain ways to the process of interviewing. If you display a lack of understanding of what is expected, your judgment may be called into question. It is important for you to take seriously the behaviors you exhibit at the interview and realize that they take on a much greater significance in an interview than they would in any other business situation.

THE DYNAMICS OF INTERVIEWING

After working with hundreds of students and professionals in developing interviewing skills, I have found that there are four different aspects of interviewing that influence how well an interview goes. These dynamics include: exchange of information, sales presentation, social occasion, and theatrical performance. The dynamics are flexible and change throughout the interview. We will examine each of these dynamics separately.

An Exchange of Information

The first and most important dynamic of the interview is that it is an *exchange of information*. The era of going into an interview and being willing to accept anything offered is gone. Interviewing for a job is more like dating than it is getting married. You certainly wouldn't want to marry every person you date, and you definitely wouldn't want every job for which you interview. Your task is to learn as much as you can about the job, the organization, the people, and the work. That means using your powers of observation and sensitivity during the interview. The interview is also the time to ask any questions that you need answered to make the decision about whether to accept the job if it is offered. Everything you learn about the interviewer and the organization will help you determine whether the job will be a good fit for you.

A Sales Presentation

The sales presentation is the dynamic of interviewing with which you are probably most familiar. Part of interviewing well is selling yourself and your skills to the interviewer. An interview is, in some respects, a *sales presentation*. As in any sales presentation, you will be showcasing information about yourself that makes you a strong candidate for the position and de-emphasizing those aspects of your background that conflict with the employer's assumptions. It is important to be "fast on your feet," reinforcing your strengths and enthusiasm to encourage the employer to offer you the job. To do that, you have to know what the employer needs and draw attention to the ways you can meet those needs.

A Social Occasion

Even though an interview is usually businesslike, sometimes even formal, it is also a *social occasion*. People who are likable get job offers. People who are not, don't. Interviewers need to assess whether you will "fit in" with their present team; you can make them feel comfortable by being friendly and warm during the interview. This is not easy for everyone. Some of us are naturally open and friendly; others of us struggle to smile. Take advantage of your assets when you interview and, without question, the ability to smile and respond warmly is a key factor.

A Theatrical Performance

The fourth dynamic in the interview is that it is indeed a *theatrical performance*. You are being observed by an audience of one, the interviewer. Think about how you will answer the interviewer's probable first question, "How are you today?" In all likelihood, you will answer with the expected response, "Fine, thanks." If you have a headache or nervous stomach, you will probably keep that to yourself and *act* as though you feel fine. Most often, job seekers work at appearing confident. It helps to look confident and comfortable during an interview, but nervousness is actually not the worst trait you can display. Nervousness can even be interpreted favorably. It shows the employer that you care about the outcome of the interview and that your behavior is authentic and genuine. Above all, you will be trying your best to act the role of competent professional.

Interviewing well and taking into consideration these four dynamics is a complex and difficult task. You may make friends with the employer but feel that you did not *sell* yourself well. You may convey the attitude of a professional but be unable to connect with the interviewer. Since you have limited control over most of the externals that dominate an interview—the time, the location, the person interviewing you, or the tone of the interview—interviewing is always a challenge. (It may help to remember that others interviewing for the job face these same challenges and may be less prepared!)

Remember, you do have control over some very important variables. What do you control and how can you use these variables to your advantage? We'll start with the things over which you have the most control and proceed from there.

ASPECTS OF THE INTERVIEW YOU CONTROL

Many of the factors that affect the circumstances of the interview may be outside your control, but that doesn't necessarily determine the outcome. The variables you control have a much greater influence on the outcome than any of the externals. Knowing what you can do to influence the interview will help you feel more comfortable with interviewing as a whole and help you focus your energy productively.

Variable 1: Your Appearance

Your appearance is one variable over which you have great control. Your dress, haircut or style, makeup, and accessories all contribute—or detract—from the image you project. The image you want to confirm in the employer's mind is that of a competent, credible professional. To do that, you need to dress the part. Dressing the part can also influence how you behave. If you *look* the part, you will find it easier to convey a professional demeanor. If you doubt that the way you dress has an impact on your behavior, just think of teenagers in their prom formals and tuxedos. Notice any differences in their behavior?

Conventional wisdom has emphasized that the first 30 seconds of the interview are the most critical to success. The first impression created by the image you project can have a substantial effect on everything that follows.

Although some organizations have adopted casual dress in the workplace, interviewing still requires your most polished appearance. Traditionally, the standard uniform for interviewees has been the business suit for both men and women. Men are typically expected to wear dark suits, white cotton shirts, and dark ties. Women are to be similarly attired in dark suits and light blouses. But this doesn't mean that a woman wearing a red suit is immediately disqualified from consideration. It may mean that she has to work a bit harder to convince the employer that she respects all of their

8.1 Take a Closer Look

MIRROR, MIRROR ON THE WALL . . .

Before your interview appraise yourself in the mirror, from head to toe. Remember, you are trying to convey confidence and professional poise. Go through the following checklist and assess how you look.

_____ Is my clothing appropriate for a professional business meeting?

_____ Is it in keeping with the typical business dress of the profession that I am seeking to enter?

_____ Are my accessories (jewelry, footwear, makeup, fragrance) minimal and appropriate?

_____ Is my hairstyle conventional and neat?

_____ Does my appearance fit the culture of the job and convey professional competence?

Some of you may be wondering how you can afford to wear clothes just to accommodate the employer's expectations. From my experience, it is worth the investment to buy one good wool/wool-blend suit for interviews. Dressing well for an interview boosts your confidence and creates a favorable impression.

conventions. If you are interviewing in the ultraconservative professions of accounting or banking, these rules are especially true.

The remaining details of your appearance should also be considered carefully and reflect the nature and attitudes prevalent in the profession you wish to enter. Shoes should reflect the same traditional look as the suit you wear. Dress shoes are the preferred choice for both men and women. Sandals or athletic wear are not appropriate and will project a negative impression. Don't let the trend in casual office dress fool you. For interviews, casual dress does not apply.

Accessories for both men and women should be kept to a minimum and, again, very traditional. Avoid frilly blouses, jangly bracelets, or athletic watches. Women should use makeup sparingly and avoid cologne. You also may wish to leave your purse at home or bring a leather portfolio instead.

Hairstyle is an important part of your image and should reflect the same classic look. Be sure your hairstyle is neat and businesslike. Men with mustaches or beards may want to trim them before an interview.

Although the above advice is meant to set guidelines, you may find that some professions are more flexible than others. Art, advertising, construction, and information technology professions are less focused on appearance and image than are the fields of banking or finance. Conventional wisdom suggests dressing two levels above the job that you want. That means if you are seeking a carpenter's position, you would apply wearing clean denim jeans, a work shirt, and steel-toed shoes. If you were to show up in a suit, you might convey the image that you didn't know what was expected of you on the job.

Knowing the culture of the occupation you are entering will give you insight into the expectations of your interviewer. Will you be working independently, expected to take initiative and produce on your own? Or will you be working closely with other team members, expected to take direction from a manager or team leader? The more autonomous your role, the more latitude you may be given in the way you present yourself.

Variable 2: Questions and Answers

Every interview includes questions you will be expected to answer specifically. You can't control what you're asked, but you can control your answers. Part of your preparation must include anticipating the different types of questions you might be asked and thinking in advance about how you will answer them.

Many of the questions will be *skills questions*. These are "What can you do?" type questions related to technical or academic knowledge. These questions can cause you unnecessary anxiety. Because they tend to deal with how much you know, you might feel that the interviewer will find a weakness in your knowledge, thereby eliminating you from the competition.

In reality, skills questions are a great way for you to showcase what you can do and, for the most part, the easiest. Most employers would not be interviewing you if you didn't have the background they were seeking, so the chances are good that you will know how to answer these questions. If you don't know the answer, don't try to cover up by saying just anything. Instead, say "I'm not familiar with that particular issue but I have had some experience with . . . ." Let the employer know that even if you don't know the answer to a particular question, you do feel secure about your background. The *Chicago Tribune* reports that studies of American managers have found that skills questions are a secondary determinant in candidate acceptability. The more important factor is attitude.

Attitude questions are another type of question that you can expect. These are the "What will you do?" questions that employers might ask to gauge your motivation; how you feel about overtime, weekend work, night work, working with women or men, minority group members, coworkers with a disability, and so on. Try to answer the questions in a straightforward, sincere manner that accommodates the employer's needs. Sometimes questions like these can alert you to an employer's hidden agenda or an issue with which the company might be struggling. Questions about overtime might mean that the company is chronically understaffed and covers their employee shortage by expecting people to pick up the extra workload. Listen carefully and see if you can detect what is implied by the question. In most cases, you should respond positively to the interviewer. Signs of lack of commitment or bias will be viewed negatively. Most employers are looking for "can-do" employees.

Some interviewers will use *scenario questions*. These questions typically describe a situation and then ask you to provide your ideas on how you would handle it. Sometimes employers might be looking for specific answers and sometimes they might simply be looking at how you make decisions and solve problems. These are difficult questions to prepare for, so use your best judgment and be thoughtful and creative. You will probably do better than your competition given your knowledge of the field and your preparation.

Occasionally, just as with applications, employers may ask questions that would be considered illegal, usually relating to private information protected by law. Unfortunately, if you point out the impropriety, you will do little to endear yourself to the interviewer. These questions must be handled delicately. You have a right to privacy so disclose only information you believe to be pertinent to the job. Try to answer with a "non-answer" if possible. For instance, if an interviewer asks how many children you have, you might ask how that relates to the job. If you are asked if you plan on having any more children, you might simply state that you are happy with the size of your family. These types of questions tell you a lot about the employer you would be working for; that alone might be a warning about whether you would be comfortable working in that organization.

A type of interviewing that is increasingly used by employers is called *behavior based interviewing*. This approach focuses on the skills required by the position and asks you to respond very specifically to events from your experience that reflect those skills. The circumstances of the event, how the skills were used, and the resolution are all part of exploring how you have actually performed in similar situations. The approach for this type of interview is based on the belief that past behavior is the best predictor of future behavior. Preparing for this type of interview offers distinct advantages, even if your interviewer doesn't use this approach. Being able to showcase situations from your experience in which you have demonstrated a high level of skill is a powerful way of responding to an employer's questions. Exercise 8.2 is designed to prepare you to respond to an interviewer in a meaningful and substantive way.

8.2   Take a Closer Look

TELLING, NOT BRAGGING

Identify five to ten experiences or events in which you feel you demonstrated exceptional skill with good results. These should be accomplishments that required you to use skills related to the position for which you are applying—a valuable way to "show off" your expertise.

Describe the events using a model that divides the experience into four components:

Event: Describe the challenge you or your team (in work or school) faced in factual terms. Make sure the event was one that showcased a skill relevant to the position.

Skill: Use details to create a picture for the employer that allows them to "see" you using the skill that they are seeking.

Solution: Relate the resolution of the situation, highlighting your role.

Results: Make sure you include the results of your highlighted event. Nothing is as impressive as getting concrete, positive results.

Event 1:

_____

_____

_____

Event 2:

_____

_____

_____

Event 3:

_____

_____

_____

Event 4:

_____

_____

_____

Event 5:

_____

_____

_____

Use additional sheets if you have more than five events to describe.

After completing this exercise, you will be able to use the information about these events to respond factually to questions about specific skills and abilities. You needn't wait for the interviewer to ask; look for opportunities to introduce the kind of information that "sells" you. When you sense an opening, you might start with a question related to your relevant skill such as, "Do you use Microsoft Excel?" Regardless of the interviewer's answer, you can continue your dialogue by citing your mastery of that particular package (and others if applicable) and the situation in which you used it to meet a need successfully.

Be yourself in an interview, answering questions genuinely and authentically. Ask a friend to critique your grammar and usage so that you can sharpen your communication skills. A complaint that employers have related to me as a career services professional is that young people as a group don't possess strong communication skills, especially in terms of speaking standard English. Your ability to articulate your thoughts in an understandable way gives you a competitive edge that will reach far beyond the interview. Also, don't hesitate to clarify the question before you respond. Simply ask if you can restate the question in your own words to ensure that you understand what is being asked.

Aside from being prepared for specific skills and attitude questions, there is a standard group of questions that most interviewers use as a way to establish baseline information about you. Exercise 8.3 is a way to prepare yourself for these typical questions.

Take a Closer Look 8.3

SAMPLE INTERVIEW QUESTIONS

Look over the following list of questions. Think of how you might respond, and be conscious of any hidden agenda in the questions. Have a partner from the CA Café or your class ask you the questions in a role-playing dialogue to see how your answers sound.

Tell me about yourself.

Keep your answer focused on the skills and your interest in the field. Stay away from family and personal information.

What are your strengths and weaknesses?

You can take advantage of the strengths question to reinforce your suitability for the job, especially in the skill area, but be careful of the weakness part. Don't tell anything that is damaging to your image as a dedicated worker. My favorite is "I find that sometimes I can't say 'no' to an opportunity to do something if it needs to be done." Avoid answers such as "I don't get along with people" or "Sometimes I'm late." The interview may continue but you will probably be out of the running.

What brings out your best?

The single best answer to this is "A challenge." Go on to describe what that means to you.

How do you work under pressure?

You know what to say here.

Why should I hire you?

Again, there is only one answer: "Because I know I can be an asset to this organization." Tell how.

Why do you want to work here?

Try to say something that indicates you are looking for a place where you can use your skills to good advantage.

What was your favorite class in college?

Name one that was related to the skills associated with the job.

What was your least favorite class in college?

Name one that was unrelated to the job.

What did you like the best in your last job?

Focus on the similarities to the job you're seeking.

What did you like the least in your last job?

Come up with an answer that reinforces your interest in facing challenges that might have been absent in your last job.

Describe a situation in which you made a mistake. How did you handle it?

Everyone makes mistakes. Ensuring that you handled it well—keeping your focus, coming up with plan B, facing consequences with poise—will satisfy any employer.

Where do you see yourself in five years? Ten years?

This is a goals question, so project forward a few years and emphasize your commitment to growth and becoming a better employee. Be careful though. You don't want to sound as if you have your sights set on taking over the company or the interviewer's job.

A word about 'trick' questions . . . sometimes employers may use questions that seem innocent enough but actually mask an intention to get past the professional persona you have worked so diligently to create. Questions related to other jobs you are in competition for or your preparation for the interview may seem relevant, but they probe in ways that invite you to let your guard down. Now is when that side of you—the consummate professional—rises to the occasion. Never answer in a way that reveals anything that does not contribute to your image as the trusted new associate of the organization. Keep your focus and continue to offer responses that support the notion that everything you have done to this point has prepared you for the position they have and for which you are now interviewing. Keep that in the front of your mind and you will know how to handle any question.

Discuss your experience in the role-playing dialogue when you visit the CA Café or with the class.

Variable 3: Nonverbal Cues

Surprising as it may seem, one variable that you may have difficulty controlling is your nonverbal communication. While you might be very conscious of what you tell an employer verbally, you might find it a challenge to monitor the information you communicate nonverbally. Nonverbal cues are habits and behaviors of which we are largely unconscious. An employer can learn a lot about you—positive and negative—by observing your nonverbal communication.

You may be sitting in the lobby of a company waiting to be called to your interview and thinking about what you will say to the interviewer. You may be completely unaware that you are tapping your foot, jiggling your leg, and picking lint off your suit. These relatively innocuous behaviors may communicate to others your anxiety about the interview. Your nonverbal behavior can tell the employer more than you might want her to know.

Your goal should be to control and modify your nonverbal communication to support the overall positive impression you are striving to convey. Convince the interviewer that you are confident and at ease, eager to respond openly and sincerely. The best way to create this image is to focus on the ways you can connect with the person interviewing you. As the interviewer greets you, step forward with your hand extended, a warm smile on your face. Shake hands firmly, make eye contact, and greet the interviewer with a pleasant "Happy to meet you, Ms. Payne." Make sure you say the interviewer's name. It establishes the appropriate tone of a business meeting. Don't call the interviewer by her first name unless invited to.

When you get to the interviewer's office, wait to sit until after the interviewer takes her seat. Maintain your warm demeanor while you get comfortable. Try to relax and observe the room. You might chat about the weather or perhaps an item in the interviewer's office that sparks your interest, but keep small talk to a minimum. Casual conversation is a good way to start off, but the interviewer will want to move along.

When seated, keep both feet on the floor or crossed at the ankles. Sit up straight and relax your hands in your lap. Try not to appear rigid or stiff. Continue making good eye contact—this is the best way to connect. When you are talking, be expressive and enthusiastic. Have a pleasant look on your face, smile easily, and use gestures that are appropriate to what you are saying.

Vary your tone of voice when you convey your ideas. Try to avoid saying "ums" to fill in silences. Also, be aware of verbal habits you might not realize you may be using such as "like" to, like, make a point. Vocalized pauses and habitual behaviors such as twirling your hair or bouncing your leg can be extremely distracting and conflict with the image of a professional you are trying to confirm in the employer's eyes.

If you begin to feel more comfortable, you will better be able to communicate your enthusiasm about the job opportunity. Stay businesslike even if your interviewer behaves quite informally. Exercise 8.4 will help you assess how your nonverbal cues support you in the interview.

Take a Closer Look   8.4

HOW AM I ACTING?

Ask yourself these questions as a way of becoming sensitive to how you are communicating nonverbally.

_____ Do I look comfortable and friendly when smiling?

_____ Is my handshake firm without being too strong?

_____ When seated, are my feet crossed at the ankles or next to each other flat on the floor?

_____ Is my posture correct without being stiff?

_____ Are my hands folded in a relaxed manner in my lap?

_____ Am I comfortable gesturing appropriately when my remarks call for it?

_____ Can I refrain from fidgeting?

_____ Can I look at my interviewer in a confident manner, making eye contact without "staring" him down?

_____ Is my diction clear and verbal tone pleasant?

Discuss the challenge of monitoring your nonverbal cues when you drop in at the CA Café or with the class.

Variable 4: The Interview's Tone

My experience has led me to believe that formal, high-stress interviews are less common today. Interviewers have found that putting candidates under stress can intimidate interviewees. The goal of the interviewer is to help you feel comfortable so you will reveal as much of yourself as she needs to know to determine whether you are a viable candidate for the position. That most often translates into friendly behavior. Be careful to distinguish friendliness from friendship. The interviewer is *not* your friend. While he may not wish you any ill, the interviewer is paid to qualify people for further consideration. Anything that might make you a risk could disqualify you. The recruiter or interviewer is the organization's gatekeeper. Stay focused on your goals, your skills, and what you can do for the organization.

Variable 5: It's Your Turn to Ask

Gathering information about a job also requires you to formulate questions to ask your interviewer. Many of your questions about a position and the organization may already be addressed during the interview. If not, be prepared to bring them up at an appropriate point.

Typically, the questions you might like to ask are the very ones to avoid in a first interview. I'm referring to questions about salary and benefits. The interviewer is focused on how you meet the organization's needs and wants to believe that is your focus as well, although you are both aware that this is a job for which you will be paid. Save the money and benefits questions for a later date. If you are offered the job, a salary will then be discussed. If not, you may be better off not knowing what might have been.

Most often questions should focus on the nature of the work to be performed, the work team, the company, the industry, and future growth. Sometimes you might find that your interviewer is not giving you a chance to tell what you can do. In that case, use the questions you have prepared to highlight the skills you think make you the ideal choice for the position.

The best questions tell the employer that you have done your homework on the company and the industry. The first option for learning about a company is the Internet. Use your web browser to research the organization. Most sites will have general information about the organization but many will have a link to 'Careers' which will offer information you can use to prepare. The information available might go well beyond the products and services offered to philosophy or policy. The Better Business Bureau and the local chamber of commerce also offer information about member organizations.

If your college has a ongoing relationship with the organization—it recruits regularly at your campus—then it may have a library of data available for you to review and, more importantly, the staff of the career center may be able to advise you on how to best prepare for this opportunity based on success stories of prior candidates like you.

If those resources are not as detailed as you need, try some online resources that offer more background data. *Standard & Poor's, Thomas's Register of American Manufacturers,* and *Dun & Bradstreet Reference Book* are a few resources that might offer information about a company. Frequently these sources are available only through a subscription, so check with your library reference center or university career center to see if access is available. You might want to call the company with which you will be interviewing and ask the receptionist if you can drop by and pick up a brochure or an annual report. Most companies are happy to accommodate such requests. An added benefit is that you get the opportunity to "dry run" your visit to the company. Being well prepared for the interview is a strong statement of your willingness to go the extra mile to reach your goals, a definite plus with any employer.

Always leave an interview with a clear understanding of the next steps in the process. Follow up by sending a thank-you note to the interviewer. A brief, positive email or traditional note shows your appreciation, reinforces your candidacy, and brings the interview to an appropriate close. An email is increasingly taking the place of the hard-copy note, primarily due to timeliness. Some type of thank you is a necessary courtesy. If you have not heard from the interviewer in a reasonable amount of time, be sure to follow up with a phone call.

Use Exercise 8.5 to think about the questions you might ask your interviewer.

Take a Closer Look   8.5

PREPARE YOUR QUESTIONS

The best candidates are ready with questions, so take advantage of this opportunity to practice asking some of the more typical ones.

What is the career path for this position?

What is the person who performed this job doing now?

Are there opportunities for professional growth in this position?

Are there training opportunities in this position?

For whom would I be working?

Could you tell me about the team of people with whom I would be working?

What skill would you say is critical to the performance of this job?

What are the most critical challenges I may encounter in this position?

What do you see as the most significant challenges and opportunities faced by this organization?

Why did you choose to become a part of this organization?

How could I best prepare myself were I to be selected for the position?

What do you see as my strengths for this position?

What is the next step in the process? When would you like to schedule our next meeting? May I follow up with you?

Come up with questions of your own. Remember: Save your questions about salary, vacation, or benefits until a later time.

TELEPHONE AND ONLINE INTERVIEWING

The use of telephone and online interviewing has been adopted by many organizations as a proven method of screening for employment. While many job seekers believe that telephone and online interviews are easier than face-to-face interviews, there are factors that can make it more difficult to convey your value. Although sitting in your living room talking on the phone may feel more comfortable than going one-on-one with someone you've just met, the pitfalls of these interviews are more numerous than for the conventional interview. Telephone and online interviews don't allow the opportunity to build rapport and connect with the interviewer. Additionally you can't always assess how your responses are registering with the interviewer as effectively when you're talking on the phone. Frequently technical factors like response delays and echoes may throw off your timing. One interviewee who responded to a question with a humorous quip was panicked when his light remark drew blank stares and silence. He was relieved when the group interviewing him by Skype laughed appreciatively a few moments later.

If you are asked to participate in a pre-screening interview by phone or online, here are some things to keep in mind as you prepare:

- Be as prepared for this interview as you would be for a face-to-face interview. Prepare talking points that prompt you to mention your specific value to the organization and remind you of the questions you wish to ask. Have your documents (resume, cover letter, etc.) and the list of accomplishments/skills that you developed for your interview close at hand.
- Practice the interview with a friend and solicit feedback on your performance.
- Before the scheduled call, engage in a relaxation exercise. Make a note of the names and titles of everyone participating in the call.
- During the interview, speak clearly and assertively. Smile when responding. Your interviewer will "hear" your smile even if the interview is over the phone.
- Listen carefully and don't speak over or interrupt the interviewer.
- If you pause to think over a response, explain the gap in the conversation.
- Provide the interviewer with specific examples that support your accomplishments. Offer additional supporting information if necessary.
- Make sure you know what the next phase of the hiring process will be and make sure that the interviewer hangs up before you do.
- After the interview, send a thank-you note, just as you would after a formal face-to-face exchange.

KEEP YOUR FOCUS

Keeping your focus can be a challenge. You may understand the individual dynamics of interviewing well, but juggling all the different variables can be overwhelming. Set your goals before you go into the interview and stay focused on them. Try not to be consumed by anxiety or nerves. Say to yourself "I'm so excited." You must be an attractive candidate to have gone this far, so be proud of yourself. You are exactly where you want to be—one step away from your goal.

One way to keep your focus is by visualizing beforehand how you would like to see yourself perform in the interview. World-class athletes use visualization to inspire performances that win them the championship or the gold medal. You can do the same. Try Exercise 8.6 to see how visualizing helps you feel ready for the interview. Then simply imitate the images of yourself doing well.

Take a Closer Look   8.6

VISUALIZE YOUR SUCCESS

Take 30 minutes daily for a week before your interview and imagine yourself going through the entire interview experience. Close your eyes and see yourself driving to the interview. You are the model of professional dress and personal power. You are calm and have been preparing for this meeting for a long time. You are obviously better prepared than any other candidate for this job.

You are in the office now, shaking hands with the interviewer. You are smiling, happy to be there. Your handshake confirms your confident, open approach to the world. The interviewer likes you and wants you to do well. You answer questions thoughtfully, taking whatever time you need to feel comfortable. Your interviewer thinks your answers are excellent. You are poised and comfortable and ask questions that impress the interviewer. Your interviewer closes the session, expressing regret that there isn't more time to explore your views on the position and the company. You are also disappointed that there isn't more time to share your thoughts but are pleased to have had the chance to meet your interviewer regardless of the outcome.

You leave the interview and return home to send an email that reinforces the ideas discussed in the interview and expresses appreciation for the opportunity to meet the interviewer.

If you have worked through the exercise diligently, you should feel relaxed, uplifted, and totally prepared for your interview.

Discuss how the visualization exercise worked for you when you visit the CA Café or with the class.

YOUR INTERVIEW GOALS

As you prepare for the interview, you may feel like a programmed robot. "Sit straight. Feet flat. Smile. Shake. Answer. Question. Leave." You may feel that trying to integrate all the suggestions here is going to have you spinning like a top. The intent of this chapter is to offer you methods of communicating that have been proven to be successful. Ultimately, to be genuine and sincere, you must be yourself. If you want to strengthen your interview skills, set some goals that you want to achieve for each interview you schedule. Assess the variables and choose one or two areas in which you want to improve your performance. Integrate these improvements into your presentation until they become a part of you and you no longer have to think about them.

Keep in mind that your primary goal is to get the job offer. In the past, students may have been agonizing over an interview for a job they're not sure they want. My advice is always the same. If you go into an interview with any doubts, you will convey them to the employer. If you find out halfway through the interview that it is your dream job, your doubts may have already eliminated you from consideration. So go into the interview with the goal of getting the offer and let the employer tell you about the job.

It's important to recognize that for every question the interviewer asks you, there are two answers . . . the one you want to give and the one he wants to hear. If the job is a good fit for you, the distance between the two answers may be small to negligible. If you find, however, that the answers are far away from one another on the continuum, then it is a strong sign that the job may not be the right one for you. Don't be disappointed—be glad you found out now. It will save you time and a hundred heartaches if you simply withdraw your candidacy or turn the job down.

8.7   Take a Closer Look

PULLING IT ALL TOGETHER

Before you go to your first interview, check this list to make sure you are prepared.

_____ Does my appearance (dress, shoes, hair, accessories) present the image that is appropriate for a business meeting for the field in which I seek employment?

_____ Have I thought through the answers to the typical questions encountered in an interview?

_____ Have I sat down and written about my skills and accomplishments that are related to the position for which I am interviewing?

_____ Have I thought about how I will respond to attitude questions?

_____ Have I assessed my nonverbal behavior or asked someone to observe and critique my nonverbal cues so that they convey a professional image?

_____ Do I have a list of relevant questions for my interviewer?

_____ Have I practiced my interview visualization exercise?

_____ Am I excited and happy to be meeting my interviewer?

_____ Have I set my goals and know what I want to accomplish in the interview?

A LOOK BACK

This chapter has introduced you to the complex ritual of interviewing and your role in making it a productive and positive experience. It is part meeting to exchange information, part sales presentation, part friendly visit, part performance.

The interview can seem at times like a mystery over which you have no control. In fact, the variables over which you have control are those that have the greatest influence on the outcome. Your appearance is a variable over which you exert complete control and which you can use to your advantage. The answers to questions, whether about skills, attitude, or scenarios, are also under your control. Your nonverbal cues can be an important part of communicating with the employer and demonstrating a positive image. The tone of the interview, though generally set by the interviewer, can offer you the opportunity to establish yourself as a businesslike and friendly individual. Finally, you can use the questions you ask the interviewer to support your image as a strong candidate for the position and lead the interviewer to your most important skills.

You should be able to set goals when approaching the interview, with the primary goal of getting the job offer. Then prepare yourself fully by visualizing the kind of interview in which you achieve every goal and receive the recognition you deserve.

Career Adventure Café

Visit the CA Café and share the results of this phase of your job search process. The opportunity to practice interview skills is a prime advantage available through the CA Café. Perhaps some members of your group have had experiences with interviewing from which all can benefit. If you are someone who has never interviewed for positions like the one you are seeking as a career goal, the other members of your group may be able to provide you with helpful tips gained from their experiences. You might try interviewing on video and posting your videos on YouTube. The digital space of the CA Café can be a place to share the results of interviews and set up a "best-practices" model of behaviors to act as a guide to good interviews. Discuss with the other group members your thoughts on interviews and whatever concerns you may have. Here are some questions to get you started:

When do you know an interview is going well? If it isn't, is there a way to turn it around? Will you always know how an interview is going? If so, how?

_____

_____

Have the members of your group ever gotten a job offer from an interview that didn't go well? What went wrong? How did positive aspects of the interview make up for it?

_____

_____

What is the best method for relaxing and being yourself in an interview? What do the members of your group think?

_____

_____

Facebook It

Here we go! If you have had an interview, how did it go? Share your experience on Facebook and let's hear the details! If not, how has your experience seeking an interview gone? Are you getting calls or is the phone silent? If so, go back and check your resume. It may not be selling you as you deserve. Share what's going on and help each other with this challenging part. If things are slow, head to the CA Café for a chance to see what else is going on and find out if there are some things you might try to get things going.

Other Sources and Suggested Reading

Keywords to Nail Your Job Interview: What to Say to Win Your Dream Job by Wendy S. Enelow

   This book builds on the concept of using the key words associated with the position for which you are interviewing throughout the process.

Best Answers to the 201 Most Frequently Asked Interview Questions by Matthew J. DeLuca and Nanette F. DeLuca

   This is a fresh treatment by the authors at answers to specific questions.

The Best Answer: 9 Secrets to Job-Winning Interviews by Deb Gottesman and Buzz Mauro

This book focuses on responding in a genuine and authentic way that showcases your unique value to the organization in the role for which you are interviewing.

Ask the Right Questions, Hire the Best People by Ron Fry

Ron Fry is the successful author of many job seeking guides. In this book, he gives readers an insight into how managers think and what they're looking for.

Creative Visualization: Use the Power of Your Imagination to Create What You Want in Your Life by Shakti Gawain

This book focuses on tapping the power of the mind to energize growth and achievement. Regardless of your philosophical perspective, the techniques and exercises described here are useful and effective.

Case In Point: Complete Case Interview Preparation by Marc Cosentino

The type of interview that is described in this book is most associated with business positions but is increasingly being used in other fields as well. This type of interview uses a scenario that requires the interviewee to examine a case and devise a solution to the problem presented. This book is an excellent primer on the method and will provide good preparation for any type of interview.

Web Sites and Internet Resources

http://career-advice.monster.com/job-interview/careers.aspx

This is a well-known full-service site from which you can gather the latest information on interviewing techniques.

www.collegegrad.com

This is a great site with information about interviewing in all its forms. This is especially useful to recent college grads.

www.career.vt.edu/interviewing/index.html

This site from Virginia Tech offers detailed advice on interview preparation.

Developing Job Leads 9

For most of us, the prospect of finding a job feels like a mystery in which we play the clueless detective, more like Inspector Clousseau than Sherlock Holmes. Gamely we follow leads, most of which are dead ends of rejection and frustration. Finally, our persistence and preparation pay off, and we're the right person in the right place at the right time.

Too often, job seekers using traditional search methods end up feeling as helpless as a clueless detective. And too often, job seekers experience frustration and rejection as a result of traditional job-search methods. Over the years we have begun to question these traditions and come up with new approaches to achieving our employment goals.

Part of the overall philosophy of your career adventure is the expectation that *you* have the greatest influence over the goals and outcomes that you choose to pursue. You have acted on this belief in each different portion of this text. The same philosophy is reflected in the final part of your adventure—finding the right job.

In this chapter, we explore the methods and approaches that will give you control over your job search. The process won't remain a mystery. It is more like a guidebook that shows you how to move toward your goals. This is hard work, so be prepared to throw out any fixed notions of what success means when looking for a job.

THE HIDDEN JOB MARKET

The most frustrating part of finding a job when using traditional methods is *waiting*. You see an ad, you write a letter, you send a resume or post it on a job-seekers Web site, you wait . . . and wait . . . and wait. Without question, waiting is more discouraging to job seekers than any other single aspect of job seeking. Now, with the advent of online job postings and resume distribution, you can engage actively in electronic job search. You may even feel that if you spend hours clicking on links and uploading your resume, you've been productively engaged. It is important to recognize that those activities may be necessary to finding a job but they are only one aspect of job seeking. You still have to use the conventional methods that distinguish you from the competition.

You should be actively engaged in developing new leads and pursuing new possibilities. If you want a job, *you* must find the employer, not the other way around. Too often, job seekers think that employers should look for them, either through ads, agencies, or career center postings. Those methods may work at times, but not often, and not for everyone.

You have probably heard of the "hidden job market." Perhaps it isn't as well hidden as it has been in the past. The hidden job market refers to the process by which thousands of jobs are filled. The primary method used to fill jobs in the hidden job market is networking. You are already familiar with networking from the material in Chapter 5. The networking that employers use when filling a position is only slightly different.

Imagine you are Matt, the manager of accounting in a small company. Everything is going well until your ace accounting associate, Chloe, comes in and tells you that she is going back to school full time and is giving you two weeks' notice. It's February and the April 15 tax deadline is looming. You try to talk Chloe into postponing her departure. She's firm, however, so you accept the decision. Chloe is telling you about her college schedule, which begins at the end of March, but you aren't hearing a word. You are mentally scanning your current staff to determine who might be able to pick up her workload. With difficulty, you acknowledge that the staff isn't up to absorbing her work and you will have to hire someone new. Experienced accounting people are scarce this time of year. Slowly, you mentally return to the office, and you ask her if she knows of anyone who might be able to take her place.

Boom! That is how the hidden job market works. Now imagine that you are a good friend of Chloe's—you are someone with comparable ability and dedication but unhappy in your current position. Chloe knows you are available and just happens to have your resume with her. It would be difficult to find a better way to be introduced to an employer. The trick is becoming "Chloe's friend."

You may be surprised to know that you already are "Chloe's friend." Somewhere in your existing network, there may be a Chloe who is in a position to recommend you to her boss the next time a vacancy occurs. Your responsibility is to let Chloe and everyone else in your network know that you are available for a job and that you have particular skills that their organization can use.

The process of alerting your network to your goals and availability is a great way to start your job campaign. It is an opportunity to practice your sales skills before you get to the interview. Here are some ways to get started.

ALERTING YOUR NETWORK

In Chapter 5, you spent some time making contact with people you knew and some you didn't to discuss careers and jobs. Those people are bona fide members of your network now. You are a member of *their* network as well and, as such, you can rely on one another for information or assistance when necessary.

At this point in your job search, it is important that all the people in your existing network are aware that you are seeking employment. Not just any job, though. Uncle John at the automotive plant might know about an opening that is coming up in maintenance. That doesn't mean that you are qualified for or interested in it. Uncle John also may know someone in design at the same plant. If design is an area in which you have an interest, it is up to you to let Uncle John know that he can help you.

Contacting Uncle John will probably be easy. Friends and family members are accessible and often happy to assist you. All you need to do is give them a call. That call is important, though. Don't take for granted that Uncle John will automatically understand what you want from him. Make your intentions clear to everyone you contact.

When calling someone in your network, have a statement prepared that capsulizes your request in a straightforward manner. First let them know you are looking for a job and you need their assistance. Describe your skills and the job you are seeking. Most important, let them know what they could do for you that would help. It might not always be obvious, so be as specific as you can.

Just as you did in Chapter 5, compile a comprehensive list of people who could help you. Then get on the phone and let them know you need them to be your eyes and ears in your job hunt. Not everyone will be able to channel your resume. The most valuable help you can receive is information about a possible opening and whom you might contact. As a matter of fact, research has shown that the most valuable referrals come not from sources close to you, with whom you share the same circle of acquaintances, but from sources with whom you have more distant ties because they are aware of opportunities you have no exposure to. Any help at all can be a welcome advantage over your competition.

Exercise 9.1 will help prepare you to ask the people in your network for assistance.

Take a Closer Look 9.1

ENLIST YOUR NETWORK'S SUPPORT

During your initial contact with those in your network, let them know in exact terms what you believe their role is. Choose your words thoughtfully. Your statement should cover four issues:

1. The fact that you are looking for a job:

    "I'll be graduating in June and I'm starting to look for a job."

    "I've decided to make some changes and my career is one of the things I'm thinking of changing."

    "I'm eager for a chance to do something that's related to my major so I'm looking for a new job."

2. Why the person might be in a position to help:

    "You work in the field I'm interested in and probably hear about things before anyone else."

    "I enjoyed working with you at the plant and thought you might know what's happening in the field."

    "You were a big help to me before and I am hoping that you might be in a position to help me out again."

3. What skills you bring to the job:

    "I have a good background in business with special skills in the use of Excel and Access."

    "I've written ad copy for a number of local firms and have some experience in public relations."

4. What the person can do for you:

    "Can I use your name as a reference?"

    "Have you heard of any jobs that might be available in this area? Do you know someone specific I could contact about a job? Could I use your name when I contact that person?"

Use the following space to develop your own statement that tells the person in your network what he could do to give you a boost into your career.

Networking Statement

_____

_____

This statement will change depending on the person with whom you are talking and what that person might be able to do for you. Work on perfecting your delivery in a calm, self-assured manner. Remember, your current network of friends, family, college acquaintances, and work associates will be the easy ones. Take advantage of this type of networking contact to see what it feels like to "sell yourself" both in person and over the phone.

Try the dialogue out with a partner in the CA Café or the class and then discuss how it might feel to ask for someone's assistance.

ACCEPTING SUPPORT

For some job seekers, asking for help from the people in their network causes great anxiety and discomfort. Sometimes asking someone you know for assistance is more difficult than asking a stranger.

Based on what you learned in Chapter 5, you know that using the telephone or email to contact people can result in obtaining valuable information about careers and organizations. The process of networking for a job is similar. You are not asking for a job. You are recruiting the people in your network to provide you with support through information and referrals. None of us would mind helping someone if we could. It is a win–win situation. It solidifies and reaffirms our relationships with one another and offers us a chance to do something worthwhile with minimal effort. When the time comes, you will provide the same support to someone else, whether it is the person who helped you or someone new. Anyone who provides information to someone that results in a job offer will likely have a favor returned to them at some time in the future. The network continually renews itself through everyone's efforts. Now it's your opportunity to become a part of a network that could be a continuing asset in your career for many years.

MARKETING YOURSELF

You are ready to start your all-out, full-court-press marketing campaign. You have informed all your initial contacts and may have been able to generate some leads from that effort. In what other ways can you market yourself?

The most important aspect of marketing yourself is constantly being on the lookout for an opportunity to sell your skills. Every person you encounter during this time is a potential resource of information and referral. Let everyone you meet, even through a chance encounter, know what you are looking for and ask them to help. One of the simplest ways to do this is to carry index cards with your name, address, phone numbers, and a brief statement of your skills and the job you want. Better still, create your own business card with your vital information using affordable templates found at most office supply stores or from Web sites that specialize in reasonably priced cards like Vistaprint. Bring them with you wherever you go, and if you do happen to run into someone you haven't contacted yet, just pull out a card. Every time you leave your home is an opportunity to extend your network a bit further.

If you intend to use the newspaper to seek employment, go beyond the classified ads. Read the paper from front to back looking for any information that could lead you to your future employer. An article that mentions a company's new contract, the expansion of an organization, or a promotion can mean that the company will soon need to hire a new person. There is no reason why it shouldn't be you.

Now is also the time to go back to the resources you accessed in Chapter 4. Look at the online directories or the ones in the library that detail information about companies in your field of interest. The same directories you used in Chapter 8 when you were researching companies offer job seekers information about companies that provide a host of employment opportunities. Local resources such as the chamber of commerce and the yellow pages can be valuable in your exploration of the job market. Specialized publications such as Gale's *Job Seeker's Guide to Private and Public Companies* or the *Job Hunter's Sourcebook* focus on a wide range of information about companies and sources for leads.

Using the traditional methods of finding employment is a good start—you also want to include any other avenues you can. The conventional approaches represent only 20 percent of the jobs that need to be filled and are usually found in the newspaper ads or the online ad sources offered by media outlets. At first glance, the ads can seem to offer a wealth of possibilities. However, you have no way of knowing who will read your resume or with whom you are competing. Sometimes ads that seem to describe you to a T will be the ones you enthusiastically write to but never hear from. Did the employers have a candidate in mind already? Did someone better qualified than you apply? You will never know.

Other times, jobs that seem like a long shot will be the ones for which the employers are dying to interview you. Essentially, there is no logic to the process, so don't even try to understand it. Do try everything.

Internet sites may be useful. Most organizations now have a "Careers," "Jobs," or "Employment" tab on their Web sites that you can click. Health care institutions, government agencies, public utilities, and colleges frequently offer such options to explore available positions. Each will have specific requirements for submitting your credentials including uploading your resume, letters of reference, transcripts, and any other required documents. These sites may make you feel like you are using your time productively and may even result in a job, but this type of job seeking is comparable to the use of want ads in the newspaper. You have no control over who sees your application, and you can spend an enormous amount of time inputting information with no return. Job seeking like this has the potential to be a huge time and energy drain. You can use these sites but don't rely solely on these options. Continue to use your face-to-face network as your primary path to finding the opportunity that is right for you.

Another approach to job seeking is the growing use of the *career fair* as a job-seeking tool. These events are typically focused on a particular career emphasis such as health careers or information technology careers. A career fair is essentially a sales pitch from employers with immediate openings seeking potential employees with hard-to-find skills. During the career fair, organization representatives meet and greet job seekers and present the organization's opportunities. They prequalify candidates for possible further examination and, in some cases, may schedule interviews on the spot. If you are planning to attend a career fair, dress as you would for an interview. Bring several copies of your resume for distribution and be prepared to answer a few cursory questions as part of the screening process. Smile warmly, shake hands firmly, and try to stay fresh through the repetitious ritual of meeting lots of human resource professionals.

Using the career services office at your college should also be part of your search strategy. There are companies that rely heavily on college career services offices for referrals and resumes. Register for services and discuss the particulars of your search with the professionals there. Become familiar with the referral system and take full advantage of whatever information is available. The advisors are not in a position to place you in a job. Take their advice and support seriously, but remember that you are responsible for your own success.

At some point you may want to consider working with a placement agency. If you decide to pursue this avenue, do so with your eyes wide open. The people with placement agencies generally work on a contingency basis. That is, they find people for jobs, not jobs for people, and they are paid only if they deliver. Your value to them is related to how much money they can make placing you in a job. An interview with an agency person will probably be congenial since the person never knows when an employer might call and need exactly the skills you have. Don't be disappointed if you don't hear from agencies. They will call you only if an employer has called them first. If they make the placement and charge their fee, your worth could be as much as 30 percent more than if you had called the employer yourself. You are better off foregoing the services of a placement agency and marketing yourself directly to the employer.

USING THE INTERNET

Today it may be easier than ever to market yourself directly to employers, thanks to the networks that link computer users around the world. It is now possible to accomplish the following (and much more!). More information about each of these topics is presented on the following pages.

1. Research organizations and potential employers through electronic employer databases.
2. Access online job ads from around the nation and world.
3. Distribute your resume to potential employers via computer.
4. Use social networking to convey your value to potential employers.

Regardless of the career you wish to establish, the type of job you are seeking, and the geographical parameters you set for your job search, Internet resources will be of great value to you. If you wish to stay in your current location, the local newspaper may provide online job ads. If you are seeking opportunities in a wider geographic range, national job search sites like Monster or CareerBuilder will be an obvious source for information and available positions. Your first step is to investigate resources that may be appropriate to your search.

A key issue is access. Most colleges and universities now offer access to the Internet. If you do not have a personal computer, check out what access services your college or university offers students. Community colleges and commuter universities should offer various locations, including the classroom, where you can hook up. Public libraries offer free access as well so there is nothing to prevent you from accessing digital information sources. Most of us who access cable TV services can obtain Internet access through that option or through service providers who install Internet connections for a monthly fee.

RESEARCHING EMPLOYERS AND JOBS ELECTRONICALLY

With the number of career and employment Web sites currently available for review, you will probably have no trouble finding Internet sources. The real problem will be conducting your search wisely so that you avoid wasted time wading through information that is only marginally useful. As described in Chapter 4, using Internet search engines and directories is the quickest way to find Web sites that can provide you with almost any type of information you need. While there may be technical differences in what the various search engines cover, the process is similar for each. The key factor is narrowing your search to yield productive information. There are two approaches that can serve your needs:

1. *Search for specific sites.* Whether you are researching employers or seeking job postings, you can find specific sites that are dedicated to single subject areas. This requires that you choose key words that adequately narrow your search. The best approach is to review the suggestions offered by the search engines to help you narrow your search. Sometimes something as simple as phrasing ("all X not XY") will limit your search to more useful sources.

2. *Search for vertical portals and sites with links.* Certain sites offer links to other valuable sources that your original search might not have grabbed. This allows you to go to one site and then skip back and forth between your original site and the related sites offered by links. The downside of this type of search is, again, you end up with much more than you need or can use.

Virtually all organizations have their own Web sites and can easily be accessed by searching under the company name. If you wish to avoid the one-by-one process of researching employers, try one of the following sites that offers either information at the Web site or a link to the employer Web pages:

- **www.careerbuilder.com:** Employer profiles, jobs, even online job fairs make this one of the most visited Web sites on the Internet.
- **www.jobweb.com:** The National Association of Colleges and Employers Web site is a great place for all types of career information, including "Employer Profiles."
- **www.vault.com/wps/portal/usa:** This site offers comprehensive information about companies, including rankings and reviews of employers.
- **www.collegegrad.com/employer:** Rankings of employers as well as solid advice on how to sell yourself to an employer.

One online resource available to you is access to electronic employment ads. Several valuable Web sites have evolved that can give you the ability to access thousands of job ads quickly and conveniently. Conventional methods used in the past would have required you to search through dozens of newspapers from all over the country to achieve this. Now you are able to download your resume either to companies or to resume distribution services as a way of advertising your availability and responding to advertised openings. The number of ways to distribute your resume electronically multiplies every day. If you feel this service may be of use to you, you must do some research. There may be resume distribution networks and resources available specifically for individuals in your field. A good source of reference for electronic distribution will be the professional organization affiliated with the discipline to which you belong.

Many companies provide job seekers the service of classifying, storing, retrieving, and sending resumes to prospective employers. Resume information may be scanned into the database and retained either in its original form or as a standardized form produced by the computer. Sometimes the resume is synopsized into the database. The stored information is then provided to employers using the system. Resume software may offer you assistance in designing, formatting, and downloading your resume to the network that will make it available 24 hours a day to employers. Most word processing software packages now provide resume templates that will help create a compatible document.

While distributing your resume electronically is not a complete substitute for a networked face-to-face job search, it offers you as a job seeker access to a far greater number of employers than you would be able to reach using conventional methods. A list of some of the services in operation follows. Some may require a fee for access and distribution, but most are free.

- **www.indeed.com:** This site searches databases and generates a list of job openings based on a job title and geographic location.

- **www.monster.com:** This is a full service site that can offer information on a range of topics and provides information on job openings as well. The first and most successful.

- **www.ajb.dni.us:** America's Job Bank matches employers' job listings with resumes on a state-by-state basis.

- **www.jobsite.co.uk:** Jobsite UK (Worldwide) provides a sampling of jobs available in Great Britain. Check the exchange rate between British £ (pounds) and U.S. $ (dollars) before you surf this site.

A simple browser search will provide you with a host of sites that offer job listings. Within a short time you will be adept at determining which ones will provide the types of positions in which you have an interest.

Perhaps the ultimate in "posting" your resume is having your own Web site. A LinkedIn profile can provide you that. Taking it to the next level may mean having a blog. A free service for Web bloggers is available at www.blogger.com, while tools for building your Web site are available at www.wordpress.org, all for free. There are instructional videos on YouTube that offer instructions on blogging or, if you are supremely confident, you might consider introducing yourself to your employer through a short introductory video on YouTube. Be careful with this option, however. Approaches like this border on gimmickry and can backfire if not done with exactly the right tone and superior production values. Unless you are destined for a media career, leave this option to a professional.

Staying Aware of the Electronic World

New ways of applying the world of computer information systems to the field of job search are constantly and quickly evolving. Some college career services offices offer employers interactive online services that allow human resources professionals to access the resumes of registered students based on the company's hiring needs. The potential for the development of new systems to assist both employers and job seekers seems unlimited. Your challenge is to keep informed about the latest in information technology innovations so you can take advantage of every tool available to you.

A word of caution, however—in the words of legendary basketball coach John Wooden, "Never mistake activity for achievement." It may seem like time spent on the Internet clicking and surfing is more productive than the challenge of face-to-face job seeking, probably because of the sheer volume of information available. Don't fool yourself though. The Internet can absorb your time like a black hole. Set a time limit for how long you spend on the Internet and stick to it.

ENLARGING YOUR NETWORK

Now that you have activated your network, you can begin to enlarge it to include those organizations and people that might be in a position to hire you. Some of the people you contact might have been leads you obtained through others in your network. Others might be people of whom you are aware from searches online, newspaper articles, directories, or social networks like Facebook or LinkedIn. All leads have two things in common: They are all in a position to assist you, and none of them knows you.

Your challenge is to reach out to each of these people to enlist them into your network. There are two basic ways to accomplish this. The first is the conventional method of launching an email campaign. Develop a standard email that attempts to persuade the person to contact you to discuss possible employment opportunities. This method can be productive, but you typically get responses from a small percentage of those contacted. That means you must send out 100 emails to get one or two calls. And that is if the email gets through the spam filters. To boost the possibility of results, you can include a line letting the person know that *you* will be contacting *her* on a particular date at a particular time to follow up. You might get a few more interviews so be sure to follow up with the phone call and not squander that lead.

A more productive method is the telephone campaign. Think back to Matt, the desperate accounting supervisor. Suppose Chloe tells him that she doesn't know anyone who can help him. Just as she leaves his office the phone rings. You are calling to tell him that you are graduating soon. You are skilled in corporate accounting and tax work and would like to schedule an appointment with him. Not only will Matt clear his calendar to accommodate your schedule, but he'll also consider you an exceptional candidate based on your skills, initiative, and self-confidence.

Landing a job is, of course, the ideal telephone campaign result. You might be surprised to know that it happens regularly to people who employ these methods. Why is this approach so successful? Because people know the right people to call and what to say.

It is usually counterproductive to contact the human resources department. The people there may not necessarily know about relevant job vacancies and can be very skeptical about people applying for employment. Just as you did in Chapter 5, contact the person who works in the field that you wish to enter. If it is accounting, call and ask for the name of the person who manages accounting. Managers are more willing to meet with and talk to potential employees than are human resources professionals. If a manager has an opening, he will be eager to meet you. If you do well in the interview, you will meet the human resources personnel when they help you fill out the paperwork necessary to hire you.

Just as in the networking process, approach potential leads and employers with caution. A large percentage of these people may not have an immediate opening. They might have an interest in you, so convey your enthusiasm without being too aggressive.

Try not to scare them off. Attract their interest by telling them immediately what you can do for them. Then ask if you could drop by for a brief chat about opportunities at their organization. Many of the people you contact by phone will tell you right away that they don't have anything. That's okay. Then you can ask if they are aware of anyone who is looking. Even a telephone call that doesn't result in an interview can offer you useful information.

The most difficult part of a telephone campaign is picking up the phone the first time. With each successive call it becomes easier. You save a great deal of time by calling instead of emailing and waiting, and the results are much better as well.

That brings us to the second key for your success. You must know what to say. I mentioned briefly some of the points to touch on. Exercise 9.2 details the information you need to include in your phone conversations.

9.2   Take a Closer Look

GENERATING INTERVIEWS

The most important part of contacting people for job leads is to mention your specific skills related to the field. Sometimes this is referred to as your 'elevator speech,' what you would say if you were in the elevator with someone who had the power to offer you the job of your dreams. You will know when you finally make contact with someone who might have an opportunity if they begin to probe your background and ask questions. That is when the door begins to open. Lean in and start your heavy-duty marketing right there. It should result in an interview. Fill in the blanks in the following dialogue to practice your telephone campaign:

Operator: Good morning. Wayne Industries.

You: Good morning. Could you please give me the name of your (public relations, engineering, accounting) _____ manager?

Operator: Yes, that would be _____.

You: May I speak with _____ ?

Manager: _____ speaking.

You: Good morning, Mr./Ms. _____. My name is _____. I am highly skilled in the areas of _____, _____, and _____. I am wondering if I might drop by at your convenience and chat with you concerning opportunities available at Wayne Industries.

Manager: I'm sorry but we don't have anything right now.

You: Do you know of any company that might be interested in someone with my background?

Manager: Yes, I think there is an opening with Hale Environmental right now. Jean Cook is the manager there, I think.

You: May I say that you referred me?

Manager: Sure.

You: Thank you for your help. Goodbye.

Try out your telephone role play with your partner in the CA Café or in the class. Practice it until you are sure of what you are going to say and then discuss the results. This is tough stuff ... but it preps you for when you get your shot.

BE ORGANIZED AND PERSISTENT

Employers will frequently put you off during your search by requesting your resume or by telling you to call back at another time. They may be sincerely interested but otherwise preoccupied. Staying organized is essential to follow-up. You need to know when and where your interviews are, and who is awaiting your resume, a follow-up call, or a thank-you letter. Use a system that works for you, three-ring binders, index cards, electronic management tool like Business Contact Manager in Outlook, an Excel spreadsheet—whatever you are comfortable with—to keep your campaign organized and to record each contact you have made and the results of your calls. To market yourself effectively try to make at least ten calls each day to people who might be in a position to hire you or give you useful information.

Ten calls may sound like you will spend a lot of time on the phone. In reality, if you apply yourself to the task, it should take no more than 45 minutes to an hour. One especially effective way to ensure that you actually make the calls is to work with a partner in job seeking. Make a commitment to meet with your partner every morning in a private place where you won't be interrupted. Take turns making calls until each of you has completed your ten calls for the day. Monitor each other's calls, encouraging your partner when the calls are not going well and celebrating when you get results. By the end of the first week, you should be booked with interviews that will keep you busy. Don't stop making calls, however: Continue until you have a firm job offer in hand.

Anyone who is in sales will tell you that persistence is the greatest predictor of success. Your willingness to keep calling will have a greater impact on your success than any amount of luck. Make the ten calls. There is an old saying: "If breaking a rock takes hitting it ten times, you don't want to stop on the ninth time." Don't give up on the ninth call or the second or the fifth. Keep calling. There are bound to be disappointments. Don't dwell on the calls that end quickly. You're well prepared and will be successful as long as you keep trying.

Exercise 9.3 provides you with a way of organizing your campaign and gives you a taste of what marketing yourself is like.

Take a Closer Look 9.3

THE MINI-CAMPAIGN

Using the following information categories, make up a form or spreadsheet to track your job campaign.

Company

Address

Phone

Email

Contact person

Outcome

Follow-up

Using the resources mentioned throughout this text—online browser, social networks, directories, professional journals, computer databases, online newspapers—develop a list of ten new contacts. From the prior role-play exercise, develop the list and try to arrange interviews. Work with partners and conduct a mini-campaign using all the techniques available to sell yourself. Keep track of your results. If people request a resume, forward one and then follow up for their response. Even if the person doesn't offer you an interview or a job, see if you can get feedback about your resume or a referral to another source. Be polite, persistent, and flexible, and you will be gratified with the results. If you are engaged in a serious job search and not just completing a class assignment, extend your mini-campaign, making ten contacts per day until you find the position that will get you started on your career path.

Discuss with your group in the CA Café or the class the responses you received when you conducted your mini-campaign.

BEING A RESOURCE TO SOMEONE ELSE

Now that you have experienced what it feels like to pick up the phone and persuade someone to give you their time and consideration, you can hardly go back to the old assumptions about seeking employment. The techniques described here are becoming more accepted as part of an overall employment strategy. The chances are very good that at some time in the future you may get a call very much like the ones that you placed. If you are looking for someone to fill a spot in your organization, you might welcome the call. If not, please remember your own experience and greet your job seeker graciously and with encouragement. Making calls requires a high level of confidence and courage for job hunters. Your support will help them continue to pursue their goals.

9.4   Take a Closer Look

PULLING IT ALL TOGETHER

This exercise looks at your overall job-search strategy.
What are your top three skills that an employer would find most useful in the work setting?

1. _____

2. _____

3. _____

Does your statement to the people in your network highlight these skills? Are you clear about what you need from your contact?

○ Yes   ○ No

Does your statement to a potential employer focus on these top three skills?

○ Yes   ○ No

A referral can be valuable in your job search. Does your telephone inquiry mention your interest in other opportunities that might be available?

○ Yes   ○ No

What resources have proven to be most valuable in providing you with contacts?

○ Current network   ○ Job banks   ○ Computer databases

○ Social network sites   ○ Placement office   ○ Other

○ Online newspapers   ○ Professional directories

What system of organization works best for you?

○ Excel spreadsheet   ○ Organizing calendars (i.e., Outlook)

○ Index cards/forms   ○ Electronic organizer

Have your calls generated any interviews? If not, what part of your approach needs work?

A LOOK BACK

The responsibility you assume for your success is the most important aspect of your career development. The methods described in this chapter are your key to open any door—for referrals, networking support, Internet links, or interviews. The critical factor in successfully using these methods is knowing the people or resources to contact and knowing what to say or email. Emphasizing your skills and probing for referrals will create opportunities that result in job offers. Persistence in pursuing leads will have more impact on your future than relying on outside agencies and online ads. This chapter has described ways to make your job search a comprehensive, all-out marketing campaign that will take you where you want to go.

Career Adventure Café

Visit the CA Café and share the results of this phase of your job search process. You have all the tools necessary to launch a serious job search. You will be using the traditional methods, but you and the other members of your group will also go beyond those to leverage the power of the CA Café and social networks to fuel your search. The job search process will yield a wealth of information that you can share with the members of your group as you navigate to your goals together. Are all the members of the group looking in different areas or do some of you pursue similar outcomes? Can the CA Café be a digital space at which you can organize events and share information? Brainstorm with the group about how the CA Café can be a vehicle to accelerate your job search. Here are some questions to get you started:

Is there a way to get information out to the group quickly and effectively? Are there digital tools that you can incorporate into your job seeking process?

_____

_____

Are there ways to collaborate within the group that can expand your effectiveness? Would breaking into smaller groups based on career goals be more productive?

_____

_____

How can the group work most effectively to support all the members? What do the members of your group think?

_____

_____

Facebook It

Have you been busy finding new leads and working your network? Post what you have been up to on Facebook and see if your friends in the CA Café have been as productive as you have. We are getting to the end of this phase of your adventure, but you can keep visiting Facebook and the CA Café as long as you wish. Even after you are well down your career path, stay connected to your friends in the CA Café . . . they are all a part of your network now, the Friends of You!

Other Sources and Suggested Reading

College Grad Job Hunt, 6th Edition by Brian D. Krueger
> This perennial favorite of college grads offers techniques for job hunting that have been tested and proven successful.

Guerilla Marketing for Job Hunters 3.0: How to Stand Out from the Crowd and Tap Into the Hidden Job Market Using Social Media and 999 Other Tactics Today by Jay Conrad Levinson and David E. Perry
> The authors incorporate the latest approaches in the use of information technology and social media in this aggressive guide to job hunting.

The Power Formula for LinkedIn Success: Kickstart Your Business, Brand, and Job Search by Wayne Breitbarth
> Using the power of the LinkedIn Web site offers job seekers an additional advantage in their job search.

Web Sites and Internet Resources

www.careermag.com
> This Web site from Career Magazine offers job listings, a resume bank, current articles on career issues, and a mobile app.

www.careerbuilder.com
> This is a full-blown network Web site that offers job postings, advice, and resources.

www.thingamajob.com
> More than a resume posting site, this site offers a variety of services for job hunters.

Continuing Your Adventure

Your career adventure has led you to many places but it is far from over. You have only begun to explore the surface of what your career will mean in your life. You will continue to learn and grow, going beyond the superficial aspects of work and success toward a deep understanding of what is meaningful and important to you.

Now is a good time to prepare yourself for any obstacles and frustrations you may encounter. And you can be sure that there will be many, whatever path you choose to take. It is important to prepare yourself consciously for what might lie ahead.

We act as though comfort and luxury were the chief requirements of life, when all that we need to make us really happy is something to be enthusiastic about.

CHARLES KINGSLEY

UNDERSTANDING YOUR EMPLOYER'S EXPECTATIONS

"And now, ladies and gentlemen, straight from his last management assignment as the safety monitor for your third-grade class, it's *your new boss!*"

Thankfully most of us will spend our entire careers without encountering anyone who acts like the third-grade safety monitor. Even so, all employers have expectations.

What *do* employers expect from us on the job? As with almost every other aspect of our society, we have seen employers' expectations affected by the increasingly competitive global economy. Employees are now expected to become "partners" with their employers in learning how to do business better and how to respond to changes in the economy.

One of my students lamented to me that he was disgusted with his coworkers at a local manufacturing plant. He was on assignment for a temp agency but he was appalled to see the employees retire to the back room to play cards after they had finished the work required by their contract. He wondered if the workers at their competitors' plants were playing cards during their shift.

Companies that have to carry workers such as the card players won't be able to absorb the economic losses that are sure to result. The company in which this incident took place has been closed down and is now shuttered. The global economic reality has fostered a new understanding of employers' expectations.

The New Rules for Workplace Survival

1. Self-starters will survive. Take responsibility for your career and what you accomplish each day. Don't wait for your boss to come over and tell you what to do next.

2. Be a contributor. If your company is a winner, then you will be, too. If you cheat your company, arrive late, steal office supplies, or "goof off," you hurt the company and, in the long run, yourself.

3. Don't become too comfortable. If you get in a rut and find yourself playing it safe, push yourself by taking on a new project or new idea. Employers are listening intently today to their best assets, their employees.

4. If you become frustrated and do not find the opportunities to grow that you seek, don't whine and assign blame. Look for something that is a better fit for you.

5. Every new project is an opportunity to acquire new skills, new knowledge. Look for ways to expand capabilities in different areas by taking on tasks that challenge you in new ways.

The new rules are actually an update of some old rules that still hold true. Here's a quick review of guidelines that will help you keep your job.

Tried but True Rules for Keeping Your Job

1. Arrive on time!
2. Stay focused on your task and don't distract your coworkers.
3. Accept change willingly and work hard at learning new things.
4. Watch the details. Avoid repeating the same errors.
5. Demonstrate that you can work without supervision.
6. Make sure your work is done on time and is complete.
7. Don't procrastinate. Plan your work and stick to your plan.
8. Work hard at communicating effectively.
9. Seek opportunities for growth.

As the global economy has expanded and diversified, most employees now accept responsibility for their own success and recognize the competitive nature of the labor market. They've internalized the reality of today's workplace and taken steps to secure their future on their own. That may translate to moving on when salary or opportunity no longer appeal or judiciously planning the next step in a systematic and methodical way. As our culture continues the transition to digital operations, relying on the "brain power" of its workers, employees with the right skills will become the value centers of their organizations.

THE WORLD OF HUMAN CAPITAL

Careers are no longer straightforward choices, and you must know what's ahead before you venture down a career path. Yet, predicting the future has always been a tricky endeavor. It can be frustrating or exciting depending on how you approach the task.

The best way to plan for career success is to experience growth one step at a time. Use the research techniques you've learned. Actively seek the information you need to make a decision. Plan your steps to your goal. Have faith in your ability to handle the obstacles. And then work, work, work to make your goal a reality.

See the value in any job you do, regardless of the visibility or recognition associated with the job. Pay attention to the details of your job and perform to the best of your abilities. You may have many more capabilities than the job gives you a chance to use; accept the fact that you will have to earn the right to move into a more rewarding position. Keep your mind and your eyes open, and eventually you will see a job that represents the next step in your career growth. It may be one that you've always wanted or it could be something brand new. Then plan for how you will get to that next step.

The instability in the career marketplace may be seen as a source of anxiety by those who are ill-equipped for the rigors of managing their own progress. If you have stuck with the formula outlined in this text, then you know that, despite any lack of guarantees, you are well-prepared to take responsibility for your own success. Yes, the path may be winding, but you have acquired the skills and human capital value to stay way ahead of the competition.

WIGGLING AROUND

Building your career step-by-step is what I call "wiggling around." It is impossible for you to anticipate what you may encounter as your career progresses. It is almost as difficult to project the ways in which you will grow and change over the years. Locking yourself into a career path or goal that doesn't let you breathe and blossom could be a mistake. Give yourself room to grow, stay flexible, and wiggle your way into the career that offers you what you need to have a happy and meaningful life.

Does this mean that you will automatically take any promotion offered? Or that your path will always be straight up—with no excursions on interesting side streets? Who knows? You will make those decisions when you get there. What you must do is stay in touch with the voice that guides you today, the one you have been in touch with throughout your career adventure. That inner voice will tell you which path is best when the time comes. If you are fortunate you may find a career that offers you the opportunity to consistently challenge yourself, build your skills, and continually grow. This state, called "flow," when everything seems to fit and fall into place, is the path to lasting career satisfaction. As one of my students put it, "If I can find the right career, one that makes me consistently try to do my best, and helps me develop to meet the challenges, then I'll never work again."

YOUR CAREER: A WORK "IN PROCESS"

A remarkable woman, Maya Angelou has been tested in her lifetime and has found the things that she knows about herself and what they mean to her. She is far from finished with creating the person she is, however. She refers to herself as a work "in process."

If you listen closely to the voice within, you will find, as has Maya Angelou, that not only can you do some things with grace but also that within you are flashes of brilliance—perhaps even a brilliance that will light the world for those around you.

Your career adventure will be one of self-discovery and evolution. Always follow where it leads. Your career is a work "in process" that will mirror your growth and change, a vehicle to give you profound knowledge of yourself and the world. If you value your talents and the way you use them, your career will offer you satisfaction and meaning. Most important, pay attention to the brilliance that lies at your core. Finding a way to reveal that quality is part of the challenge of the career adventure. I hope, as a result of this process, you are ready for the adventure to continue. If you are fortunate, it will never end!

Career Adventure Café

Well, here we are . . . back in the CA Café. This might seem like the end of a process, but everything you shared and created in the CA Café is a part of you now. Make no mistake, you are connected with your group through the experience you have shared, and you will be available to each other as you continue your career adventure. As you visit the CA Café this time, check with the members of your group to see how you might continue to work together in the next chapter of your life.

Have you found the CA Café a good space to meet and share your thoughts? If so, how can you keep it going?

_____

_____

It may be that working in a smaller digital space will allow greater focus. Have you found anyone in the group whom you can work with in a small group (two or three members)? If a "table for two (or three)" would work better for you, do you know whom you might invite? Or would it make more sense to post an invitation and see who responds?

_____

_____

How can you keep your connections to the members of the CA Café group vibrant? What do the members of your group think?

_____

_____

Appendix

Samantha Fields

587 Sandalwood Road
Santa Barbara, CA 93107

Residence (805) 567-2499
Cell (805) 673-0756
sfields22@netzone.net

PROFILE

Experienced nursing professional; specialized training in an acute care setting

EDUCATION

The University of California at Los Angeles
Bachelor of Science/Nursing
Graduated 2012, magna cum laude. GPA: 3.8

EXPERIENCE

UCLA Medical Center, Los Angeles, CA
Med-Surg Nurse, June 2012 to present
Responsible for full range of patient care for five to seven patients; focus on primary care

CLINICAL EXPERIENCE

UCLA Medical Center, Los Angeles, CA
Student Nurse, September 2011 to June 2012
Provided nursing services through clinical training in variety of departments

COMMUNITY EXPERIENCE

South Central Free Clinic, Los Angeles, CA
Volunteered on weekends through special program in conjunction with UCLA Medical Center

LICENSURES

California Licensure, June 2012
Southern California Regional Board, June 2012
National Board Certification, May 2012

FUNCTIONAL/ACHIEVEMENT

Thomas McCrary

tmccrary1@aol.com

2367 Golden Lane
Cincinnati, OH 45204

Residence (513) 473-5898
Cell (513) 244-6371

CAREER PROFILE

Strong analytical, financial, and interpersonal skills; acknowledged leadership capabilities; highest performance standards

SUMMARY OF ACCOMPLISHMENTS

Analytical and Financial

Proven analytical and financial skills as indicated by the following accomplishments:

- Researched and initiated the use of cost accounting software that increased assignment efficiency by approximately 35 percent over the prior year
- Prepared financial statements for various corporations, including multinationals
- As treasurer of a social collegiate organization, undertook management and accounting of all financial transactions

Interpersonal

Exceptional interpersonal and communications skills:

- Organized and monitored a successful United Appeal Executive Prospector Program at Ernst & Young, which resulted in pledges in excess of $57,000 during the 2011 campaign
- Received highly favorable commendation based on client comments regarding work on a particular auditing assignment

WORK EXPERIENCE

Ernst & Young, Internship, August 2011 to December 2011

EDUCATION

Bachelor of Science degree, 2012, Accounting (cum laude), GPA: 3.7
The Ohio State University, Columbus, OH

HONORS

Who's Who in American Colleges and Universities
National Dean's List
Dean's Honor List

Sherry Campbell

1002 Princess Anne Street   CELL (540) 368-5532
Fredericksburg, VA 22401   scampbell@hotmail.com

SUMMARY

Recognized specialist in assessing and responding to customer needs; aggressive self-starter.

WORK EXPERIENCE

2006–2009   Policyholder Services Representative (PSR)
                   Progressive Insurance

                   Provided customer service support to policyholders, sales representatives, and other interested parties primarily through telephone and Internet transactions; furnished information and responded to inquiries on billing, coverage, and rating criteria

                   Major Achievements:
                   ■ Exceeded new policy sales quotas five quarters; awarded PSR
                     'Excellence in Service' award, June 2007 and February 2008
                   ■ Revised PSR response form to facilitate communication between
                     customer and PSR, resulting in annual savings of approximately
                     $1,080

EDUCATION & TRAINING

2009–Present   George Mason University, Washington, DC
                   Currently majoring in Business Administration
                   GPA: 3.2

Other Training: Policyholder Services Representative Training, 2006
                   Customer Service Seminar, 2007

Amy Lieseberg

2242 Springmill Road	(920) 457-9045	Green Bay, WI 54303

September 23, 2012

Ms. Donna Jaques
Mark-It Labeling Company
633 Courtney Road
Green Bay, WI 54304

Dear Ms. Jaques,
Bill Browning, an associate of yours at Mark-It, suggested I contact you concerning the possible expansion of your design engineering department.

As a recent graduate of Purdue University, I am currently exploring opportunities in which my education can be utilized more fully. My college degree is in design engineering with a special emphasis in mechanical design. In addition, my internship with Monarch Marking in Dayton, Ohio, gave me an excellent chance to gain hands-on experience in this field.

My conversation with Bill confirmed my favorable impressions of your company. Mark-It's leadership in the areas of design and cost control has set a recognized standard for excellence. My ability to work hard and to earn my place on a team has always been one of my strongest attributes. I am convinced I could become a valued member of your design team and would welcome the opportunity to discuss further how we might work together.

My resume is enclosed for your consideration. I am available at your convenience for a personal interview and look forward to hearing from you.

Sincerely,

Amy Lieseberg

Amy Lieseberg
Attachment

Chloe McCann

34 NARROWS TRACE   ●   Woodbridge, VA 22192   ●   (703) 264-5588

July 17, 2012

Mr. Jerre Pavey
Advertising Fresh
39 Arundel Drive
Reston, VA 20195

Subject: Account Representative (*Washington Post Online;* July 16, 2012)

Dear Mr. Pavey,

Your Requirements	*My Background*
■ Strong communication skills	B. A. in Communications, *Summa cum laude*
■ Full service client orientation	Sales account manager, *Clarion* Student Newspaper
■ Detail-oriented, well-organized	Worked full-time while carrying full-time class load
■ Proven collaborative creative capabilities	Acted as creative lead in student ad campaign for successful Guinness Book of World Records Pillow Fight

As you can see from my resume, my background is ideally suited for the account representative position you are seeking to fill. My current work setting is fast-paced and deadline oriented. It requires the skills of a juggler with the nerves and balance of a high-wire artist. I've been "walking the wire" for two years now and have loved every minute of it!

I'm ready to raise the wire to a new level. I believe I have the combination of dedication and aggressive creativity your organization seeks. I've enclosed my resume for your consideration and look forward to hearing from you. Please don't hesitate to call if you have any questions.

Sincerely,

Chloe McCann

Chloe McCann
Attachment

References

CAREER PLANNING CHART

Brooks, Kate. July 12, 2004. "Liberal Arts Career Services." University of Texas. Retrieved January 6, 2004, from http://www.lacs.utexas.edu/student/careerplanning/roadmap/freshman.

"Career Services." Oct. 7, 2004. Wright State University. Retrieved Oct. 7, 2004, from http://career.wright.edu.

Noel, Renee. 2004. "The College Plan." Career Planning. Retrieved January 6, 2004, from http://www.thomas_more.edu/career/collegeplan/freshman.html.

Path, Rich. 2004. "Career Services." Edgewood College. Retrieved January 6, 2004, from http://www.edgewood.edu/src/career/planning/freshman.htm.

Richey-Suttles, Stephen. July 1, 1998. "Career Resources." University of Dayton. Retrieved July 29, 2003, from http://www.udayton.edu/cc/career.

"University Career Services." 2004. The Ohio State University. Retrieved December 23, 2003, from http://www.careers.osu.edu.

CHAPTER 1

Brown, Chris, Roberta George-Curran, and Marian Smith. "The Role of Emotional Intelligence in the Career Commitment and Decision-Making Process." *The Journal of Career Assessment* 11 (November 2003): 379–392.

Emmerling, Robert J., and Cary Cherniss. "Emotional Intelligence and the Career Choice Process." *The Journal of Career Assessment* 11 (May 2003): 153–167.

Maddi, Salvatore. "Hardiness: An Operationalization of Existential Courage." The Journal of Humanistic Psychology 44(3). (2002): 279–299.

Young, Cheri A. 1996. "Emotions and Emotional Intelligence." The Web Center for Social Research Methods. Retrieved November 11, 2003, from http://www.socialresearchmethods.net.

CHAPTER 2

Bengis, Ingrid. April 1993. "Sunbeams." In *The Sun*. Chapel Hill, NC.

Bolles, Richard Nelson. 2001 ed. *What Color Is Your Parachute?* Berkeley, CA: Ten Speed Press.

Brown, Duane, and Linda Brooks. 1991. *Career Counseling Techniques*. Boston: Allyn & Bacon.

Dictionary of Occupational Titles. 1991. Washington, DC: U.S. Department of Labor.

Gordon, L.V. 1975. *The Measurement of Interpersonal Values*. Chicago: Science Research Associates.

Hall, Brian P. 1976. *The Development of Consciousness: A Confluent Theory of Values*. New York: Paulist Press.

Hanson, Marlys, Merle E. Hanson, and Arthur F. Miller, Jr. 2002. *Passion and Purpose: How to Identify and Leverage the Powerful Patterns That Shape Your Work/Life*. Atlanta, GA: Pathfinder Press.

Hart, Gordon M. 1978. *Values Clarification for Counselors*. Springfield, IL: Charles C. Thomas.

Huitt, William G. February 2004. "Maslow's Hierarchy of Needs." *Educational Psychology Interactive*. Retrieved May 14, 2013, from http://www.edpsycinteractive.org/topics/conation/maslow.html.

Jay, Meg. 2012. *The Defining Decade: Why Your Twenties Matter and How to Make the Most of Them Now*. New York: Grand Central Publishing.

Maslow, Abraham. 1954. *Motivation and Personality*. New York: Harper & Row.

Maslow, Abraham. 1968. *Toward a Psychology of Being*. New York: Van Nostrand Reinhold.

McNeil, Elton B., and Zick Rubin. 1977. *The Psychology of Being Human*. New York: Harper & Row.

McWilliams, John-Roer, and Peter McWilliams. 1991. *Do It!* Los Angeles: Prelude Press.

Rokeach, Milton. 1973. *The Nature of Human Values*. New York: The Free Press.

Rokeach, Milton. 1979. *Understanding Human Values: Individual and Societal*. New York: The Free Press.

Ryckman, Richard M. 1978. *Theories of Personality*. New York: Van Nostrand Reinhold.

Sher, Barbara. 1996. *Live the Life You Love*. New York: Delacorte Press.

Zunker, Vernon G. 1986. *Using Assessment Results in Career Counseling*. Monterey, CA: Brooks/Cole.

CHAPTER 3

Aspen Institute. 2010. *Skills for America's Future*. Retrieved February 11, 2012, from http://www.aspeninstitute.org/policy-work/economic-opportunities/skills-for-americas-future.

Black, Sandra, and Lisa M. Lynch. 1996. *How to Compete: The Impact of Workplace Practices and Information Technology on Productivity*. Washington, DC: U.S. Department of Labor.

Brown, Duane, and Linda Brooks. 1991. *Career Counseling Techniques*. Boston: Allyn & Bacon.

Drapela, Victor J. 1987. *A Review of Personality Theories*. Springfield, IL: Charles C. Thomas.

Department of Labor. 2009. *New and Emerging Occupations of the 21st Century: Updating the O*NET®-SOC Taxonomy.* Retrieved February 11, 2012, from http://www.onet center.org/reports/UpdatingTaxonomy2009.html.

Department of Labor. 2012. *O*NET Online: Content Model.* Retrieved February 11, 2012, from http://www.onet center.org/content.html/1.A#cm_1.A.

Department of Labor. 2012. *CareerOneStop: Industry Competency Models.* Retrieved February 11, 2012, from http://www.careeronestop.org/CompetencyModel /pyramid.aspx.

Department of Labor. 2012. *O*NET Online: Skills Search.* Retrieved February 11, 2012, from http://www.onetonline .org/skills.

Holland, John L. 1997. *Making Vocational Choices: A Theory of Vocational Personalities and Work Environments.* Lutz, FL: Psychological Assessment Resources.

Jeffries, William C. 1991. *True to Type.* Norfolk, VA: Hampton Roads Publishing.

Jobs, Steve. 2005. *Commencement Address.* Palo Alto, CA: Stanford.

Jung, C.G. 1971. *Psychological Types.* Princeton, NJ: Princeton University Press.

Keirsey, David, and Marilyn Bates. 1998. *Please Understand Me II: Temperament, Character, Intelligence.* Del Mar, CA: Prometheus Nemesis.

Kroeger, Otto, and Jane M. Thuesen. 1989. *Type Talk.* New York: Dell.

Kroeger, Otto, and Jane M. Thuesen. 2002. *Type Talk at Work: How the 16 Personality Types Determine Your Success on the Job.* New York: Delta.

Learning a Living: A Blueprint for High Performance. A SCANS Report for America 2000, Part 1. 1992. Washington, DC: U.S. Department of Labor.

Levy, Frank, and Richard J. Murnane. 1996. *Teaching the New Basic Skills: Principles for Educating Children to Thrive in a Changing Economy.* New York: The Free Press.

Lore, Nicholas. 2012. *The Pathfinder: How to Choose or Change Your Career for a Lifetime of Satisfaction and Success.* New York: Touchstone Books.

Sharp, Daryl. 1987. *Personality Types: Jung's Model of Typology.* Toronto: Inner City Books.

Tieger, Paul D., and Barbara Barron-Tieger. 2001. *Do What You Are: Discover the Perfect Career for You Through the Secrets of Personality Type.* New York: Little, Brown.

CHAPTER 4

Berkman, Robert. "Internet Searching Is Not Always What It Seems." *The Chronicle of Higher Education* (July 28, 2000): B9.

Bhagwati, Jagdish. "Why Your Job Isn't Moving to Bangalore." *The New York Times* (February 15, 2004).

Calvert, Robert, Jr., ed. "Ready for Work in 2023? What to Anticipate." *Career Opportunities News* (October 2000).

Carnevale, Anthony, P., Stephen J. Rose, and Ban Cheah. *The College Payoff.* Washington: Georgetown Center on Education and the Workforce.

Challenger, John A. "The Coming Labor Shortage." *The Futurist* (September–October 2003).

Coates, Joseph F., Jennifer Jarrett, and John B. Mahaffie. 1990. *Future Work.* San Francisco: Jossey-Bass.

College Board. 2011. *Book of Majors.* New York: Macmillan.

Dictionary of Occupational Titles (4th ed.). 1992. Washington, DC: U.S. Department of Labor.

Dohm, Arlene. "Gauging the Labor Force Effects of Retiring Baby-Boomers." *Monthly Labor Review* (July 2000).

Farr, Michael, LaVerne Ludden, and Leonard Shatkin. 2005. *Guide for Occupational Exploration* (4th ed.). Indianapolis, IN: JIST Works.

Farr, Michael, and Laurence Shatkin. 2003. *Best Jobs for the 21st Century* (3rd ed.). Indianapolis, IN: JIST Works.

Florida, Richard. 2002. *The Rise of the Creative Class.* New York: Perseus Books.

"High-Paying Occupations With Many Openings, Projected 2004–14." *Occupational Outlook Quarterly* (Spring 2006). Retrieved from http://www.bls.gov/opub/ooq/2006/spring /oochart.pdf on March 1, 2012.

Kleiman, Carol. "Employers Make Office a Great Place." *The Chicago Tribune* (September 21, 1997).

Kristof, Nicholas D. "Watching the Jobs Go By." *The New York Times* (February 11, 2004).

Kunde, Diana. "Job Sharing Gives Clients, Employers Double Benefits." *Dallas Morning News* (September 21, 1997).

Lenox, Richard A., and Linda Mezydio Subich. "The Relationship Between Self-Efficacy Beliefs and Inventoried Vocational Interests." *The Career Development Quarterly* 42 (June 1994): 302–313.

Lieta, Carole. "Evaluating Internet Resources: A Checklist." *InFoPeople Project.* Institute of Museum and Library Services. 1999. http://www.infopeople.org.

Luzzo, Darrell Anthony, Dylan P. Funk, and Jason Strang. "Attributional Retraining Increases Career Decision-Making Self-Efficacy." *The Career Development Quarterly* 44 (June 1996): 110–125.

Ferguson Publishing. 2010. *Encyclopedia of Careers and Vocational Guidance, 15th ed.* Chicago: Ferguson Publishing.

Naisbitt, John. 1994. *Global Paradox.* New York: Morrow.

Northdurft, William E. 1989. *SchoolWorks.* Washington, DC: The Brookings Institute.

Occupational Outlook Handbook, 2011–2012, 5th ed. 2011. New York: McGraw-Hill.

Rayman, Jack R. 1990. "Computers and Career Counseling," in *Career Counseling Contemporary Topics in Vocational Psychology,* W. Bruce Walsh and Samuel Osipow, eds. Hillsdale, NJ: Lawrence Erlbaum Associates.

Samuelson, Robert J. "The Specter of Outsourcing." *Newsweek* (January 14, 2004).

Samuelson, Robert J. "The Value of College." *Newsweek* (August 31, 1992).

Simkin, Joyce. 2011. *American Salaries and Wages Survey* (11th ed.). Detroit, MI: The Gale Group.

Thurow, Lester C. 1996. *The Future of Capitalism: How Today's Economic Forces Shape Tomorrow's World*. New York: Morrow.

Weise, Elizabeth. "One Click Starts the Avalanche." *USA Today* (August 8, 2000).

Winefordner, David W. 1978. *Worker Trait Group Guide*. Charleston, WV: Appalachia Educational Laboratory.

Woodard, Eric. 2011. *Your Last Day of School*. Seattle: CreateSpace.

CHAPTER 5

Azrin, Nathan H., and Victoria A. Besalel. 1980. *Job Club Counselor's Manual*. Austin, TX: PRO-ED.

Bjorseth, Lillian D. 2009. *Breakthrough Networking: Building Relationships That Last* (2nd ed.). Lisle, IL: Duoforce Enterprises.

The Career Guide 2003 D&B® Employment Opportunities Directory. 2002. Bethlehem, PA: Dun & Bradstreet.

Darling, Diane. 2010. *The Networking Survival Guide: Practical Advice on How to Gain Confidence, Approach People, and Get the Success You Want* (2nd ed.). New York: McGraw-Hill.

Fine, Debra. 2005. *The Fine Art of Small Talk: How to Start a Conversation, Keep it Going, Build Networking Skills—and Leave a Positive Impression*. New York: Hyperion Books.

Granovetter, Mark S. "The Strength of Weak Ties." *The American Journal of Sociology*. (May 1973).

Informational Interviewing. 2004. Dayton, OH: Sinclair Community College/CPPC.

Jecker, J. and D. Landy. "Liking a Person as a Function of Doing Him a Favor." *Human Relation* 22 (1969): 371–378.

Zack, Devora. 2010. *Networking for People Who Hate Networking: A Field Guide for Introverts, the Overwhelmed, and the Underconnected*. San Francisco: Berrett-Koehler.

CHAPTER 6

Arnold, John D. 1978. *Make Up Your Mind!* New York: AMACOM.

Bartone, Paul D., Ross H. Pastel, Mark A.Vaitkus, and David A. Rubenstein. 2010. *The 71F Advantage: Applying Army Research Psychology for Health and Performance Gains*. Washington: National Defense University Press.

Carroll, John S., and Eric J. Johnson. 1990. *Decision Research*. Newbury Park, CA: Sage.

Golden, Bonnie, and Kay Lesh. 2001. *Building Self-Esteem*. Upper Saddle River, NJ: Prentice Hall.

Goza, Barbara K. "Graffiti Needs Assessment." *Journal of Management Education* (February 1993).

Hammond, John S., Ralph L. Keeney, and Howard Raiffa. 2002. *Smart Choices: A Practical Guide to Making Better Decisions*. Cambridge, MA: Harvard Business School Press.

Hankin, Sheenah. 2008. *Complete Confidence: The Handbook*. New York: William Morrow.

Hastie, Reid, and Robyn M. Dawes. 2009. *Rational Choice in an Uncertain World* (2nd ed.). Newbury Park, CA: Sage.

Kahneman, Daniel. 2011. *Thinking Fast and Slow*. New York: Farrar, Straus and Giroux.

Kanchier, Carole. "Using Intuition for Career Decision Making." *Counseling Today* (February 1997).

Lenox, Richard A., and Linda Mezydio Subich. "The Relationship Between Self-Efficacy Beliefs and Inventoried Vocational Interests." *The Career Development Quarterly* 42 (June 1994): 302–313.

Luzzo, Darrell Anthony, Dylan P. Funk, and Jason Strang. "Attributional Retraining Increases Career Decision-Making Self-Efficacy." *The Career Development Quarterly* 44 (June 1996): 110–125.

Martino, R. L., and Elinor Svendson Stein. 1969. *Decision Patterns*. Wayne. PA: MDI Publications.

McKowen, Clark. 1986. *Thinking About Thinking*. Los Altos, CA: William Kaufmann.

Mezirow, Jack, and Edward W. Taylor. 2009. *Transformative Learning in Practice: Insights from Community Workplace and Higher Education*. San Francisco: Jossey-Bass.

Miller-Tiedeman, Anna. 1988. *Lifecareer: The Quantum Leap into a Process Theory of Career*. Vista, CA: Lifecareer Foundation.

CHAPTER 7

Bolles, Richard Nelson. 2004 ed. *What Color Is Your Parachute?* Berkeley, CA: Ten Speed Press.

Boston College. 2012. *Career Center: Resume Action Verbs*. Retrieved July 2012 from http://www.bc.edu/offices/careers/skills/resumes/verbs.html.

Brown, David. 2012. *Preparing and Managing Your Career Portfolio* (Kindle Edition). Seattle, WA: Amazon Digital Services.

Brown, Lola. 2006. *Resume Writing Made Easy* (8th ed.). Upper Saddle River, NJ: Prentice Hall.

Criscito, Pat. 2005. *e-Resumes: Everything You Need to Know About Using Electronic Resumes to Tap into Today's Hot Job Market*. New York: Barron's Educational Services.

Enelow, Wendy. 2003. *Best Key Words for Resumes, Cover Letters, and Interviews: Powerful Communication Tools for Success*. Manassas Park, VA: Impact.

Greene, Brenda. 2008 *Get the Interview Every Time: Fortune 500 Hiring Professionals' Tips for Writing Winning Resumes and Cover Letters* (2nd ed.). Chicago: Dearborn Trade.

Hackett, Ann. 2003. "15 Tips for Writing Winning Resumes. Part 2." *CrossRoads Newsletter*. Net-Temps Career Development Web site. Retrieved April 2003 from http://www.net-temps.com/careerdev/crossroads.

Kennedy, Joyce Lain, and Thomas J. Morrow. 1994. *Electronic Job Search Revolution*. New York: John Wiley.

Levene, Donald, and Blythe Cozza. 1996. *Resume Magic: Master Resume Writer's Secrets Revealed.* Westbury, NY: Sharp Placement Professionals, Inc. http://www.liglobal.com /b_c/career/res.shtml.

Marriott, Jessica R. 2004. "Resumes: 5 Essential Steps That Work." *CrossRoads Newsletter.* Net-Temps Career Development Web site. Retrieved May 2004 from http://www .net-temps.com/careerdev/crossroads.

Neal, James E. 2009. *Effective Phrases for Performance Appraisals.* Perrysburg, OH: Neal Publications.

Parker, Yana, and Beth Brown. 2012. *The Damn Good Resume Guide: A Crash Course in Resume Writing* (5th ed.). Berkeley, CA: Ten Speed Press.

Richardt, Joan. 2003. "Career Portfolios: Telling Your Lifework Story." *CrossRoads Newsletter.* Net-Temps Career Development Web site. Retrieved July 2003 from http:// www.net-temps.com/careerdev/crossroads.

Robbins, Carolyn R. 2002. *The Job Searcher's Handbook* (2nd ed.). Upper Saddle River, NJ: Prentice Hall.

Walker, Deborah. 2004. "Is Your Resume Lost in the Great Internet Void?" *CrossRoads Newsletter.* Net-Temps Career Development Web site. Retrieved August 2004 from http:// www.net-temps.com/career-advice/#axzz2TVeVgcBJ.

Wetfeet Staff. 2012. *Killer Cover Letters and Resumes!* San Francisco: Wetfeet.com.

Whitcomb, Susan Britton. 2010. *Resume Magic: Trade Secrets of a Professional Resume Writer* (4th ed.). Indianapolis, IN: JIST Works.

Williams, Anna Graf, and Karen J. Hall. 2005. *Creating Your Career Portfolio: At a Glance Guide for Students* (3rd ed.). Upper Saddle River, NJ: Prentice Hall.

CHAPTER 8

Bolles, Richard Nelson. 2004 ed. *What Color Is Your Parachute?* Berkeley, CA: Ten Speed Press.

Cosentino, Marc. 2011. *Case In Point: Complete Case Interview Preparation.* Needham, MA: Burgee Press.

Deluca, Matthew, and Nanette F. Deluca. 2010. *Best Answers to the 201 Most Frequently Asked Interview Questions* (2nd ed.). New York: McGraw-Hill.

Enelow, Wendy. 2004. *Keywords to Nail Your Job Interview: What to Say to Win Your Dream Job.* Manassas Park, VA: Impact Publications.

Fry, Ron. 2010. *Ask the Right Questions Hire the Best People* (3rd ed.). Franklin Lakes, NJ: Career Press.

Gawain, Shakti. 2008. *Creative Visualization: Use the Power of Your Imagination to Create What You Want in Your Life.* Novato, CA: New World Library.

Gottesman, Deb, and Buzz Mauro. 2006. *The Best Answer: 9 Secrets to Job-Winning Interviews.* New York: Berkley Trade.

Jackson, Tom. 1978. *Guerilla Tactics in the Job Market.* New York: Bantam.

Levenson, Lisa. "High Tech Job Searching." *The Chronicle of Higher Education* 41, no. 44 (July 14, 1995): A16–A17.

Magnuson, Lisa. 2003. "The Job Interview: Opportunity or Dreaded Event?" *CrossRoads Newsletter.* Net-Temps Career Development Web site. Retrieved June 2003 from http://www.net-temps.com/careerdev/crossroads.

Neece, Michael. 2004. "Questions You Ask During the Interview." *CrossRoads Newsletter.* Net-Temps Career Development Web site. Retrieved March 2004 from http:// www.net-temps.com/careerdev/crossroads.

Neece, Michael. 2004. "Second Interviews & First Interviews." *CrossRoads Newsletter.* Net-Temps Career Development Web site. Retrieved March 2004 from http:// www.net-temps.com/careerdev/crossroads.

Questioning Applicants for Employment. Brochure. June 1985. Columbus, OH: Ohio Civil Rights Commission.

Stafford, Diane. 2012. "Asking for a Job? Ask Good Questions." World News, Inc. Web Site. Retrieved March 2012 from http://article.wn.com/view/2012/03/20/Diane _Stafford_Asking_for_a_job_Ask_good_questions_2.

Stucker, Hal. 2000. "Rethinking the Interview." *Impress.*

TD Strategies. 2003. "Telephone Interviews." *CrossRoads Newsletter.* Net-Temps Career Development Web site. Retrieved February 2004 from http://www.net-temps .com/careerdev/crossroads.

Thomas Register of American Manufacturers. 2004. New York: Thomas Publishing.

Walker, Deborah. 2003. "Win Your Next Job With Three Essential Interview Skills." *CrossRoads Newsletter.* Net-Temps Career Development Web site. Retrieved June 2003 from http://www.net-temps.com/careerdev/crossroads.

Zielinski, Jennifer, ed. 2000. *Dun and Bradstreet and Gale Industry Handbook.* Detroit, MI: The Gale Group.

CHAPTER 9

Azrin, Nathan, and Victoria A. Besalel. 1980. *Job Club Counselor's Manual.* Austin, TX: PRO-ED.

Azurin, Regine P., and Yvette Pantilla. 2003. "Effective Networking for Personal Success." *CrossRoads Newsletter.* Net-Temps Career Development Web site. Retrieved November 2003 from http://www.net-temps.com /careerdev/crossroads.

Bolles, Richard Nelson. 2004 ed. *What Color Is Your Parachute?* Berkeley, CA: Ten Speed Press.

Branscum, Deborah. "Life at High-Tech U." *Newsweek* (October 27, 1997).

Breitbarth, Wayne. 2011. *The Power Formula for LinkedIn Success: Kickstart Your Business, Brand, and Job Search.* Austin, TX: Greenleaf Book Group.

Brown, Lola. 2002. *Resume Writing Made Easy.* Upper Saddle River, NJ: Prentice Hall.

Calvert, Robert, Jr. October 1997. "Why Pay for Something That's Free?" *Career Opportunities News.* Chicago: Ferguson Publishing.

Carroll, Joe. 2010. *How to Get a Job in 90 Days or Less.* Corona del Mar, CA: Triad Group.

Donlon, Kevin. 2003. "4 Job Search Questions." *CrossRoads Newsletter.* Net-Temps Career Development Web site.

Retrieved November 2003 from http://www.net-temps.com/careerdev/crossroads.

Eakins, Daniel. September 2004. Press Release. "Outsourcing & Offshoring." Minneapolis, MN: Capella University.

Freeman, Skip and Michael Garee. 2010. *"Headhunter" Hiring Secrets: The Rules of the Hiring Game Have Changed . . . Forever!* Seattle, WA: CreateSpace.

Job Hunter's Sourcebook. 1991. Detroit, MI: Gale Research.

Job Seeker's Guide to Private and Public Companies. 1992. Detroit, MI: Gale Research.

Kennedy, Joyce Lane, and Thomas J. Morrow. 1994. *Electronic Job Search Revolution.* New York: John Wiley.

Kennedy, Joyce Lane, and Thomas J. Morrow. 1995. *Hook Up, Get Hired! The Internet Job Search Revolution.* New York: John Wiley.

Kramer, Marc. 1997. *Power Networking: Using the Contacts You Don't Even Know You Have to Succeed in the Job You Want.* Lincolnwood, IL: VGM Career Horizons.

Kreuger, Brian D. 1998. *College Grad Job Hunter* (6th ed.). Avon, MA: Adams Media Corporation.

Levinson, Jay Conrad, and David Perry. 2011. *Guerilla Marketing for Job Hunters 3.0: How to Stand Out from the Crowd and Tap Into the Hidden Job Market Using Social Media and 999 Other Tactics Today.* Hoboken, NJ: Wiley.

Miller, Gordon. 2003. "Research 101: Checking Out a Prospective Employer." *CrossRoads Newsletter.* Net-Temps Career Development Web site. Retrieved July 2003 from http://www.net-temps.com/careerdev/crossroads.

Regan, Michael P. "What's Your Major? Shifting Market Make(s) It Key Query." (September 27, 2004).

Ringo, Tad, and ed. 1996. *World Wide Web Top 1000.* Indianapolis, IN: New Riders Publishing.

Stromp, Steve. "Weak Ties Could Be the Missing Link in Your Job Search." *Dayton Daily News* (August 22, 2004).

CHAPTER 10

Angelou, Maya. 1997. *Even the Stars Look Lonesome.* New York: Random House.

Csikszentmihalyi, Mihaly. 1990. *Flow: The Psychology of Optimal Experience.* New York: Harper & Row.

Holmstrom, David. "The Voice of a Writer 'In Process.'" *The Christian Science Monitor* (October 20, 1993).

Kingsley, Charles. "Sunbeams." *The Sun* (February 1994).

Kleiman, Carol. "College Grads Get a Dose of Reality." *The Chicago Tribune* (January 24, 1994).

Kleiman, Carol. "New Rules Key to Survival in the Workplace." *The Chicago Tribune* (March 21, 1994).

Korry, Elaine. December 11, 1997. "Regaining Employee Loyalty." *National Public Radio.*

Romac & Associates. Undated. "Survey: Employers Versus Employees: What the Other Half Thinks." Romac & Associates.

APPENDIX

Sorgen, Carol. 2003. "Cover Letter Do's and Don'ts." *CrossRoads Newsletter.* Net-Temps Career Development Web site. Retrieved June 2003 from http://www.net-temps.com/careerdev/crossroads.

Sweeney, Jimmy. 2004. *Top Ten Secrets of the . . . World's Greatest Cover Letter.* Retrieved July 2013 from http://www.perfectediting.com/cover_letter_tips/worlds_greatest_cover_letter.pdf.

Index